AMERICAN SHEIKHS

AMERICAN SHEIKHS

TWO FAMILIES, FOUR GENERATIONS, AND THE
STORY OF AMERICA'S INFLUENCE IN THE MIDDLE EAST

BRIAN VANDEMARK

Prometheus Books

59 John Glenn Drive
Amherst, New York 14228-2119

Published 2012 by Prometheus Books

Cover images © American University of Beirut/Library Archives
Tile border © 2007 by Dover Publications, Inc.
Jacket design by Grace M. Conti-Zilsberger

Inquiries should be addressed to
Prometheus Books
59 John Glenn Drive
Amherst, New York 14228–2119
VOICE: 716–691–0133
FAX: 716–691–0137
WWW.PROMETHEUSBOOKS.COM

16 15 14 13 12   5 4 3 2 1

Library of Congress Cataloging-in-Publication Data

VanDeMark, Brian.
    American sheikhs : two families, four generations, and the story of America's influence in the Middle East / by Brian VanDeMark.
        p. cm.
    Includes bibliographical references and index.
    ISBN 978–1–61614–476–0 (cloth : alk. paper)
    ISBN 978–1–61614–477–7 (ebook)
    1. American University of Beirut—History. 2. American University of Beirut—Influence. 3. Bliss, Daniel, 1823–1916. 4. Dodge, Bayard, 1888–1972. 5. Middle East—Civilization—American influences. I. Title.

LG351.A72V36 2011
378.569'25—dc23

2011037541

Printed in the United States of America on acid-free paper

To my beloved son, Grey

CONTENTS

INTRODUCTION:
THE BLISSES AND
THE DODGES

They were the "first family" of Americans in the Middle East for more than a century and created the finest university in the region. The university was founded by American missionaries in 1866 as the Syrian Protestant College. Later renamed the American University of Beirut, AUB grew to become the most influential institution of higher education in the Middle East and a powerful symbol of America's presence and influence in a critical part of the world. AUB produced countless leaders and legislators, ambassadors and educators, scientists, doctors, and businessmen—both Arab and Jewish—whose lives and accomplishments wrote much of the modern history of the region. The university has had an enormous impact throughout the Middle East, and it continues to affect regional and global affairs to this day.

The Blisses and the Dodges created AUB in Lebanon. With its diversity of religions and ethnicities, the political and religious passions (and possibilities) that mark the Middle East as a whole—past, present, and future—manifest themselves in Lebanon in their most vivid and enduring forms. Its capital, Beirut, is strikingly heterogeneous and sophisticated. East literally meets West in Beirut. It is a crossroads of people and ideas and interests that make it a microcosm of the Middle East and, in subtle but important respects, of the world. In Lebanon, the most pressing contemporary issues in the Middle East, including the rivalry between Iran and the United States, the tension between Israel and its Arab neighbors, and the ever-present prospect of sectarian friction spilling over into overt conflict, play out dramatically every day in the streets and make headlines around the world.

A missionary from Vermont, Daniel Bliss, and three generations of his descendants created and led the university during all but a handful of years from its founding in 1866 until 1997. Daniel's son Howard led the school as AUB's second president, and Howard's son-in-law Bayard Dodge served as AUB's third president. Bayard's son, David Dodge, like his father, grandfather, and great-grandfather before him, also became president of AUB. Over four generations and 131 years, the Blisses and the Dodges made AUB into the preeminent symbol of American culture and values in the Middle East and a leading influence in the region.

But AUB is more than just an exceptional institution. The story of AUB is also a metaphor for something bigger and more important. Enduring themes of American mission, nationalism, and idealism, along with America's encounter with imperialistic politics and American frustration as a great power in the region, have all played out in vivid and dramatic detail through the lives of four generations of the Bliss and Dodge families. The story of their efforts to build a great school with alternating audacity, arrogance, generosity, paternalism, and vision is indeed an allegory for the larger history of the United States in the Middle East.

The Blisses and the Dodges built AUB because they felt called on a mission to the Middle East, just as their Puritan ancestors had felt called on an errand into the wilderness to build a "city on a hill" in seventeenth-century New England. They believed Providence had given them a special responsibility to spread the blessings of liberty, democracy, and equality to others. The Blisses and the Dodges went forward to preach the American Gospel under the banner of Manifest Destiny. They considered themselves to be chosen people, called to fight for enlightenment and justice. Driven by unshakeable confidence and fortified by extraordinary endurance, Daniel Bliss and his descendants sought to transform the Middle East. It seemed as if the finger of Providence had pointed to them. "Hold up the Stars and Stripes," Daniel Bliss wrote in 1862, "for our country is the model for the world."[1] This sincere (if naïve and, some say, arrogant) belief purported that what is good for America is good for the world, that it is America's beneficent calling to save mankind. This belief remains potent to this day.

So many momentous changes have swept the Middle East over the last 150 years—the end of Ottoman rule, the First World War, the era of British and French colonialism, the awakening of Arab nationalism, the creation of the State of Israel, America's rise as a global power, the emergence of Islamic fundamentalism, the coming of the War on Terror—and yet AUB's intimate connection with all of them is not well known. It is an unfamiliar story because it does not conform to prevailing narratives of America in the Middle East that center on oil, Israel, and security. Amid today's constant staccato of news reports of violence in the Middle East, we can lose sight of a visionary institution in the region that symbolized cross-cultural enlightenment and coexistence. Now, when the United States is deeply involved in the region, tracing the motivations, achievements, and failures of those who created its greatest university seems appropriate and instructive. Their story reveals another, deeper dimension of America's long encounter with the Middle East and reminds us that unexpected truths can be found in the engagement between two seemingly irreconcilable worlds.

Understanding this story requires recapturing the texture and intimacy of bygone years. AUB's roots hark back to the days when American missionaries came into closer contact with the Arab world than did American military and diplomatic officers or merchants. Ambassadors and admirals came and went and knew little of the people or the language or the culture, but missionaries were masters of all three. They spoke the language and knew the people as few Americans ever did. They remained for years the chief source of information and knowledge of the region. Their endeavors also fundamentally shaped how Middle Easterners came to view and understand the United States and its purposes in the region.

Daniel Bliss went to the Middle East as a missionary when doing so was courting real danger, and not only from Islamic extremists. He first traveled there to evangelize for Christianity. But time and experience changed him and the university he had created. Contrary to most American missionaries of his generation, Bliss decided the most effective way to reach and, therefore, influence Middle Easterners was by enlightening them rather than proselytizing them. The Blisses and the Dodges pursued this goal by cooperating with—rather than challenging—the dominant local religion of Islam. They did not view their strategy as a lack of faith or conviction about their own beliefs. The families simply believed it was the best way to help others. They were far ahead of their time. As an observer put it, "They were Peace Corps types before the Peace Corps."[2]

The possibilities AUB opened up to generations of Middle Eastern men and women fostered a revolution. The Blisses and the Dodges provided an education that challenged long-held values and structures by elevating equality over hierarchy and civic responsibility over family, clan, and religious loyalty. AUB infused its students with a new sense of social responsibility and service. It also provided them with a new understanding of democracy and progress. The struggle between the weight of custom and tradition and the yearning for political and cultural change—a struggle that continues to this day—had been joined. The university helped facilitate growing literacy, cultural consciousness, and opportunities for women, and all of these things, together with the focus on rationalism and modernization that AUB instilled in its graduates, fueled Arab nationalism, cosmopolitanism, and the emergence of a modern Middle East. Arabs who received their education from AUB sought to blend their heritage with the best of Western culture. Ironically, the Blisses' and the Dodges' greatest impact lay in their spread of secular—not religious—ideas.

The story of the Blisses and the Dodges is not an unbroken story of success. Until World War II, many Middle Easterners viewed AUB as an engine of positive change because they saw the United States as a benign force in the region. After 1945, when the United States replaced Britain and France as the predominant political, military, and economic power in the Middle East, things changed. AUB now found itself buffeted by increasing winds of nationalist frustration, anti-Zionism, and eventually Islamic extremism. Middle Easterners became more dubious about America's purposes and began to see AUB less as a cradle of learning and more as an agent of undesirable Western interests.

AUB's ups and downs, from its founding in 1866 to the present, reflect the ups and downs of the larger story of America's encounter with the Arab world. Both the Bliss and Dodge families' experiences in the Middle East and the United States' experiences there were motivated by idealism and arrogance, tempered by the realities and constraints of experience, buoyed by success and influence, and burdened with disappointment and frustration. Private and public history converge.

In this book, I try to convey both the family saga and the wider historical themes. Using collections of letters, author interviews, biographies, and other reliable sources, I have reconstructed the activities and experiences of the Blisses and Dodges to provide a coherent and dynamic narrative of their unique family history. Their story is full of meaning for us as we wrestle with the hard issues of today. By analyzing how the Blisses and the Dodges attempted to shape the Middle East, where they succeeded, and where they failed (and why), we may hopefully open up new perspectives on the history of American involvement in the Middle East and draw lessons that point the way to improving relations between Americans and the Muslim world. It is time to reclaim the past for the benefit of the future.

PROLOGUE:
SAILING TO BEIRUT

Amherst's wintry snow lay far from the sunny Levant as the young missionary Daniel Bliss and his bride, Abby, bumped along the coach road to Boston in early December 1855 on the first leg of their long journey to a new life in the Middle East. He welcomed the prospect of breaking away from the quiet, serene provincialism of his New England education, denying himself and his new wife the security of family and friends, to risk the perilous journey into the foreboding unknown. They reached Boston, the Puritan mecca, on Tuesday, December 11. The next morning, Daniel and Abby boarded a small, three-masted bark named the *Sultana*, tied to the wharf in historic Boston Harbor. As missionaries, they could not afford to travel on an expensive steamer, so the newlyweds had booked passage on a less expensive but swift clipper bark—the only type of ship running to ports in the eastern Mediterranean—that sailed during the stormiest time of the year. In addition to its passengers,[1] the *Sultana* carried dozens of barrels of New England rum destined for British troops fighting in the Crimea. A cargo of missionaries and rum.

The weather was bitterly cold. A biting wind mixed with snow flurries blew hard from the northwest. Officials of the American Board of Commissioners for Foreign Missions (ABCFM) assembled on the *Sultana*'s deck to say farewell. One of them, a grizzled veteran of many overseas missions, stomped his numb feet, pointed to Abby Bliss, and muttered to another official under his breath, "the Board ought not to send such a feeble-looking lady to a foreign land; she will not live a year."[2] There was a good chance none of them would ever be seen again.

Everyone joined in a religious service, broke bread from an open barrel of "hard-tack" biscuits on deck, sang the hymn "Jesus Shall Reign," and closed with a brief prayer offered on this occasion with unusual intensity.

Then, right at noon, the ship's captain, a Dane named Charles Watson,[3] ordered the well-wishers ashore, the *Sultana*'s sails raised, and the ship underway. The destination was Smyrna, an Ottoman city on the Anatolian coast of the Aegean Sea and the center of American commerce in the eastern Mediterranean.[4]

The *Sultana* had barely cleared Boston Harbor when the bark began to pitch and roll. The Atlantic crossing was rough—snow, sleet, and biting wind, day after day. Captain Watson said it was the harshest weather he had encountered in twenty-five years at sea. The *Sultana* encountered icy gales for two weeks. The northwesterly wind blew with such fiendish intensity that when the waves began to crest, the wind sheared off their tops like a knife, filling the air with stinging salt spray. It felt like standing at the foot of a briny Niagara Falls. Ropes and lines in the *Sultana*'s rigging formed a floating musical instrument in the wind. The sound was terrific—"soul thrilling music," "a harp of a thousand strings."[5]

Daniel and Abby were young and healthy, but they still suffered during the voyage. They could not stand on deck without being lashed to rigging or a rail of the heaving bark. The ship rolled side to side, and they rolled with it. It pitched up, then it plunged down. Each time, their stomachs seemed to drop with it. Below deck, damp cold penetrated the whole ship. Their tiny cabin—barely large enough to hold a table and chairs—lay in the stern of the ship over the rudder. Seawater leaked through their porthole, soaking their mattress and bedding. They tumbled constantly against the close walls and creaking cabin door, getting covered with bruises. Even with racks on the table, they found it difficult to eat, so they took most of their meals reclining on their berths. All of the passengers washed from a single bowl filled once a day with cold seawater. Headache, dizziness, and seasickness afflicted them in an endless cycle of misery. Another passenger wrote in his journal:

> Sea sickness! Who shall describe it? Who can bear it? For eight long days and restless nights I have hardly left my berth, rolling and tossing with the heaving deep, too sick to converse with the well ones in the little saloon, unable to raise my head without giddiness, hardly caring whether the sun ever rose or set again. I did not care to live. I cared for nothing. The idea

of motion became a horror. The thought of our running on a rock would have made me happy, for a rock does not move. I longed for rest. Oh, if this bark would only stop and stand still five minutes, but no—roll, roll, roll, reel, reel, reel and I might say rile, rile, and no rest.[6]

Eight days out, the northwesterly winds dogging them since Boston picked up. On the morning of December 21, the barometer plunged and the gale became a hurricane. The wind screamed and the waves seemed like rolling mountains. The *Sultana* rose to the top of an immense wave as though it were on a high summit, then it crashed into a deep trough, like a shock, a concussion. The ocean flooded over the bow, burying the forward and quarter decks with a mass of water eighty feet long, thirty feet wide, and ten feet deep, weighing hundreds of tons. The *Sultana* shuddered, sank for a moment, then slowly righted itself—it seemed like an eternity—with an awful groan as seawater rushed out the scuppers. The fore-topsail and the staircase from the main deck to the quarter deck had been swept away. Every remaining beam and plank on the ship creaked and quivered. The next monstrous wave might break apart the little bark. The sober Captain Watson and his crew looked anxious. Daniel Bliss and his fellow missionaries looked serene. There was no murmuring, no sign of fear among them. They confidently believed God held the winds in his fist and the waves in his hand. He would protect them.

This unshakable determination and self-confidence gave Protestant missionaries the fortitude to endure adversity to a much greater extent than other American merchants, travelers, and diplomats. Indeed, they gloried in hardships. In their minds, surviving such hardships safeguarded their redemption. They acted as they looked: fearsome, ascetic, and daunting. They went abroad ingrained with notions of superiority common to Westerners of the time. They felt blessed with special talents and, thus, special responsibilities. It is what made them different, a breed apart. They had a *mission*. Lest any of them doubt or question what that mission to the Middle East meant, the ABCFM spelled it out for them in a list of axioms given to Daniel Bliss and his brethren on the day they boarded the *Sultana*:

- Don't expect American-built air castles to stand Syrian siroccos.
- Build solidly upon the Rock.
- Don't expect to find Lebanon all leveled to your hand on arriving. If you get fatigued in your work, don't get tired of it.
- Don't count upon too much fragrance in bouquets of Sharon roses, until the roses have had time to blossom.
- Don't expect to convert a soul by talking a foreign language badly, when you could not convert one by talking English ever so glibly: but remember that abroad, as here, sufficiency is of God.
- Let not the juvenile expect to be eloquent in Arabic in three months. Juveniles did not learn their English so quickly.
- Stammer, trip, blunder, but keep talking.
- Don't expect natives to be aware of your superiority all in a day, and don't believe them if they profess to be.
- Remember that it is human, and not merely American, to believe that one's own peculiar race is the best ever fashioned.
- Remember you go to win, not to browbeat or ridicule, nor yet to fail, but to win souls.
- Remember how many years passed before you would consent to love God.
- Don't be more careful to keep fleas out of your house, than to get Arabs in.
- Don't condemn every building which is not of American shape nor all costumes and customs not fashionable in New York.
- Some things can, and may, be done as well as others.
- Prove all things—Hold fast the good—Fret not thyself because of evil doers.
- Remember that you dwell in houses of clay, and that it is an unwise zeal which kills a missionary before he can save a single soul.
- Walk in the way you point out to others. Tricks of ventriloquism, throwing your voice where you do not go, will not deceive those before whose eyes you are evidently standing still.
- Asiatics will detect your weak side sooner than recognize good and godly characteristics.

- Envy is one of the oldest inhabitants of Asia, but Master "God's peace" is a stranger and must not expect to be recognized.
- You will have need of patience, that after you have done the will of God, you may receive the promise.
- Remember in prayer those whom you expect to remember you.
- Remember to write to your near relatives methodically, not everything at once, but to write regularly on some given week in every month.[7]

* * *

The storm finally broke as they passed north of the Azores Islands and made for Cape Saint Vincent. Almost instantly, the Atlantic's waters turned from an angry, gunmetal gray to a calm, indigo blue and began to yield its wonders. Porpoises and whales played in the waves and occasionally frolicked at the surface. This created great excitement among the passengers, who remembered Herman Melville's recent novel *Moby Dick*. "Do whales ever attack ships?" they asked. "Will they come up again?" At sunset, wavy and gleaming light danced magnificently across the water's surface for an instance as the sun dropped into the sea. Clouds assumed a mellow, watery softness. At night, phosphorescence caused light streams to trail from the rudder like a luminous string of stars slowly vanishing in the distance. At times, the sea's surface shined as though reflecting a full moon. Daniel and Abby raised their eyes in wonder to see if the moon was not really there.

The *Sultana* sighted Cádiz on the Spanish coast at first light on New Year's Day 1856. The yellowish-white cliffs along its shore came as a welcome sight. At eight o'clock, they passed Cape Trafalgar. Running with a fair wind, they reached the Strait of Gibraltar and the Pillars of Hercules at noon. A brilliant rainbow arced over the Rock of Gibraltar on their left. On their right loomed Apes Hill on the Moroccan coast. Seventeen days passed between when they left Boston and when they entered the Mediterranean— the Sea of the Greeks, as Arabs called it.

After sailing slowly eastward against a headwind for ten days, the *Sultana* reached the rocky island of Malta. The ship dropped anchor alongside twenty British warships in the harbor of Valetta, a British-controlled port guarding the route to India and the staging point for Western missionaries heading to the Middle East. Houses and walls of cream-colored limestone set off by windows and balconies painted blue and light green gave everything in Valetta a bright, cheerful look. Adding color to the scene were twelve thousand Redcoats, just back from fighting Russians in the Crimea, who filled the port city's narrow cobblestone streets. Everything about Valetta seemed particularly beautiful after the missionaries' long ocean voyage.

Abby described what happened next in a letter to her uncle back in Amherst:

> After we dropped anchor, a little boat came alongside the vessel, into which we descended by a ladder, and were rowed to the shore. . . . There are very many English families residing here. . . . The English seem to keep up their old prejudice against the Americans! At table they quite ridiculed our army and asked [her husband] Mr. B. what could be done, where there was no standing army. He replied there were millions ready to stand up for the defense of their country. They then said our soldiers were perfectly undisciplined—and many other things rather impolite under the circumstances—"What should you do?" said they, "if your country she be invaded again?" "Oh," said Mr. B., "I suppose we should do about as we did in the Revolution!" They changed the subject.[8]

On January 15, Daniel visited the British and Foreign Bible Society (BFBS), the headquarters of Western missionary activity in the Middle East. The BFBS ran a college and printing press on Malta, and also distributed an old Arabic translation of the Bible.[9] But the Malta Protestant College (MPC), founded in 1846, was the BFBS's main focus. Educating young men from throughout the Ottoman Empire, the MPC offered a variety of courses in Latin, French, English, and Italian. Touring the MPC gave Bliss the notion of founding an American college in the Middle East one day. The thought inspired and exhilarated him. Here was something worth striving for, thought the ambitious young missionary.[10]

The next day the *Sultana* set sail for Smyrna, a bustling Ottoman port on the coast of Anatolia and home to many Western merchants and missionaries. Flying the American flag, the little bark cruised through the Aegean archipelago over the next seven days, and Daniel revived his memories of biblical history. It made him reflect. He thought of Paul, who had planted churches on these islands' mountaintops 1,800 years before. How would he compare? Daniel wondered.

The *Sultana* reached Smyrna on January 22. After a week's rest, Daniel and Abby transferred to a French steamer, the *Menton*. The *Menton* sailed by the islands of Patmos, Rhodes, and Adalia, to Mersin near Tarsus—Paul's birthplace—then to Alexandria, Latakia, and Tripoli. Daniel and Abby marveled at the dramatic scenery that unfolded before them. The snowy peaks of the purplish-blue Taurus Mountains paralleled the coast for miles before fading away in the soft and mellow light of sunset. Just as the sun dipped below the horizon, they caught their first glimpse of the northern-most coast of the Ottoman province of Syria. What had brought Daniel and Abby Bliss on this long voyage that now neared its end?

Chapter 1:

DANIEL BLISS AND AMERICAN MISSION

Daniel and Abby Bliss's odyssey to the Middle East began in the college town of Amherst in western Massachusetts. Founded in 1821 to educate indigent students to become missionaries, Amherst College sat atop a rise in the broad Pioneer Valley. Its neoclassical buildings self-consciously evoked the culture of ancient Greece. The centerpiece was Doric-columned Johnson Chapel, whose square tower afforded an unsurpassed view of the surrounding towns and the distant Berkshire Hills. Flanking Johnson Chapel stood South College and Middle College, austere Georgian brick piles built by residents of the town as a demonstration of support for Amherst College. The school grew rapidly and by the 1830s had become the second largest college in the United States, behind only Yale.

Daniel Bliss, a frontiersman born in Vermont's Champlain Valley who migrated as a thirteen-year-old boy to Ohio by covered wagon and by boat on the Erie Canal and grew up as a barefoot farm boy craving education, entered Amherst in 1848. At twenty-five, he was much older than most freshmen. He had been forced to quit school at age sixteen to work because education had become a luxury his father could no longer afford. This experience set Daniel apart from the well-connected people whose company he kept in later years. He knew the life of ordinary people. He did manual labor. He milked cows; he became an apprentice tanner; he pruned fruit trees. But he yearned to make something of his life and to make a difference—he was a typically restless and ambitious American. He transformed his deferred dream of education and learning into the story of his life. Daniel Bliss resolved to become a missionary.

Religion held a central place in the culture of antebellum America. Alexis de Tocqueville, the precocious French aristocrat who had toured the United States the decade before and had written a brilliant analysis of American society based on his travels, observed in *Democracy in America* that "the religious atmosphere of the country was the first thing that struck me on arrival in the United States." Tocqueville went on to write:

> Religion in America takes no direct part in the government of society, but it must be regarded as the first of their political institutions; for it does not impart a taste for freedom, it facilitates the use of it. Indeed, it is in this same point of view that the inhabitants of the United States themselves look upon religious belief. I do not know whether all Americans have a sincere faith in their religion—for who can search the human heart?—but I am certain that they hold it to be indispensable to the maintenance of republican institutions. This opinion is not peculiar to a class of citizens or to a party, but it belongs to the whole nation and to every rank of society.[1]

Religion dominated the life of Amherst. The school's motto was *Terras Irradient* (Let Them Give Light to the World). Amherst's charter proclaimed its purpose to train men for "civilizing and evangelizing."[2] Prayers preceded every breakfast and followed every dinner. Sunday chapel was mandatory. Every Monday night the college president, Reverend Edward Hitchcock, gathered students in his home where he solemnly imparted the bedrock Calvinist principles of "The Elect," the centrality of "good works," and the conviction that doing right represented man's duty to God while doing good represented man's duty to his fellow man. The human story had a purpose, Hitchcock told students. It was not enough to avoid sin; one must actively do good. An all-powerful God endowed human beings with the ability to understand—and a mission to shape—the world they lived in. God acted through his believers to right the world's wrongs. God had chosen Americans to lead his work at this stage of history. Missionaries represented the leading edge of God's plan. And missionaries would not be true to themselves unless they tried to change the world.

Hitchcock and other Amherst faculty did their jobs extraordinarily well. The college produced supremely self-confident and self-sacrificing young men for whom a life abroad in mission work represented the highest ideal of service and status. Each year during these antebellum decades, Amherst graduated more missionaries than any other college in America.[3]

Daniel Bliss arrived at Amherst in the fall of 1848 with sixty-five dollars in his pocket for the entire year. To make ends meet, he prepared most of his meals on the wood-burning stove that heated his dormitory room. He also sawed and toted firewood to fellow students' rooms, rang the college bell in Johnson Chapel each dawn, sold textbooks, tutored local grade-school children, and did haying on nearby farms to earn extra income. "The way looks dark, but I must, and will, press on," he wrote in his personal account book that first year.[4]

Amherst's atmosphere—far removed from the rough, profane world of the Ohio frontier he had known as a boy—struck a deep and resonant chord in Bliss. Gifted teachers brought abstract ideas to life, explained biblical passages in sonorous tones, and confidently lived their faith. In the way of an impressionable young man, Bliss partook of that idyll. He returned to his dormitory room each night full of enthusiasm and admiration for the eloquence and fascinating humor of his professors. Their example appealed to Bliss's idealism and his longing for purpose in life.

His favorite professor was William Tyler, who taught Greek at Amherst for sixty years. Although Tyler was a devout Congregationalist, he was no starched shirt—he was ironic, urbane, and sophisticated. He was also patient and gentle, relying on persuasion more than discipline. He knew how to bring out the best in others. Faculty colleagues considered him too popular; students considered "Old Ty" wonderfully human. Bliss grew close with Tyler and remained so for forty years. Tyler taught Bliss how to learn and, more importantly, how to teach.

A strikingly handsome young man with a strong face, Daniel Bliss looked like the missionary he aspired to be. A prominent Roman nose and thin lips anchored hawk-like blue eyes, all framed by a thick mane of brown hair. "It was a visage straight out of a Grant Wood painting," a perceptive writer later noted, "harsh and angular, the clear New England eyes radiating a dead certainty and belief leavened by an attitude of benevolent superiority."[5]

While at Amherst Bliss met, courted, and fell deeply in love with a beautiful and vivacious young woman seven years his junior named Abby Wood, who would become his wife and constant companion. "If I did not succeed in finding the philosopher's stone in college," Bliss wrote years later, looking back, "I certainly obtained a very precious jewel from the town."[6]

Born in Westminster, Massachusetts, and nicknamed "Westminster Abby" by friends, she had been orphaned as a child and grew up in the care of her maternal uncle and aunt, Luke and Abby Sweetser of Amherst. Uncle Luke, as her guardian, initially opposed the romance between Abby and Daniel. He thought his niece foolish to fall for a young man who proposed to go halfway around the world as a missionary. Uncle Luke put up lots of obstacles. Courting Abby "required more courage than 'bearding the lion in his den' or facing a Goliath with a sling, or storming a fort or meeting a bear robbed of her whelps," recalled Daniel, who dubbed Uncle Luke "the flaming sword."[7] But Daniel persisted—he knew what he wanted and how to get it—and Uncle Luke eventually blessed the match.

Abby was quite a catch. She had fine brown hair and a porcelain complexion set off by radiant blue eyes. Physically frail and frequently sick, she nonetheless possessed spirit and a sharp mind—traits she shared with her close neighborhood friend, Emily Dickinson. The Sweetser house was perched on a hill amid a grove of tall oaks west of the campus. Just down the hill sat the home of Edward Dickinson, treasurer of Amherst College, and his family. His daughter Emily had yet to become the reclusive poet of later fame.

The 1840s marked a golden age of American letters and made Amherst a regular stop on the antebellum New England literary circuit. No speaker or writer achieved more popularity than Ralph Waldo Emerson, the celebrity of transcendentalism. Emerson challenged Puritan orthodoxy with the ideal of humanitarianism. He did so in ways that dazzled his audience. He had been trained in rhetoric, and eloquent sentences streamed from his mouth and pen. One observer, Walt Whitman, said Emerson's sonorous speeches and essays had "the quality of the light of day. . . . You cannot put your finger upon it yet there is nothing more palpable, nothing more wonderful, nothing more vital and refreshing."[8] A former preacher, Emerson taught that God could be found by striking out into the world:

Every spirit builds itself a house, and beyond its house a world, and beyond its world, a heaven. Know then that the world exists for you. . . . What we are, that only can we see. . . . Build therefore your own world. As fast as you conform your life to the pure idea in your mind, that will unfold its great proportions.[9]

Emerson had an intensity of purpose, a grandness of vision, and a wellspring of energy that made him intensely charismatic. He was an insistently optimistic and confident dreamer who addressed himself and his audiences to a future of possibilities. He preached progress and limitless faith in the individual. It was a contagious evangelism.

The evangelical revivals of the period, known as the Second Great Awakening, also shaped Bliss. It was an era of excitable idealism. People in New England at the time struggled with religion. Many had fallen away from the traditional Puritan faith, and so a religious revival movement swept the area, bringing people back to the church. Evangelical camp meetings attracting tens of thousands of "witnesses" sprouted up across western New England in towns like Amherst. Ministerial spokesmen of the Second Great Awakening redefined preaching from an esoteric calling to a humanitarian service. "Only the extension of Christian love," Reverend Samuel Hopkins explained, can "bring nearer to humankind the millennium that would wipe out poverty, injustice, and oppression."

This message reflected antebellum America's dynamism and self-assurance. It fired aspiring missionaries like Daniel Bliss who saw their country as the salvation of the world and saw themselves as its agents. Glorifying God meant improving people's lives not just in America, but everywhere. God had given Americans a mission, and their country's future—indeed, the world's future—depended on fulfilling it. In a commencement address to his fellow Amherst graduates in the spring of 1852, Bliss called for permanent "agitation" in religion and politics, since there would be "no finality this side of the gates of the New Jerusalem" until enlightenment and "liberty like day breaks" out everywhere in the world.[10]

Investing themselves with the purest motives, Bliss and other missionaries-to-be unselfconsciously thought of themselves as the "choicest grain" of God's most "privileged garden," destined to rescue the heathen world. Such beliefs made the nineteenth-century American missionary, in the memorable words of Randolph Bourne, writing in 1917, at once "the most unselfish and the most self-righteous of men."[11]

After graduating from Amherst, Bliss enrolled at Andover Theological Seminary. Founded in 1807 as part of Philips Academy in Andover, Massachusetts, it was the oldest seminary in America and a bastion of New England Congregationalism. At Andover, Bliss continued his study of a moralistic Calvinism, energetically engaging the great issues of the day.[12] Religious idealism combined with a political activism and intensified by intellectual introspection dominated the seminary's atmosphere. Andover taught that God saw Americans as his new chosen people. Missionaries bore a special responsibility for fulfilling God's purposes on earth by answering the call to regenerate and redeem the world. Every missionary kept one question constantly in mind: What good can be done? The missionary would have to face severe tests, but he should *never* give up and *never* be deterred by adversity.

Bliss finished at Andover in the spring of 1855. Along with his diploma came ordination as a Congregationalist minister. Bliss immediately applied for a position with the ABCFM. A powerful, influential missionary society headquartered in Boston and headed by Reverend Rufus Anderson, the ABCFM sponsored half of all overseas American missions.[13] Most ABCFM missions were in the Middle East—many more than in South Asia, Africa, or China—because there was a well-established American trade presence in the Mediterranean and because the Holy Land was the land of the Bible. Most nineteenth-century Americans knew the Bible intimately. The Old and New Testaments presented a vivid panorama of the Middle East replete with ancient pyramids and temples, shimmering oases, and sublime deserts. Many young Americans from the frontier, including Daniel Bliss, dreamed of seeing such spectacles themselves. The seductive allure of overseas work was no different then than it is now. It offered the possibility for prestige and glory in the name of God, as well as a way to find adventure and improve one's social status.[14]

The ABCFM operated in many respects like America's first international nongovernmental organization. It solicited donations from thousands of small donors. It deployed staff and resources within the United States (among Native Americans) and to the four corners of the world. It published books and technical journals, and it rigorously selected candidates for its missionary work. It required postgraduate seminary education at a time when only 2 percent of Americans attended college. The ABCFM sought ambitious, adventuresome clergymen with courage and common sense, who were also adaptable and patient, preferred cooperation to confrontation, and could settle for gradual results. It wanted missionaries who could stir up people but could also learn from them.[15] Yet the ABCFM's mission was explicit, unequivocal, and uncompromising: to "civilize" through what they reckoned to be disinterested and compassionate Christian service. This ethnocentric humanitarianism reflected the prevalent nineteenth-century Western attitude of the "White Man's Burden" that viewed all non-Europeans as racially and culturally inferior to Anglo-Christians, whose duty it was to uplift "pagan heathens," delivering them out of their long night. At its core, American evangelical Christianity harbored an unquestioning sense of superiority vis-à-vis other lands and religions and the justice of its expansionist world view. There was light—and darkness—in the hearts of missionaries.

Daniel Bliss shared these assumptions before he set out for the Middle East. His first sermon as an ordained minister, at Boston's famed Park Street Church in the summer of 1855, conveyed an air of moral superiority and self-confident presumption typical of nineteenth-century Americans. Bliss said missionary work demanded the strongest and most skillful men because they "must contend against a strong error," "communicate Christian truth in language fitted to the conceptions of a heathen mind," and "lay the foundations of all social reform and of religious doctrine." His voice booming from the pulpit, he finished, "I had rather go twice five miles, and stand all day in the door of the house of God, than to hear the wail of a lost soul, which had perished because I chose to live at ease in Zion."[16] Bliss got his wish when the ABCFM assigned him to Syria. What would he find in himself and in the land when he got there?

Chapter 2:

AMERICA ENCOUNTERS THE MIDDLE EAST

T he view of Beirut from the vessel was perfectly enchanting," Abby Bliss wrote at sunrise on February 7, 1856.[1] Beirut hugged the north shore of a cape jutting five miles into the Mediterranean Sea, where a coastal plain broadened out at the mouth of a river flowing down from the legendary Lebanon Mountains. Stunning scenery extended in all directions. Olive trees, orange groves, and almond trees colored the land. In fields, daisies and poppies mingled with small yellow dandelions and clumps of rose-pink cyclamen. To the east stood the snowy summits of the Lebanon range, with their legendary cedars, running from Tripoli in the north to Sidon in the south. Picturesque villages of stone houses and terraced vine-yards hanging at the edges of precipices interspersed among pine forests and limestone rocks dotted the lower elevations. Streams snaked their way from the mountains to the sea through steep valleys and the dramatic Dog River gorge. To the west, the homeric wine-dark seas of the legendary Mediter-ranean faded to an infinite horizon and afforded spectacular sunsets.

Life in Lebanon followed a daily rhythm. Cackling hens, crowing roosters, and braying donkeys greeted each new dawn. Women set off for the kitchen to begin preparing the main meal of the day, a stew made of vegeta-bles and small chunks of meat cooked in olive oil with browned onions and garlic, while men set off for a day of work. Neighbors, relatives, and friends stopped by throughout the day to trade gossip over dried fruit and tea and coffee in tiny cups made by potters, who propelled their wheels by foot amid the fragrance of wet clay. Water existed in abundance, but people used it sparingly because it had to be transported from wells in heavy jars on don-keys' backs or women's heads. Used for cooking and washing first, it then got recycled to scrub floors, flat terraces, and porches.

Beirut in 1856 was a modest port on the coast of the Ottoman province of Syria, which stretched from the Taurus Mountains in the north to the Euphrates River in the east to the Sinai Peninsula in the south. Small boats anchored in its harbor bore oranges and tangerines from Haifa and Jaffa, and sugar cane and lemons from Sidon and Tyre. Passenger ships from the mighty seaport of Alexandria called there, too, before sailing on to Turkish, Greek, and Italian harbors. The scene echoed ancient times, when Egyptian and Phoenician triremes plied the Lebanese coast trading gold jewelry and purple cloth, and Roman, Hellenistic, and Byzantine galleys brought warriors to the colonial port of Berytus.

One of the oldest and most beautiful settlements in the eastern Mediterranean, Beirut nonetheless remained a small city with gates that closed at night. Simple houses with jasmine gardens enclosed by cactus hedges lined streets. Sidewalks of hard-packed earth were shaded by citrus trees whose heavy fragrance filled the air in spring. The city comprised a tapestry of ethnicities and religions from across the Mediterranean and Near East that traded with the great desert caravans originating in nearby Damascus and stretching all the way to China. In addition, Beirut merchants specializing in the silk trade[2] operated as far away as France. Quick, receptive, adaptable, and sharp judges of character, the Lebanese reflected the traits of their illustrious Phoenician forebears, adventurous seafarers of an ancient kingdom on the Mediterranean seaboard. It was a cosmopolitan and richly mannered society steeped in history.

The Ottoman Turks had ruled this social stew from the imperial capital of Istanbul since 1517. Britain and France, rising world powers with competitive ambitions in the Middle East, sought influence in Lebanon by exploiting antagonisms among its factions. There were many: Sunni and Shiite Muslims; Orthodox and Catholic Greeks; Syrian Catholics with longstanding ties to the West—France in particular—dating back to the Crusades, known as the Maronites; Catholic and Orthodox Armenians; a small community of Jews; and the Druse, a reclusive religious community with its origins in Shiism concentrated in the Shuf Mountains and distinguished by a special Arabic dialect, a warrior aristocracy, and a secret dogma. The

Ottomans, facing growing pressure from expanding European empires, strived to maintain a tenuous stability among this dizzying array of proud and fiercely independent factions that represented a microcosm of the Middle East itself.

The first American missionaries to Lebanon had arrived a generation before the Blisses, in the 1820s. Unlike European missionaries of the period, they arrived without military backing or government support, nor even many economic resources. Utterly presumptuous, they came as evangelical entrepreneurs with no knowledge of Arabic or the local culture. They were strangers, as one historian wrote, in a land "they recognized but did not know."[3] They settled in Beirut because, as a commercial port, it already had some Western residents; it was the home of a British consul (and therefore offered the protection of the Royal Navy); it afforded good communication with Europe; and it lay near Mount Lebanon, which could be used as a refuge in times of crisis. The American Mission House in Beirut, built by Isaac Bird in 1830, was the largest building outside the city walls.

The boat carrying the Blisses from the *Sultana* struck bottom before reaching shore, so Daniel climbed out, and a boatman carried Abby through the surf to the beach. After retrieving their baggage tossed on the fish-smattered quay, they proceeded through customs with its babel of languages, then hired a porter and headed for the American Mission House. They made their way along narrow, winding streets lined with banks, baths, coffeehouses, and cabarets tightly crammed together. Men wearing fezzes and women wearing veils crossed their path. Camels, horses, and donkeys added to the cacophony of exotic sights, sounds, and smells. Onlookers followed the Blisses with their eyes as they passed. In a region whose inhabitants had become well acquainted with Europeans by a long association dating back to the Crusades, they wondered at these Westerners wearing plain black clothes and stern expressions. They seemed peculiar, even a bit outlandish.

Daniel and Abby did not impress the other Western missionaries whom they met upon their arrival in the city. One veteran sent back a report to ABCFM headquarters in Boston that began, "The Blisses have arrived. Mrs. Bliss will not live a year and Mr. Bliss is not a practical man."[4] It was not just an idle put-down. The experience of missionaries abroad in the nineteenth century was as harsh as that of pioneers on the American frontier. Many never made it back home, their lives cut short by the hazardous travel, disease, and persecution.

The Lebanese and their Ottoman rulers looked upon Daniel and Abby (and all other Western missionaries, for that matter) as "foreign infidels."[5] Their leaders thundered against Westerners and those who aided them as locusts determined to destroy the true faith. They feared missionaries would weaken communal allegiance and religious identity. They grudgingly accepted the education of Muslim students in missionary schools in order to acquire necessary scientific and technological know-how, but emphasized that Muslim students should be on their guard in these schools and not fall prey to missionary indoctrination. Students should be faithful to their Islamic faith and identity.

Middle Easterners tolerated missionaries because they saw a need for the learning provided in the missionaries' schools. They graduated well-educated students, and education had become urgently important in Middle Eastern society. Napoleon's arrival in Egypt in 1798 had awakened Egyptian ruler Muhammad Ali (and then the imperial Ottomans) to the rising power of the West in the Middle East. The Ottomans felt compelled to adopt Western ways in order to modernize and, therefore, survive. They initiated a series of reforms to make their empire competitive with the rising European powers. Western educational methods such as critical analysis and independent thinking seemed much more dynamic than traditional Middle Eastern education, which stressed rote learning and educated only a small portion of society.[6] Paradoxically, and yet understandably, the Ottomans believed Western missionary education would provide Middle Eastern society with the insights it needed to protect itself against growing Western influence and pressure.

American missionaries engaged the Middle East's population in a serious and sustained manner. They wanted to change the Ottoman world, not merely experience it. The missionaries also served as a conduit between cultures. They sought not just to introduce the Ottoman Arab world to American values and customs, but also to introduce Americans to a world unknown to them—to become, in effect, ethnographers of Arabs to Americans. They aspired to know, to describe, and, most importantly, to evangelize the Arabs.[7]

No Protestant community existed in Lebanon, so the American missionaries' only way to gain followers meant converting Eastern Christians (e.g., Armenians, Maronites, Nestorians, and Orthodox Greeks)—not Muslims. Protestant missionaries did not proselytize Muslims because Muslim conversion to another faith was deeply antithetical to Islamic culture—despite the fact that Muslims avidly proselytized themselves. The Ottomans permitted Western missionaries to proselytize Eastern Christians, but Eastern Christians viewed the missionaries as arrogant, uninvited, and unwelcome upstarts. "We had the Gospel before America was born," one Eastern Christian patriarch sniffed to a Protestant missionary. "We don't need you to teach us."[8]

Daniel Bliss's initial attitude was no better. In an October 1856 letter to the *Missionary Herald*, a popular journal that updated Americans with reports on the conditions and prospects of overseas missions, Bliss observed that "every man, woman and child in this land is a living, speaking, acting argument for the total depravity of the human heart." The following year he equated the Lebanese with petulant children: "We knew that they were but Babes in Christ, and that their opinions and feelings should not be too much regarded," he condescendingly told readers back home.[9]

This outlook made it difficult for missionaries like Bliss to connect with local people. Bliss had never met a Muslim before he arrived in Beirut. He accepted the missionary ethos of the equality of all people before God, and he contradictorily accepted his generation's belief in the superiority of American culture that fueled its drive to evangelize "heathens." Slowly, Bliss shed his preconceptions. He began to understand the self-limitations imposed by his arrogant, racist outlook and to see that Muslims were just as human as Christians. Some were lazy and proud and stupid—just like Christians. Some were trustworthy and hardworking and thoughtful—just like Christians. Lecturing them soon gave way to listening to them and, thus, learning from them. Bliss changed in the crucible of encounter between American and Middle Eastern cultures.

During this period of Daniel Bliss's education, a fierce (and decidedly un-Christian) competition developed between American Protestants and

French Catholics to enroll Eastern Christians in their schools. This competition resulted in the creation and funding of dozens of missionary schools in Beirut and the surrounding villages. For villagers resolved to spare later generations the harshness of their own lives, schooling offered their children a way out.

Shrewdly, Protestants operated their mission schools according to local manners and customs. Instruction was in Arabic—not English. By teaching in this way, Protestants hoped to reach the people and therefore win the battle against the Catholic Church for the Middle Easterners' hearts and minds. But ABCFM headquarters in Boston made preaching—not teaching—its priority,[10] and American missionaries were dispatched to Lebanon with little or no knowledge of Arabic. Daniel had to learn Arabic before he could teach.

Shortly after arriving in Lebanon, he and Abby moved to the mountain village of 'Abeih, a hamlet of clay tile roofs 2,500 feet up the seaward slope of Mount Lebanon, twenty miles south of Beirut. 'Abeih housed a seminary for native preachers that earlier missionaries had also made into a language school to provide instruction for newcomers like the Blisses. Daniel and Abby's home in the village, made of rough-hewn stone four feet thick and bare wood ceilings, had a majestic view of the Mediterranean, even though it lay miles from the coast. One could see faraway Cyprus on a clear day. Luxuriant rose bushes grew in a front courtyard. They loved the solitude and pristine beauty.

Now situated in his new surroundings, Daniel tackled Arabic by studying with a tutor five hours every day. His tutor was a brilliant and energetic Lebanese Christian linguist named Butrus al-Bustāni. A village boy raised in the hill country at the foot of majestic Mount Lebanon, Bustāni had traveled far beyond the hard circumstances of his impoverished family. Enrolling in a Catholic seminary, he had done so well the monks had selected him for a scholarship at the Maronite College in Rome. His widowed mother begged him not to go away. Bustāni honored his mother's wish, befriended the first generation of American missionaries in Beirut, converted to Presbyterianism, and became the preeminent teacher of Arabic at the seminary in 'Abeih.[11]

Daniel supplemented Bustāni's tutorials by reading the Bible in translation and strolling 'Abeih in the evening, listening to tales told in the square by the *'ayn* (the village well), absorbing the social and political facts of Lebanon.[12] Poetic and demanding, Arabic incorporated unusual gutturals, a unique syntax, and so much difference between the written form (used in formal discourse) and the spoken form (used in daily conversation) that learning written and spoken Arabic effectively meant learning two languages. Lacking a natural gift for languages, Daniel made painfully slow progress. But he kept at it—he would not be deterred by any obstacle—and gradually became proficient in the language. In time, he was entertaining local guests by telling long and amusing stories in Arabic.

Daniel and Abby spoke Arabic to each other in order to learn it more rapidly. For Abby, learning Arabic also meant learning to understand and respect a different culture. She struggled to make a real connection. "They have a great many salutations all of which have their appropriate answers. I am learning these very slowly," she wrote from 'Abeih in September 1856. "Sometimes after a woman has been here half an hour—and everything has been said which we can think of—she will rise, touch her forehead and breast, and go through all the salutations again. I have hard work to maintain my gravity."[13] Abby was condescending, but she was also compassionate about the subjugation of Arab women. "My heart is full upon this subject," she wrote:

> Every influence—social or civil—is to degrade them. . . . Before they know how to walk or talk, they are often betrothed—and married from the ages of twelve to fourteen. Then they are perfect slaves to their husbands. If they offend him, they are beaten like children . . . a man has only to say "Go home to your father's house"—and she is divorced. . . . The wives of the governors can never leave their houses save at night, enveloped from head to foot, and even then a man goes before to see if any men are in the way.[14]

Abby's sensitivity to this issue increased with the birth of her daughter Mary in January 1857.

After completing language study, the Blisses moved to another mountain village, Sûq al-Gharb, where no missionary had been stationed before.

Sûq al-Gharb was a stern, rocky hamlet perched on the edge of a dramatic precipice 2,800 feet above the Mediterranean. Most of the villagers were Orthodox Christian Arabs who received the Blisses with polite coldness, the closed custom of a mountain people. Physically isolated and feeling unwelcome, Daniel broke the ice by practicing the other, practical roles he had learned as a missionary: diplomat, architect, carpenter, even doctor. His theological education had not dulled his frontier pragmatism. He understood the best way to reach people was to help them.

Bliss's main duty, however, involved running a girls' school—the first of its kind in Syria when American missionaries opened it in 1834—that had recently been relocated from Beirut. His own boyhood pain of being deprived the benefit of schooling sensitized Bliss to the schoolgirls' eagerness to learn. He intuited the intensity with which they craved an education and a feeling of independence. These schoolgirls became Daniel's and Abby's hope for the females of what they termed "this dark land."[15] Teaching the girls gradually melted their parents' reserve. So, too, did the birth of the Bliss' first two sons in the village of Sûq al-Gharb: Frederick in January 1859 and Howard in December 1860.

That same year—in 1860—the biggest outburst of sectarian violence in the history of Ottoman Syria erupted. Tension had always existed in the mountain villages of Lebanon, where strong-willed people of diverse faiths squeezed a living out of the harsh soil. *Zagals* (folk ballads) celebrated local heroes, denigrated their adversaries, and told of timeless suffering. Family and tribal loyalty and "belonging" reigned supreme. Villagers fiercely protected their communities and were quick to settle scores. When they closed ranks against rivals or outsiders, as they often did, they shouted "*hadduni*" ("restrain me") as a plea to their friends and a threat to their foes. It was a region of brooding, insular, and unforgiving politics. A latent fury waiting to be ignited lurked beneath a thin veneer of tranquility.

The Ottomans mediated this tension by balancing central state power and regional autonomy while maintaining equilibrium among religious groups. But Ottoman power was weakening and European influence and interference in the area was growing. Rival European powers began to look upon local sects as their clients and protégés, which contributed to polarization. Russia backed the Orthodox Greeks; Britain backed the Druse; France backed the Maronites. On all sides, local activists seeking greater autonomy and local extremists seeking revenge took advantage of the situation and per-petrated massacres that claimed fourteen thousand lives and aroused reli-gious sectarianism to a murderous pitch. The Ottoman garrisons stationed in Syria were too weak to restore order once the fighting spiraled out of con-trol. Violence spread from villages to monasteries and mission schools. The situation quieted later in 1860, when France landed troops to protect Euro-pean expatriates, the Ottoman government agreed to prevent the killing of Lebanese Christians, and the European powers agreed to keep a certain dis-tance from their local allies.[16] In name, Lebanon became an autonomous province that formally remained a part of the Ottoman Empire. In reality, it had become a protectorate of the rival European powers, particularly France.

Daniel Bliss and other American missionaries who had been caught in the maelstrom of 1860 wondered how to maintain the tenuous peace among Lebanon's rival communities once it had been restored. Bliss believed educa-tion was the answer; it would foster toleration and thereby inhibit destructive sectarianism. Education would persuade young Middle Easterners to widen their social and political horizons. In Bliss's ambitious and fertile mind, this meant establishing a college that would instill in its graduates a commitment to civic duty, political cooperation, and social responsibility over distrustful and competitive tribalism and sectarianism. It would make Beirut a great city where Islam and Christianity met and fashioned a society of compromise. Knowledge would lead to enlightenment, and enlightenment would lead to communal peace. That was Bliss's hope.

* * *

The events of 1860 changed Lebanon. Its new status as a European protec-torate within the Ottoman Empire brought a surge of Western influence and prosperity. European merchants, travelers, teachers, and missionaries flooded into Beirut. The medieval city walls came down. French engineers built a carriage road and then a railway from Beirut to Damascus that opened up the Lebanon Mountains. Enterprising villagers flocked to the coastal city. The port and its docks expanded dramatically after the completion of the Suez Canal in 1869. Trading vessels of all shapes and sizes—from little coastal barks to great ocean-going steamships—now crowded the picturesque harbor of St. George's Bay, the best anchorage in the eastern Mediterranean. The city's population skyrocketed from 8,000 in 1830 to 22,000 in 1856 to 120,000 by 1900.[17] Beirut rapidly transformed itself, tilting toward the West as it had long ago during Phoenician, Roman, and Byzantine times.

Travelers noted this startling transformation. Mark Twain stopped in Beirut during his journey to the Holy Land in the late 1860s. He described a "beautiful city" with "bright, new houses nestled among a wilderness of green shrubbery spread abroad over an upland that sloped gently down to the sea."[18] Another Western visitor to Beirut in the mid-1870s wrote:

> [The] sense of entering a place no longer Eastern in its full meaning is new to us. The neat house-fronts, the red tiles, the blooming verandah, said it; the smoke from many a dwelling spoke only of Europe; and the great sea, which laughed and caressed the keels of the many ships, said it too.[19]

"The world of Beirut," in the words of Fouad Ajami, "was being re-cast in the image of Europe."[20]

Beirut's tilt toward the West dramatically altered the population of the city. A rough balance between Muslims and Christians existed up through the mid-nineteenth century. By 1865, however, Christians comprised two-thirds of the city. This large new influx of Maronites and Orthodox Greeks (and some Sunni Muslims) created a growing demand for Western-style education in law, medicine, science, engineering, and finance, and for the greater opportunities for wealth, office, and influence that education promised them in a rapidly Westernizing Lebanon. The few Lebanese and other Arabs in the 1860s with a Western education had received it in Europe, where many of them had remained after they graduated.

* * *

Bliss sensed an opportunity. He saw an opening for a Western college, open to all Middle Eastern races and creeds and run on New England's best standards, that would provide a practical and liberal education; "a college that shall be a great and lasting benefit to Arab lands."[21] Bliss wanted to change Middle Eastern society from *within*, through education, rather than from without, through politics like the British or the French. Recalling his primary alma mater, Amherst College, Bliss envisioned a college that educated not only the offspring of the elite but also deserving indigent students like he had been. The potentialities were enormous. He predicted big things in a letter to his favorite Amherst teacher, Professor William Tyler. "If the Institution is favored of God and of man it *shall be* the Amherst or the Yale of the Orient," predicted Bliss.[22]

Bliss brought up the idea at the annual Beirut gathering of American missionaries stationed throughout Syria on January 23, 1862, and received his colleagues' hearty endorsement. On February 4, he wrote to ABCFM headquarters in Boston proposing the establishment of the Syrian Protestant College (SPC), the first American college in the Arab world. It was a bold idea but had bad timing. The Civil War had begun the previous spring. Amid national confusion and general uncertainty, contributions to the ABCFM had fallen drastically. The board cut overseas spending by one-third and insisted on using what funds remained on its unswerving goal of converting Middle Easterners through preaching rather than uplifting them through teaching. Boston wanted its missionaries to train local Protestant ministers—nothing else. It flatly opposed "expensive educational institutions for general education to prepare young men for secular and worldly pursuits."[23]

Five years of missionary work in the field had been a mellowing and instructive experience for Bliss. It had made him less confrontational and more conciliatory in his approach. It also had allowed him to do some soul-searching and to consider more judicious strategies less offensive to local mores than preaching. "The most discouraging thing in our mission," he candidly wrote ABCFM secretary Rufus Anderson, "is the fact that it has been in existence a third of a century and there is but *one ordained preacher from the Lebanon* and he is not in connection with us." The unspoken implication was devastating: Boston's strategy of conversion through preaching simply didn't work. On the other hand, argued Bliss, "men of little education can do a great deal of good by going from house to house talking, praying with the people and reading to them."[24] He had emerged with a clear view of what was needed. Evangelism should give way to education. It was less obtrusive and, hence, more effective than preaching. It *would* work. Before the "gospel candle" could be lit, Bliss believed, the candle of education had to "burn in the wilderness."[25]

Despite these differences—or perhaps because the distance between Boston and Beirut made enforcing any disagreement with Bliss difficult— the board grudgingly gave Bliss permission to proceed. But Boston made clear its misgivings. "An institution . . . which in its practical tendencies shall hinder you in laying the foundations of a simple, contented, independent native pastorate all over your field, and of self-governed, self-contained churches," warned ABCFM secretary Anderson, "will be a fruitful source of mischief."[26] The board's skepticism became clear when it left fund-raising for the new college entirely up to Bliss.

Anderson's letter reached Beirut in late April 1862. Bliss immediately began planning his return to the United States to lobby the board and raise money for the school. ABCFM rules required missionaries to obtain written permission from the board before returning home. But mail moved slowly across the Mediterranean and the Atlantic, and Bliss didn't want to miss the board's crucial annual meeting to be held in October. So he decided to depart Beirut without authorization. Accompanied by Abby and their three small children, he sailed for the United States on August 14 to begin the arduous task of raising funds for the school.

* * *

It was a tough time to start shaking the tin cup. The day the Blisses arrived back in New York, September 17, the bloodiest battle of the Civil War broke out 250 miles south near Sharpsburg, Maryland. The Battle of Antietam saw nearly five thousand soldiers killed and more than eighteen thousand wounded in savage fighting that day. The Civil War had settled into a costly, protracted struggle consuming more and more American lives, attention, and resources.

Bliss was undaunted. Within days of arriving back in the United States, he traveled to the board's annual meeting in Springfield, Massachusetts, to drum up support for his undertaking in Beirut among friends on the ABCFM. Bliss also delivered a dramatic speech sketching his ambitious educational vision. His fearsome and haggard appearance—he had not rested from the long journey from Beirut—only accentuated his words' effect. Here was a charismatic and committed missionary just back from a far-away land, reporting about his experiences with an intimacy and urgency that left the audience spellbound.

The next speaker on the program that day, a wealthy New York businessman named William E. Dodge, was captivated by what he heard. "When our young brother was speaking," gushed the fifty-six-year-old Dodge to the audience when his time came, "I was so moved that there was not a dry thread in my shirt."[27] The audience roared. Known somewhat caustically in Wall Street circles as the Christian Merchant, Dodge had cofounded the lucrative metals-importing firm of Phelps, Dodge & Company. The business had made him very rich. But Dodge was not just a rich man—he was a Puritan. Born in Hartford, Connecticut, into a founding New England family,[28] Dodge shared the Puritan commitment to education. Puritans valued education so highly because it brought literacy to the masses, which enabled them to read God's word for themselves without mediating institutions or individuals—a bedrock tenet of Protestantism dating back to Martin Luther. The Puritan ethic of work and industry strongly appealed to him as well. Dodge had steered his own son, twenty-six-year-old Reverend Stuart Dodge, away from a business career and toward missionary work. He belonged to the American plutocracy and the American missionary establishment, an interlocking elite in the nineteenth-century United States.[29]

Dodge and Bliss hit it off instantly. The two men, along with Stuart Dodge and their wives, dined together at Massasoit House in Springfield that evening and found plenty to talk about. The elder Dodge was older and vastly wealthier than Bliss, but they understood and liked each other. Both were ambitious, assured, and driven by Puritan zeal. Both were energetic and resourceful men who dreamed big dreams and wanted to build things. And both saw the other as the means of achieving their common goal of spreading

Protestant enlightenment. At the end of their dinner, Dodge said to his son, "Stuart, that seems to me to be a good thing; we must look into it."[30] It was the beginning of a long and decisive friendship with implications for generations to come.

Bliss and Dodge put their talents together to raise a mountain of money for the school. Dodge and his wife started things off by donating $25,000—an enormous sum at the time. Having contributed so generously, Dodge didn't hesitate to ask his well-off friends to do the same. He gave a blue-chip list of contacts to the indefatigable Bliss, who did the legwork assisted by Stuart Dodge. Together they crisscrossed New York, Pennsylvania, and New England, logging seventeen thousand miles over the next two years. They spoke at churches, gave newspaper interviews, and called on nearly three hundred potential donors. Their calls followed a pattern. Bliss and the younger Dodge rarely directly solicited donations. Instead, they enthusiastically described the future college, then the two men gave their host a "subscription list" showing other notables who had already generously contributed and gently invited them to add their name to the list. It was a smooth and effective sales pitch.

"I am fishing in deep waters, for large fish," confided Bliss.[31] His catch included Mrs. Franklin H. Delano, a New York City Brahmin, heir to the Astor family fortune, and great-aunt of future president Franklin Delano Roosevelt. Another host was a very prominent man who had a dozen people waiting to see him. Each caller sent in a card and waited his turn. Bliss's finally came, and he went in. He handed the host a letter of introduction from a mutual acquaintance describing Bliss as a modest man of God. After listening to Bliss's pitch, the host said, "Well, I will give you two thousand dollars." Bliss knew the wealthy man could give a lot more. "Can't you make it five?" suggested Bliss. The man brought his hand down heavily on his desk. "Good God!" he said. "I shall write my friend that Reverend Bliss is not a modest man!"[32] But Bliss got the extra three thousand dollars. Not only Social Register members contributed money. The first cash contribution to the college endowment came from an anonymous resident of Jewett City, Connecticut, who donated a gold dollar coin on August 21, 1863. "Enclosed is a brick ($1) for the proposed Syrian College, if such a small sum is accepted. I wish it were a thousand instead of one."[33]

Such gestures made Bliss work harder at his task. So, too, did the fact that he felt the hot breath of the Jesuits. A Catholic order with its own extensive missionary enterprise, the Jesuits rivaled the ABCFM for influence in the Middle East. There was no love lost between them. Bliss' fellow missionary Henry Jessup summed up the American attitude toward the Jesuits as "those enemies of a pure Gospel, those masters of intrigue and duplicity and perverters of the human conscience. . . . Their education is showy but deceptive."[34] Bliss had heard troubling rumors before leaving Lebanon that the Jesuits planned to establish a rival college in Beirut first.[35] This must not be. He was ready.

Bliss understood the fund-raising appeal to anti-Catholic prejudice among American Protestants sparked by recent waves of Irish immigration, and he blatantly pandered to this prejudice. "The enemies of Christianity, professed Infidels as well as Papists, fully alive to the advantages to be gained from the present state of the country," the prospectus declared, "are adopting bold and energetic measures to forestall Protestants in becoming educators of the vast population of Syria."[36] A large donation to the SPC would counteract these nefarious efforts.

Bliss and Dodge shamelessly exploited religious prejudice to raise funds for the SPC, yet, ironically, they fully intended to make religious tolerance a hallmark of the school. The paradox became apparent when William Dodge traveled to Beirut to lay the cornerstone of the main building on December 7, 1871. "This college is for all conditions and classes of men without regard to color, nationality, race or religion," Bliss declared on the occasion. "A man white, black, or yellow, Christian, Jew, Mohammedan, or heathen, may enter and enjoy all the advantages of this institution for three, four, or eight years; and go out believing in one God, in many Gods, or in no God."[37] Funded through appeals to sectarian bias, the SPC would become a bastion of sectarian inclusiveness.

Bliss and Dodge's fund-raising appeal, along with Dodge's list of contacts, Bliss's talents as a salesman and promoter, and Beirut's status as a European protectorate—all made the SPC appear attractive and safe to potential benefactors. Donations flowed in steadily despite the American Civil War. One step remained: At Bliss's urging, Dodge used his powerful political connections to arrange for the college's incorporation by the New York state legislature. Incorporation in New York would make—and later keep—the SPC independent of the Massachusetts-based ABCFM's control. Dodge retained a prominent Manhattan attorney named Samuel J. Tilden to draft the school's charter.[38] The New York legislature approved the charter on May 4, 1864, and even granted an exemption in its endowment limit.[39] Tilden's friend Governor Horatio Seymour signed the bill into law ten days later. Soon thereafter, the SPC Board of Trustees, controlled by Dodge as treasurer—a position he held for the rest of his life—elected Bliss as the school's first president.

* * *

Everything was now in place. Bliss and Dodge had raised an endowment of $100,000, a substantial sum in mid-nineteenth-century America. But inflation caused by the Civil War had seriously eroded the dollar's value. The federal government had gone off the gold standard in order to fund the increasingly costly war effort. By 1864, $240 in Union "greenbacks," as dollars were known, was worth the equivalent of only one hundred dollars in gold. The depreciated dollar posed particular problems abroad, where the money would be spent.

So Bliss and Dodge turned their sights to Britain. Britain in the 1860s was at the height of its imperial power—and the vast wealth its empire generated. It was the greatest industrial, trading, and banking power in the world. The British were not only wealthy but Protestant and therefore might support the SPC. Yet British donors expected to control what they supported with their money. Bliss, however, had no intention of ceding them control over the SPC. "I don't like . . . depending upon England," he privately wrote. "The College—in order that we may control it, and that it may not work against us—*must be American*," he added. He and his missionary colleagues had already devised a plan. "It was thought best to have Trustees incorporated by American law, and funds collected *first* in the U. States, even if the amount was small. Then all donations from England would be given to an existing Institution and even if the funds from that country were much more than from the U.S. there would be no claim for controlling power."[40] Bliss was a devoted man of God, but he was also a very practical man of affairs who knew how things worked and how to get things done.

Armed with an A-list of names from Dodge, Bliss sailed for London on September 10, 1864. When he arrived two weeks later, he took a room on Adam Street in the Strand and set out on his task. He faced serious obstacles: American missionaries supported the Union, while most British aristocrats sympathized with the Confederacy. Moreover, the British-run Malta Protestant College (MPC) that Bliss had toured on his maiden trip to Beirut nine years earlier had many backers in England who viewed the SPC as a rival for funding and students. To make matters worse, the MPC's first president, Samuel Gobat, who had become Anglican Bishop of Jerusalem, publicly disparaged the SPC on a return trip to England shortly after Bliss's arrival there. "It seems," the Bishop sneered, "that the peculiar organization of our dear American brethren is not fitted to the wants of the East."[41] Gobat's "pious words" infuriated Bliss. They "can hardly be reconciled with fair dealing, to say the least, unless we suppose him more ignorant in regard to facts than a man has a moral right to be," he confided in a letter to Rufus Anderson. [42]

Bishop Gobat's campaign against the proposed college threatened to fatally undermine Bliss' fund-raising efforts in Britain. Then, a twist of fate changed everything. While Bliss was in England, the MPC went bankrupt and closed its doors. The way was now wide open for Bliss. An entrepreneur at heart, he seized the moment by approaching the chairman of the board of the defunct MPC, Anthony Ashley Cooper, the Seventh Earl of Shaftesbury.

Educated at Harrow School and Christ Church College, Oxford, sixty-four-year-old Lord Ashley looked every inch the aristocrat. His tall, erect frame, prominent nose and chin, mutton-chop whiskers, and bushy eyebrows that curled at the ends like question marks exuded authority and self-confidence. Like many British aristocrats who enjoyed a life of secure privilege, Lord Ashley was independent-minded, eccentric, nonconformist, and a bit of a rebel. Although a Tory Party member, as a young MP (Member of Parliament) in the House of Commons in the 1830s (representing a pocket borough under the control of the Shaftesbury family) he had taken up the liberal cause of factory reform as much from dislike of parvenu factory owners as from compassion for factory workers. But he was also a deeply committed humanitarian reformer who campaigned tirelessly to limit the working hours of children in mills and mines and to create "ragged schools" for the poor. Lord Ashley often said he would rather be president of the ragged schools than of the Royal Academy.

Lord Ashley's passion for social justice and opportunity for the under-privileged derived largely from his religious outlook. "There are not two hours in a day but I think of the second advent of our Lord," he once said. "That is the hope of the church, for Israel, and the world. Come, Lord Jesus, come quickly."[43] On another occasion he told a friend, "My religious views are not very popular but they are views that have sustained and comforted me all through my life. I think a man's religion, if it is worth anything, should enter into every sphere of life, and rule his conduct in every relation. I have always been, and, please God, always shall be, an Evangelical."[44] He was just the man Bliss wanted to see.

Bliss met Lord Ashley at a meeting of the British and Foreign Bible Society, the British counterpart of the ABCFM, in London's famed Exeter Hall. Bishop Gobat opened the meeting with lavish and obsequious flattery of Lord Ashley. "I congratulate the Bible Society in being honored by your Lordship's presence as chairman," fawned Gobat. Bliss followed and said, "Your Lordship, I do not congratulate the Bible Society in having your Lord-ship as chairman but I do congratulate you on being allowed to preside at a meeting held to promote the distribution of the Word of God." When the meeting ended, Lord Ashley approached Bliss and warmly shook his hand. "It was refreshing to hear from you such a sensible remark," he said. "I am sick of this constant flattery." He was hooked.[45]

Bliss called on Lord Ashley the next morning in the drawing room of his posh Georgian townhouse on London's fashionable Grosvenor Square. Although the MPC had failed, Lord Ashley wanted to continue supporting missionary education as head of the British and Foreign Bible Society (BFBS). He listened intently as Bliss spoke about his grand plans for the future. Lord Ashley cheered Bliss's remarks and said he considered leading the BFBS the greatest honor of his life. He made a sizable donation and pro-moted the SPC among his network of prominent friends, including George Douglas Campbell, the Eighth Duke of Argyll, chief of the Campbell clan and the wealthiest and most powerful aristocrat in Scotland. After Bliss left, Lord Ashley wrote to a friend, "Poor dear Malta College! It must go down before the wealth and generosity of America, and the greater wealth and meanness of England."[46]

When Bliss finally sailed from Britain for Lebanon on February 13, 1866, he had raised another $20,000 for the school.

* * *

Bliss arrived back in Beirut on March 2, 1866, after being away for three and one-half years. He eagerly sought to get things underway. Nine months later, on December 3, 1866, what would become the Middle East's finest university opened in a rented four-room house with just sixteen students. The faculty consisted of two American instructors, Daniel Bliss (teaching philosophy and ethics) and Stuart Dodge (teaching English and Latin); two European instructors, John Fraser (teaching astronomy) and Maurice Vairn (teaching French); and two Lebanese instructors, Nāsīf al-Yāziji (teaching Arabic) and As'ad al-Shadūdi (teaching mathematics and science). The SPC—contrary to *madrasas* (Muslim religious schools)—stressed abstract reasoning and critical thinking over rote memorization. Its faculty did not merely fill Arab students' heads with facts; it taught them how to organize and interpret facts. Bliss knew how to reach and touch students' minds. He forced them to think aloud in class and encouraged free-wheeling debate on every issue.

Five of the original sixteen students graduated in 1870.[47] The previous year—around the time the Ottoman government in Istanbul finally granted foreigners the right to own property—Bliss set out to find a permanent home for the SPC.[48] For months, he rode around Beirut on his horse scouting locations. He finally settled on a spot he loved at first sight: seventeen acres of cactus-covered headland overlooking St. George's Bay (where the Christian saint reputedly slayed the evil dragon) known as Rās (Cape) Beirut.

Residents of the city—and even some college supporters—ridiculed Bliss for choosing so remote a site. Some cynics called it Bliss's Folly. Rās Beirut occupied a windswept promontory dotted with a few carob trees and a stony, cactus-lined mule path connecting it to the city, which used the site as a dumping ground. But it had spectacular vistas of the Mediterranean Sea to the north and west and the snow-capped peaks of the Lebanon range to the east. What is today the heart of the AUB campus sits on some of the choicest real estate in the entire Middle East, surrounded by a dense forest of condominiums and office buildings.[49]

The deed of sale, dated March 23, 1870, and signed by an Arab Christian representative of Daniel Bliss and six Muslim witnesses, identified the property "for the purpose of . . . a college for the teaching of arts and sciences to whosoever seeks to be taught from all communities."[50] Bliss shrewdly persuaded the chief Qādī (Muslim judge) of Beirut to recognize the college as a *waqf* (charitable foundation) under Ottoman law, thereby permanently securing its exemption from property taxes and customs duties on imported goods. "I am willing to undergo anything to advance the good of the College, which will yet shape by its power all the Orient," Bliss wrote.[51]

This same vision and drive Bliss applied to acquiring the land he applied to planning the campus. First he traveled to Istanbul, where he cajoled Ottoman officials into granting permission to begin construction and toured Robert College to get an idea of what structures might be built. Then he returned to Beirut and began the task. Envisioning a school of lasting beauty, he set aside one-third of the campus for groves of cypress, eucalyptus, palm, and pine trees. He also ordered masons to use lovely cream-colored sandstone quarried southwest of the city and brought to Rās Beirut on the backs of mules and camels. The beautiful buff-colored sandstone could be easily worked and was very durable.

Construction began in the early 1870s. In May 1873, Abby and their four children[52] returned to Massachusetts to visit relatives and enroll the older children in boarding schools while Daniel stayed behind to supervise the building of the campus, the curriculum, and the faculty. During the fourteen months Abby and the children remained in Massachusetts, Daniel wrote to them letters to help bridge the distance of separation. In these intimate letters, fifty-year-old Bliss discussed the problems arising from the construction work, the trials of dealing with the Ottoman bureaucracy, and his love and ambition for the school.

June 19, 1873:

My own dear ones,

Lonesome as it is, hard as it is to be left alone—away from wife and children, I am every day thankful that Providence so wonderfully opened the way for you and the children to go home. . . . We sometimes fear least our large buildings[53] are calling down upon us the opposition of the Turkish government. They, the Turk, understand us too well; we are for raising, educating the people. That policy does not suit the governing classes. We must work on in patience and in faith and the reward will come.[54]

September 18, 1873:

My dear family,

The West wind is blowing hard and we may expect rain. Let it come—the roof is tied down strong. . . . One month from today the College opens, and there is little time enough to get ready. The work of flooring, roofing, "dooring" and "windowing" is yet to be done. . . . The appearance will be fine.[55]

October 12, 1873:

My own precious Wife,

I am seated, upon this your birthday, in my own private bathroom at the new College building. I slept sweetly last night here—all alone. Not a servant or workman or a stray student was allowed in the building. It was as quiet out here on the "Ras" as it is on the mountains, and the noise from the sea imparts a cooling sound. I woke up after sunrise and enjoyed the chatter of the birds sitting on the bars of my open window and thought of the Birdie and birdlings far away over the blue sea and the boisterous ocean.[56]

December 5, 1873:

Dearest Darling—only Darling,

This is a most beautiful evening. The full moon shining out upon the glassy sea below us. The students have had a high time. . . . Their shouts sounded out as well as the shouts of Amherst in my day. . . . We are fast growing into a College Community. . . . Tell Prof. Tyler that we are making history out here very fast.[57]

Bliss guided affairs from a second-floor room in College Hall that looked out on St. George's Bay through Gothic windows. He kept busy. "I have sixty or seventy in the same building with me, and am asked questions about one thing or another every hour in the day and every quarter of an hour except between the hours of ten p.m. and seven a.m."[58] Bliss displayed firm leadership, judicious forbearance, and managerial savvy. "I never ask advice," he confided to Abby, "until the thing is so far begun that there can be no change."[59] He stayed in close touch with students by strolling campus, attending chapel, and helping with chores. He disciplined in unexpected but effective ways. "Sometimes I treated one as if he was telling me the truth when I knew he was lying to me. I cannot explain the philosophy of it, but trusting a boy makes him trustworthy."[60] When a student appeared before him for rowdiness, he said, "Who told you that you were sent out of that room as a punishment? Do you know the history of Lot?—he was sent out of Sodom." "Yes!" the student replied. Daniel noted that the student "smiled and said 'Ketter Khirak' [thank you very much] and bowed himself out." All of these qualities made Bliss a respected and beloved figure on the growing campus.[61]

Al-Kulliyah—"the college" in Arabic—made an immediate impact on Lebanon and the broader Middle East. It addressed a deep thirst among Arabs that had been ignored by the Ottomans for an educational system that addressed a sense of Arab identity and culture. Word spread through student and alumni networks that the SPC offered the best education in the Arab world, indeed, in the entire Middle East. More than any other school in the region, it stressed free intellectual inquiry, character building, and hard work—echoes of Bliss's experience at Amherst College. Applications from all over the region flooded in, rapidly increasing enrollment.

The school's speedy growth led to a major—if unanticipated—change in how the SPC pursued its mission. The school's charter mandated instruction in Arabic, and Bliss originally operated the SPC according to this principle. But the rapid expansion of the school's curriculum made it difficult to staff all of the departments with enough qualified, Arabic-speaking instructors and provide students with enough Arabic-language textbooks. So Bliss switched the college's language of instruction to English over several years, though Arabic instruction remained an integral part of the curriculum.

The medical department made the switch last. Added in 1867, the medical school had the most Arabic-speaking teachers of any department and had good Arabic-language textbooks that had been published in Cairo since the early nineteenth century.[62] The medical school had high standards: It required a four-year course of study at a time when most top American medical schools followed a three-year program, and it provided clinical experience through access to the Prussian Hospital—the best in the region. SPC notably improved the level of medical training in the Middle East and impressed Arabs with the momentous implications of modern Western technology. But it, too, finally switched instruction from Arabic to English in 1883.

As the SPC put down roots and grew, so did organizations associated with the college: preparatory schools, publishing houses, newspapers, magazines, literary and scientific societies. The college and its various organizations attracted students eager to blend traditional elements of Arab culture with modern concepts from the West. They became a crucible for debating ideas and goals, including the potent ideology of nationalism. Thus began a movement that remains a strong force in Arab politics to this day. As Daniel Bliss's great-grandson David Dodge later remarked, "The college fostered an atmosphere of free thought and free discussion which helped give birth to Arab nationalism, and allowed Arab nationalism to develop. You could almost say that Arab nationalism grew up out of the college."[63]

The SPC-inspired Arab nationalist awakening planted seeds of cultural creativity in the revived study of classical Arabic language, history, and literature. It also, however, planted seeds of cultural conflict seen in the emerging tension between a traditional, religious point of view and a modern, secular point of view that would be played out throughout the Middle East for many years to come. This tension would also be mirrored in the lives of individuals who would feel torn in two directions, between Islam and the West.

Chapter 3:

TRADITION VERSUS MODERNITY IN THE MIDDLE EAST

Creation versus evolution is a perennial debate pitting two opposing worldviews in a struggle to define human origins and the nature of man. A contentious issue even today, it reaches back to the publication of Charles Darwin's *On the Origin of Species* in 1859, and played out at the Syrian Protestant College (SPC) in 1882 (the year of Darwin's death) in a highly charged controversy known as the Lewis Affair. The Lewis Affair caused deep divisions between conservative and liberal faculty members, incited passionate student protests, and shook the young school to its foundation. It was an intense and bitterly fought culture war that the conservatives won. But their victory was only temporary. In the long run, liberals prevailed, and the affair marked the first step in the school's transition from its missionary roots to its modern, secular future as it became a crucible that transformed Arab students, generating momentous consequences in years to come. Ironically, the Lewis Affair played a fundamental role in shaping and improving the institution.

The trouble started on July 19, 1882, when Professor Edwin Lewis, whom Bliss had hired twelve years earlier to teach chemistry and geology, gave that year's commencement address before a large gathering in Assembly Hall. The forty-three-year-old Lewis, a wounded Union veteran of many bloody Civil War battles, had arrived in Beirut in 1870 not knowing a word of Arabic. But in the intervening years he had learned the language well enough to proofread the classical Arabic that his flamboyant army comrade, General Lew Wallace, had incorporated in his sword-and-sandal epic *Ben-*

Hur: A Tale of the Christ (1880), which became the best-selling American novel of the nineteenth century.[1]

Lewis was a tall, intense-looking man. His broad experience and education had made him something of a nonconformist. He was known among students as a freethinker. He was not always in his pew at the college chapel on Sunday mornings and he occasionally served wine at dinner and played the violin at foreigners' parties in Beirut. All of this angered conservative missionaries who had grown uneasy about the trend of things at the SPC. They saw a weakening of faith that jeopardized the religious roots of the school. A conservative missionary in Beirut grumbled that the SPC was not "the best means by which the mission could train laborers for Christ."[2] It did not take long for this remark to reach Stuart Dodge, the most powerful member of the conservative faction in Beirut. Dodge disliked Lewis, whom he considered opinionated, self-conceited, and subversive. "We are a *Missionary* organization," Dodge told Bliss in a letter in March 1882, and "if any one now connected with us is not in sympathy with the paramount object, the sooner someone else takes his place the better."[3] The financial support that Dodge and his father lavished on the school made his warning count.

Bliss nonetheless asked Lewis to deliver the commencement address that summer. The two men were faculty colleagues, fellow Amherst College alumni, personal friends, and occasional dinner companions. Lewis had impeccable academic credentials, having earned graduate degrees in both medicine (Harvard Medical School) and theology (Union Theological Seminary). In his address titled "Knowledge, Science, and Wisdom"—which he delivered in Arabic—Lewis distinguished between science (based on knowledge) and wisdom (based on religion). He then, fatefully, eulogized the work of Charles Darwin as "an example of the transformation of knowledge into science by long and careful examination and accurate thinking."[4] Lewis deliberately tried to avoid giving offense, pointing out that Darwin's theory of evolution through natural selection had not been proven conclusively. If Darwin's theory was wrong, he hastened to note, science would reveal it. "If, on the other hand, it is correct, man's high mental rank will not be degraded, not even by one particle, and he will not at all be deprived of his spiritual nature." Lewis then went even further, unambiguously proclaiming the superiority of wisdom over science:

Science is not wisdom and will not become wisdom no matter how much it is promoted and extended. Whatever science teaches us and whatever it will disclose to us in the future about the advancement of man in past times, it will not teach us anything about the true origin, namely that we are the sons of God. Whatever science may reveal to us about the progress of man in the future, it will not teach us anything about the great teaching, namely that we are immortal and the inheritors of an eternal kingdom.[5]

None of these careful qualifications mattered. Merely mentioning Darwin roused the fury of conservative missionaries. Darwin's theory of evolution through natural selection impaired the authority of the Bible by discrediting the Genesis story of creation, added the intellectual difficulty of coming to terms with the fossil record, and seemed to pull the props out from under religion by exploding the core concepts of original sin and morality. Critics thought it would lead inevitably to atheism. Most nineteenth-century American missionaries—though well-educated and worldly men—felt deeply threatened and therefore reacted furiously to Darwin. They considered him a dangerous heretic, a direct and mortal challenge to all they believed in and stood for. In him, they believed, the devil had found his wedge.

While most missionaries implacably opposed the theory of evolution, some sought to reconcile Darwin with Genesis while insisting that scientific investigation continue unimpeded. One of the most influential of these was Edward Hitchcock, who had been a mentor of Daniel Bliss at Amherst. An eminent geologist as well as college president, Hitchcock was the first chairman of the Association of American Geologists, which later developed into the American Association for the Advancement of Science. He had published an important work during Bliss's time at Amherst titled *The Religion of Geology*.[6] In it, Hitchcock argued for the metaphorical understanding of the Creation (e.g., interpreting the Hebrew word for "day" as "eon"). He went on to explain the geological record as a further revelation of God's purpose: "Science has a foundation, and so has religion," he wrote, "let them unite their foundations, and the basis will be broader, and they will be two compartments of one great fabric reared to the glory of God."

This attempt to reconcile science with religion shaped Bliss's outlook and marked him as a liberal on this emotional and contentious issue. Bliss was neither religiously dogmatic nor insecure. He did not fear modern science. He welcomed, indeed, he embraced it as further revelation of God's design and purpose. For this reason, Bliss may well have seen Lewis's commencement address as an indirect (and, therefore, safe) way to subtly nudge the SPC in a more liberal direction.

But this idea backfired. Lewis's address exacerbated the deep split among American missionaries about the school's purpose. Was its function to spiritually uplift students by inculcating traditional verities or to educate them by disseminating modern knowledge? Passions ran very high on this issue. Conservatives stood firmly in the former camp. Liberals, like Edwin Lewis, stood firmly in the latter camp. That Lewis had brought these simmering tensions out into the open, and not the actual content of Lewis's address, is what distressed Bliss and threatened his own standing. The night of the commencement, he confided to his diary, "Dr. Lewis' address much out of taste, an apology for Bible truth and an acceptance as science of unproved theories."[7]

While the effect of Lewis's speech dismayed Bliss, it gave conservatives a powerful new weapon with which to attack Lewis. "Resignations, springing from such grounds, will be welcomed," Stuart Dodge wrote Bliss, careful to put his objections in writing even though they both lived in Beirut. "Better run at half-speed—'slow her clear down'—than make sixteen knots with the aid of atheistic, materialistic or non-religious boiler."[8] In case Bliss didn't get the message, Dodge made his point explicitly later that summer. "If [the school] is to have any doubtful religious character," Dodge told him, "it will be closed." He reminded Bliss "what the trustees are permitted and required to do, if the [Evangelical] tendencies of this College are not such as the original founders proposed. . . . I shall do my utmost to close its doors rather than let it fail of the religious ends for which it was brought into existence."[9]

Another conservative, missionary James Dennis, opened a second front by publishing an inflammatory denunciation of Lewis's address in the student journal *al-Muqtataf*. "I am shocked and grieved," wrote Dennis, "that such a eulogy on Darwin should have come from such a professor before such an assembly." Dennis added that "Darwin had proclaimed himself to be a heretic who did not believe in the Bible, in the hereafter nor the mission of Christ."[10]

Lewis responded to Dennis's fierce attack in a calm and deliberately concil-iatory tone. "It did not occur to me that someone could misunderstand me in the way that the person did who criticized my speech in the last issue. . . . Reli-gion is a personal matter," he went on. "Darwin never denied nor attempted to deny Christianity. Furthermore, a man could be a great scientist and at the same time a Non-Christian. . . . In such a case," said Lewis, "I would still accept his science, teach it to my students and refute his religious beliefs."[11]

Dennis would not stop. He escalated the crisis by complaining to the powerful William Dodge, secretary of the SPC Board of Trustees in New York. (Dennis had a personal connection: his father, Alfred, sat on Dodge's board.) Dennis forwarded to Dodge the issues of *al-Muqtataf* containing Lewis's address and subsequent rebuttal. New York had become an interna-tional center of capital and communications after the Civil War with the advent of the newly invented telegraph. The telegraph dramatically nar-rowed the distance between New York and Beirut. For the first time in his-tory, a message could travel more rapidly than a messenger. It enabled Dodge to act directly in response to the crisis rather than rely on Bliss as his agent, as had been the custom in the past. It also demonstrated Dodge's underlying power as college benefactor, while exposing the limitations of Bliss's authority as college president.

The Puritan in Dodge didn't like any of what he read. He wrote Bliss a pointed letter: "A few marked passages indicated very clearly how Dr. Lewis was drifting," Dodge curtly noted.[12] Dodge's reaction intensified when con-servative missionaries (including his son Stuart) informed him of Lewis' ear-lier transgressions and accused Lewis of being "an evil influence" on students and a divisive force among the faculty. "The Syrian ammunition for Amer-ican action was most abundant and amply explosive," Dodge wrote Bliss.[13] He had learned enough and he decided to act. The word went out from New York to Beirut. On December 1, 1882, Dodge informed Bliss by telegram that "neither the Faculty, nor the Board of Trustees would be willing to have anything that favors what is called 'Darwinism' talked of or taught in the College." Lewis must go "at once."[14] It fell to Bliss to notify Lewis of his fate; Lewis replied that the medical school was "doomed."[15] Was it a prophecy or a threat?

* * *

Thus ended Lewis's tenure at the SPC. But this did not end the crisis, for Arab students reacted very differently to Lewis's address than the conservative missionaries. They liked his speech. "Signs of contentment and understanding were on everybody's face," a student reported on the event in *al-Muqtataf*, "and at times when the audience could not control its emotions there were bursts of applause. . . . When the ceremony was over, [students] were seen in pairs and in groups competing in praise of the speaker, particularly because he proved in this scientific speech that beyond science is wisdom, which is the fear of God."[16] Lewis's speech inspired Arab students. It showed them that belief in religion did not have to consist of sectarian zeal or theological orthodoxy, but rather an earnest desire to understand humanity's place in the world. Their teachers had taught them to believe in freedom of thought and moral courage, and they felt emboldened by this liberal, open-minded spirit.

This sense of assertiveness triggered a protest movement when students learned of Lewis's ouster on December 3. They refused to remain silent at what they considered an injustice. This was a radical departure. Students in the Arab world rarely—if ever—rebelled against authority. They lived in a culture steeped in deference and politeness. Taught from an early age to respect their elders and elites, they traditionally submitted to the edicts of elites. But their SPC education led them to question assumptions and the status quo. This encouraged young Arabs to do what they had never done before: challenge the authority of established institutions and dispute the impingement of *their* rights. It was a momentous precedent with immense social and political repercussions to be felt throughout the Middle East in years to come, and would reverberate during the historic Arab awakening that began in the spring of 2011.

The protest movement began on the evening of December 3, when faculty and students met in the chapel for recitations. When the time came for singing the first hymn, the students remained silent. The next day, the medical school students boycotted classes. Other SPC students soon joined the strike. On December 5, the protest leaders submitted an impassioned plea to Bliss and the SPC faculty:

We did not come to the College save to study with distinguished professors whom we know, and the College is to us those professors. We know
too well that some of you have shaken the foundations of our professors and
brought about the suspension of our pious and excellent Professor, Dr.
Lewis. . . . This pious excellent man have you suspended suddenly in a way
that violates his rights and ignores his excellent and pious services to the
College and country for twelve years. . . . You also have not allowed us to
know of what was coming before we entered this [academic] year, and we
entered on the supposition that Dr. Lewis was to be our Professor. . . .
What have you done in causing all these injuries to us! If you attribute the
blame to parties in a distant country [i.e., those in New York], are you not
those who informed them, and if you say not all of us are concerned, are not
some of you? . . . We therefore lay the strongest indictment against those
who have thus gone about to injure us.[17]

A liberal professor at the medical school named Cornelius Van Dyck
favored a conciliatory reply. Conservative faculty members demanded stern
punishment. This disagreement reflected the deep split over the Darwin
issue and the direction of the school. The liberal, secularizing faction among
the faculty included Edwin Lewis, Cornelius Van Dyck and his son William
(who had corresponded with Darwin in the last year of his life), John
Wortabet, and Richard Brigstocke. The conservative, evangelical faction
among the faculty and the missionary community included Stuart Dodge,
James Dennis, George Post, William Eddy, and Henry Jessup. Daniel Bliss
was caught squarely in the middle.

A charismatic and popular figure, sixty-four-year-old Cornelius Van
Dyck had trained as a physician in the United States before being swept up
in the wave of religious revivals known as the Second Great Awakening and
shipping out to Syria as a medical missionary in 1840—fifteen years before
Daniel Bliss. After arriving in Beirut, Van Dyck received ordination as a clergyman before turning to learn Arabic. Studying with Butrus al-Bustāni, Van
Dyck gradually mastered the difficult language. He learned not only to
speak Arabic fluently but also to write it gracefully. He translated numerous
works into Arabic, including textbooks on algebra, astronomy, chemistry,
geography, geometry, medicine, physics, and trigonometry. But his greatest
achievement (along with fellow missionary Eli Smith) was translating the

entire Bible into elegant modern Arabic. The twentieth-century Lebanese historian George Antonius praised his Bible translation as "probably the most valuable and effective single influence ever exerted by a foreigner in the cultural development of the country."[18] A great Egyptian scholar at al-Azhar University in Cairo later told Van Dyck's daughter: "Your father taught me, by his published writings, that it is possible to write good Arabic, correct in grammar and in idiom, in a style so simple and so clear as to be easily under-stood by any intelligent reader, whether learned or unlearned."[19] Such encomiums earned Van Dyck the Arabic honorific—rarely bestowed on for-eigners—of *al-Hakim* ("The Wise").

Van Dyck was a renaissance man. Unusual among nineteenth-century American missionaries, he was also a *bon vivant* who fell in love with Arab cul-ture and "went native" in his manners and customs. "I have left my heart in Syria," an SPC student quoted him as saying when he turned down a teaching position at prestigious Union Theological Seminary in New York City in 1867.[20] Foregoing the humorless and stern black frockcoat worn by Daniel Bliss and others, Van Dyck took to wearing traditional Middle Eastern gar-ments, including a red fez (*tarboosh*) with a thick black tassel, a short jacket with tight sleeves, a close-fitting vest, blooming trousers, and leather slippers turned up at the toes. He occasionally relaxed at night by smoking a Turkish water pipe (*nargileh*). It was all a flamboyant display that other American mis-sionaries in Beirut tolerated because they liked Van Dyck personally, appreci-ated his talents, and respected his standing among Arabs.[21]

Over the years, Van Dyck, like Bliss, came to view education and humanitarianism as the most effective forms of missionary work. Van Dyck spent little time preaching, devoting himself instead to scholarship, teach-ing, and medicine. He preferred alleviating suffering by treating outpatients at a twice-weekly eye clinic at the Prussian Hospital rather than sermonizing on Sundays. Bliss shared Van Dyck's preference for teaching over preaching, and initially sided with him in the faculty debate over how to respond to the student protests. Bliss wrote the student protestors, acknowledging their feelings and adding: "We cannot see how this should lead you to absent your-selves from your classes."[22] He persuaded a majority of the faculty to pardon the students' absences and directed them to return to classes.

All of the students remained absent from prayers the next morning, December 6. They gradually returned to classes over the next few days. But they did not drop their protest; they went public with it, informing local leaders (including the Ottoman governor and the American consul in Beirut) of the controversy in order to explain their case and win support. "Most unprecedented excitement has spread thru the city and country among natives and Franks," the Bliss's eldest son, Fred, head of the SPC's preparatory school, wrote his brother Howard in college at Amherst.[23] Tension mounted between students and faculty and within the faculty itself. "Papa has hardly slept at all," Abby wrote Howard and Willie in the States. "I write in great excitement as the rebellion goes on still."[24] Daniel presented a stoic façade toward his son Fred. "The President is magnificent, grand and strong and I pin my faith to him," Fred wrote Howard. Their father stood "like a rock."[25]

On the evening of December 16, the faculty met for four hours behind closed doors in the chapel assembly hall. Outside, students waited anxiously. One put his ear to the door, hoping to eavesdrop on the proceedings. The atmosphere inside the hall was tense. Tempers were frayed and the opposing camps were primed for a showdown. The meeting began when liberal faculty member Richard Brigstocke asked Bliss why Lewis had resigned. "If you wish to know why Lewis resigned, you had better ask him," said Bliss, "and if you wish to know why the Trustees accepted his resignation, you had better ask them."[26] Bliss's truthful answer painfully exposed his marginal role in the decisions leading to Lewis's removal.

Discussion then turned to the latest student petition, which reiterated previous complaints and further alleged that George Post, a conservative faculty member and unpopular teacher, had conspired with Bliss to oust Lewis. "We consider Dr. Post and the president as responsible for our troubles."[27] Bliss knew this wasn't true—who was behind this?—and resented what he considered the petition's aggressive and impudent tone. Angry and indignant, he persuaded the faculty by a vote of eleven-to-two to suspend the students for a month, permitting them to re-enroll in the college only after they signed an apology.

Cornelius Van Dyck denounced the suspensions, calling the conservatives (and, by implication, Bliss) "bigots."[28] Bliss raised his voice and demanded to know if Van Dyck had promised to teach the student protestors at his Beirut home if they were suspended. When Van Dyck answered yes, Bliss erupted. "Gentlemen, Anglo-Saxons, English and Americans. I ask you if this was not abetting rebellion!"[29] Van Dyck bolted from his chair and stormed out of the hall. A student who witnessed his dramatic exit recalled it later. "I saw [Van Dyck] riding away in his carriage and anger was clear on his face."[30] "A smashup was inevitable," Fred Bliss wrote his brother Howard, "and it came."[31]

* * *

The day the suspensions took effect, December 18, Van Dyck and his son William resigned their professorships. That evening Bliss ordered the thirty-nine suspended medical students out of the dormitories. It was a harsh gesture, but there was no turning back now. "The Faculty set the ball of discipline a-rolling," Fred wrote Howard, "and they can't back down."[32]

"We are in the midst of troublous times," confided Abby that night. "Better the College be given up than such men be in the Faculty. The excitement and anxiety are almost killing me."[33] Abby's health deteriorated. Daniel endured trying days and sleepless nights. Liberal faculty colleagues shunned him for abandoning Lewis and suspending the protestors; conservative missionaries engineered his removal from the Beirut Pastors' Committee. Both were painful personal rebukes. Some Lebanese accused him of racism for punishing the Arab students. A newspaper published a harsh criticism of Bliss by playing on his name. "One whose name is 'Iblis' [Arabic for devil], who turned out those who had such love for this country, is still busy about the College, while Dr. Van Dyck is teaching students free of charge in his own house."[34] The toll began to show. "Papa had his picture taken last week," Abby wrote Howard and Willie on Christmas Day, "but tho I tried to make him feel cheerful, by talking to him of his three good boys—it is a very stern, *firm*-looking picture."[35] Daniel felt besieged, bitter, and hurt. "I do wish I could banish all thought of this most wicked rebellion from my mind," he wrote his sons.[36] "We are having an awful time here," noted Abby on New Year's Day 1883.[37] Fred added that the family was in "a terrible condition. It's enough to make a man lose faith in his fellow men."[38]

A majority of the suspended students eventually signed the apology and returned to school. "The rebellion ranks are broken," noted Abby on January 17, "and the students are beginning to sign the apology." She reported a few days later, "The students are straggling back one-by-one. They seem to be surprised to find Papa is still their friend—all has been so wrongly represented to them."[39] Several of the suspended students, however, refused to sign and never returned. The Van Dycks taught them at their Beirut home until the students left for Istanbul in the spring for their certifying exam. They took the exam despite the conservatives' pressure on Ottoman authorities to deny them the chance. All of the students passed with distinction and became physicians throughout the Ottoman Empire.

Edwin Lewis left Beirut in May 1883, never to return, and settled back in the United States. He taught briefly at Wabash College and then practiced medicine in his hometown of Indianapolis until his death in 1907. The Van Dycks eventually rejoined the SPC faculty.

William Dodge died suddenly on January 8, 1883, of a heart attack brought on by the stress of the crisis. His son Stuart and other conservatives took steps to insure another challenge to what they considered the properly evangelical character of the college would never happen again. Early the following year, in 1884, they used the hiring-and-firing power of the board of trustees—which they controlled—to impose a Declaration of Principles on every member of the SPC faculty, including Bliss. The Declaration of Principles was, in effect, a loyalty oath. All professors had to pledge to uphold "Christian values" at the school or forfeit their jobs. The declaration flew in the face of academic freedom. The outcome of the Lewis Affair showed that conservative nineteenth-century Christians—not just conservative twenty-first-century Muslims—strictly and unbendingly applied their values not just to themselves but to everyone else as well.

* * *

Daniel Bliss remained silent about the crisis until the end of 1883, when he poured out his feelings in a letter to his son Howard at Amherst. "The trials of the last year wore upon me," he confessed, "but those trials are fast passing away." Some hard feelings lingered, however: "I still feel sad that those rebellious students should have been led into rebellion not from their own choice, but by such a man as Dr. Van Dyck.—poor fellows. . . . These men threatened to break up the college—*they broke themselves*. You will never know the tension that was upon myself for months—thank God we were brought through it all. It nearly killed your mother—Well the college is much stronger for the trial."[40]

Bliss never commented publicly on the Lewis Affair for the rest of his long life. He tellingly omitted even mentioning the crisis in his memoir, which was published after his death in 1920. Bliss's conspicuous silence reflected the deep emotional scars it had left. Bliss had accommodated himself to the conservatives' demands because he thought sacrificing Lewis and punishing the students best served the interests of the school he loved and to which he had devoted his life. Bliss also acted as he did because he understood his position as college president rested on the political support of the conservative missionaries and the financial support of the Dodges. Standing by Lewis and the students would have fatally alienated these two key constituencies, and this he would not—he could not—do.

Yet the year Bliss retired as college president, 1902, he publicly urged abolishing the Declaration of Principles. (The new college president, his son Howard, made its abolition a precondition of his acceptance of the post.) And a baccalaureate sermon that Daniel Bliss delivered *twice* (in 1888 and again in 1895) and whom he mentioned in it offered an indirect but very revealing glimpse into his true feelings:

> Pride is a great hindrance to many. It keeps them from learning from others. . . . Darwin in obtaining his vast knowledge of the habits of plants, fishes and animals, was aided by farmers, fishermen, hunters and shepherds. . . . Make this your rule: lay aside pride and be willing to learn from anyone, be willing to be taught by the most ignorant if he can impart any new thought, unknown to you. . . . But this is not enough. You must lay aside *self-conceit*. . . . Self-conceit hinders you because you think you know it all.[41]

The most important legacy of the Lewis Affair, however, lay in its effect on Arab students. Traditionally, Arab students had been very deferential. They went to school to receive a religious education from authority figures they never presumed to question nor challenge. But their education at the SPC—despite its missionary origins—changed them by changing their strictly obedient outlook. It revolutionized their sensibilities and their expectations.

One of the suspended students who refused to sign the demanded apology and therefore never returned to the school was Jurji Zeidan. A Greek Orthodox native of Beirut, Zeidan left Beirut for Cairo, where he founded the influential journal *al-Hilal* in 1892 and edited it until his death in 1924. Zeidan became one of the most influential Arab journalists and novelists of his generation. His expulsion from the SPC gave him reason to be bitter, but he was not. Looking back at the end of his life, Zeidan credited Daniel Bliss and the SPC with "training its students in freedom of thought, freedom of speech, and accustoming them to personal freedom, equality, and rights."[42] Their SPC education made them confident, questioning, idealistic, and assertive. It imbued them with moral courage and intellectual independence. This spirit found powerful expression in the student protests during the Lewis Affair that emboldened a new generation of Arabs to challenge authority and established institutions. Outlasting the crisis, this spirit of protest lived on, changing young Arabs who, in time, changed the Middle East.

Chapter 4:

HOWARD BLISS AND AMERICAN NATIONALISM

The Darwin controversy shook Daniel Bliss and his school, but both eventually recovered from the crisis. In barely one generation, the Syrian Protestant College (SPC) had established itself as *the* institution of higher education in the Middle East. It also had acquired considerable influence in the region through its growing ranks of alumni who had assumed influential positions in business, government, and the professions. This led the Ottoman governor of Lebanon, Rustum Pasha, to tell Daniel Bliss: "I do not know how much mathematics, nor how much of history, philosophy or science you teach at your Syrian Protestant College, but I do know this: that you make *men*, and that is the important thing. I wish I had one of your graduates to put into every office in my province. I would then have a far better government than I have now."[1]

At the same time the school's influence increased, its evangelical character diminished. The liberal "Social Gospel" movement that challenged Protestant conservatism in the late nineteenth century also transformed the SPC. The Social Gospel's emphasis on humanitarianism and the needs of this world struck at the traditional evangelical doctrine of original sin, which placed the origin of humanity's troubles and conflicts in human nature itself rather than in bad institutions. This philosophy deeply influenced young SPC faculty members, who eagerly embraced the new thinking. The Social Gospel became an integral part of missionary thought. The religious rituals required of students—compulsory prayers, Bible classes, chapel services, and Sunday school—began to fall away. Those who supported the shift (including, implicitly, Daniel Bliss) did so because they believed students would be exposed to Christian values anyway. And besides, they began to

69

ask, what good came to the region by denying the benefit of a higher education to its non-Christian young? This subtle but profound change in outlook became crystal-clear during registration one autumn. "What is your religion?" the registrar asked a student. "The religion of the SPC," answered the Muslim-raised student.[2]

This shift toward secular education led to a boom in enrollment. In its early days, SPC students came from Syria, Egypt, and other Arabic-speaking countries. During the 1890s, large numbers of Muslim and Jewish students from all across the Ottoman Empire began applying to the school. Members of the growing Lebanese diaspora[3]—particularly in North and South America—enrolled their children as well. Illiterate and semiliterate parents had no greater desire than to see their children educated. The SPC brought all of these ethnic and religious groups together in a way they never would have otherwise. On the athletic field, a team might include Druse, Jews, and one-half-dozen Christian denominations, all under a Muslim captain. It was remarkably cosmopolitan. Istanbul endorsed this nonsectarian experiment because reformers saw it as part of the modernizing trend they hoped would solve the empire's pressing social, economic, and political problems. The demonstrable and sustained effectiveness of the SPC persuaded Middle Easterners of the relevance and utility of American education as a cultural transplant.

Statistics told the story. In 1891, 196 students enrolled at the SPC. In 1901, 611 students entered the school—a more than 300 percent increase in just ten years.[4] This jump spurred the purchase of more land and the construction of more buildings for students and classrooms. Ada Dodge Hall went up in 1885, the Chapel in 1891, the Chemical Laboratory in 1893, the New Observatory in 1894, the Medical Annex in 1895, Morris Jessup Hall in 1897, Pliny Fisk Hall in 1900, and, in honor of his impending retirement, Daniel Bliss Hall that same year. Bliss Hall's imposing size and modern construction (it was the first building in Lebanon with reinforced concrete and indoor plumbing) was a fitting tribute to its namesake, who had dared to dream big dreams—and succeeded.

Much of the funding for these buildings came from Stuart Dodge, who had returned to New York after his father's death to run the SPC Board of Trustees, but continued to visit Beirut regularly until 1890. He remained intimately involved in the college's affairs thereafter until his own death in 1921. Whenever money was needed in Beirut to buy another parcel of land, to renovate a building, or to cover a deficit in the operating budget, word came from New York, "charge that to the General Fund"—which meant the account of Stuart Dodge.

Dodge's financial generosity coexisted with religious narrow-mindedness that bordered on blatant bigotry. He resented the SPC's increasing secularization and expressed alarm as the number of Muslim students continued to grow. "We have cause for a degree of anxiety in this increasing element," wrote Dodge in 1902. "They [Muslim students] cannot help importing into the midst of the Institution more or less of the atmosphere of corruption in which they mostly live. The whole problem of several existing sects in the College requires eternal vigilance to maintain our Protestant and Evangelical standard."[5]

Dodge personally interviewed every applicant to the SPC faculty at his office at 99 John Street in lower Manhattan. All of the interviews followed the same pattern: After making a few observations, Dodge asked questions that usually had nothing to do with the candidate's teaching experience. He wanted to know if the applicant understood the college's purpose and would be a good fit for the school. If successful, the candidate then received an invitation to Dodge's Manhattan home, which usually included a second interview masked as a casual chat with his very elderly, very polite, and very perceptive mother.

Daniel Bliss visited Dodge at his seven-hundred-acre weekend country estate, Bushy Hill,[6] in rural Connecticut during his final trip back to America in 1910. The two men reminisced proudly and fondly about all they had done together over the decades to build up the SPC and make it the best college in the Middle East. Their minds drifted back to memories of the early days in Beirut, as Dodge drove them along Connecticut's winding country lanes in his new-fangled automobile. "Here's a good stretch, let's have a little speed," said Bliss with a smile as Dodge pressed the accelerator. They enjoyed it, as they used to enjoy horse rides on the sandy beach below Rās Beirut with their Arab stallions in the early days.[7]

Daniel Bliss retired as college president in June 1902. The seventy-nine-year-old Bliss remained in remarkably good health for his age, but he sensed that after thirty-six years as head of the SPC, it was time to step aside—otherwise he would never know when to stop. By now, many of Bliss's former students had become influential leaders throughout the Middle East. Several of these men living in Egypt and Sudan commissioned a life-size marble statue of Bliss to show their affection for him and to commemorate his contributions to the school.[8] Bliss spoke at the presentation of the statue in the spring of 1904. He made the statue a metaphor for his work at the school: "As the workmen broke off from the block of marble all that surrounded this statue," said the white-haired Bliss, "so the College tries to break off, from young men, vanity and inventions and to leave standing the ideal man, made in the image of God." He proudly declared that his greatest achievement lay in "the character, standing and influence of our graduates and"—in a gracious allusion to the Lewis Affair—"others who were with us for a longer or shorter time. . . . We know that they are far more honored and respected by the people of their own countries than Western graduates are by their own people. . . . Who made the College?" Bliss asked in his memoirs. He answered self-effacingly by quoting Topsy in *Uncle Tom's Cabin*: "Nobody, I jist growed."[9]

After his retirement, Bliss stayed on, teaching a course on biblical ethics, which he saw as a chance to continue influencing students for good. He still walked the campus every day. And every Sunday morning he made his way from the top floor of Dorman House, where he and Abby now lived with their eldest granddaughter, to the chapel. His long, white mane made him look like a fierce Old Testament patriarch. He sat ramrod-straight in the front pew, right under the pulpit. He had trouble hearing now and he used an old-fashioned ear trumpet as an aid, though he disliked its obtrusiveness and sometimes just cupped his hand to his ear to hear the sermon. He joined in singing his favorite hymn, "Rock of Ages," in a strong and clear voice. After chapel, he presided over family supper that included his great-grandchildren and always ended with New England mince pie that Abby flavored with a few drops of "B" [brandy] "from the medicine bottle for Mr. Bliss."[10] It made for delicious mince pie. In the late afternoon, Daniel and Abby sat together on the lofty balcony, holding hands and taking in the familiar view of the city and the newer view of tramcars on the street below.[11] Neither felt a need to fill the silence. Sadly, Abby suffered a stroke and died on April 12, 1915. Daniel lived on for another year, until July 27, 1916. He was buried alongside her in the old American Mission Cemetery in Beirut, in the soil of the land they had come to love and to which they had devoted their lives.

* * *

Daniel and Abby left behind four children. Their oldest child and only daughter, Mary, wed an American missionary in Syria, Reverend Gerald Dale, and raised a family there alone after her husband died prematurely. She was an independent and accomplished woman. Daniel and Abby's first son, Fred, ran the SPC preparatory school and later joined the Palestine Exploration Fund. Their third son, Willie, stayed in America after college and practiced journalism in New York. They looked to their middle son, Howard, a minister like his father, to succeed Daniel as head of the school one day.

Daniel groomed Howard for this purpose from an early age. Howard spent his boyhood on the SPC campus, walking its pathways and absorbing its spirit. The school became fixed in his mind and memory. He loved the land and people of Lebanon, acquired an open-minded understanding of Islam, and learned to speak Arabic fluently. When the time came for college, he left for his father's primary alma mater, Amherst College, where he got to know his Sweetser relatives and fell in love with the natural beauty of New England. His father stayed in close touch with him during those years, writing about developments on campus. He wanted to keep the SPC connection alive for his son. During Howard's senior year, his father wrote, "It is not necessary for you to determine now where your future life shall be spent," then added: "It may be that your duty will appear not to be a missionary but an educator—Keep your eyes and ears open and your heart ready to respond to the call of duty."[12]

When Howard finished at Amherst in 1882, he got a taste of the American frontier by teaching school for one year in Topeka, Kansas, before returning east to study for the ministry at Union Theological Seminary in New York. There Howard met and came under the influence of Lyman

Abbott, the celebrated rector of Brooklyn's Plymouth Church and a leader of the Social Gospel movement. The head of a wealthy church that carried on extensive settlement-house work in the crowded immigrant slums of New York's Lower East Side, Abbott came into close contact with the problems of an urbanizing and industrializing America. Abbott believed man was not evil by inheritance; evil originated in poverty, ignorance, and fear. These ills—not sin—led to most social injustice. The way to mitigate injustice was for good men to take constructive action in society, bringing good out of evil, order out of chaos, and progress out of poverty.

Howard lived and studied in this climate of opinion and imbibed its beliefs. He became deeply wedded to the ideology of the Social Gospel. When he graduated from Union Theological Seminary in 1887 at the top of his class, he won a two-year fellowship at the University of Oxford in England and the Universities of Berlin and Göttingen in Germany. He returned to America in 1889 and that same year married Amy Blatchford of Chicago, whom he had met while in college. The newlyweds moved to the East Coast, where Howard worked for five years as associate pastor at Abbott's Plymouth Church, then settled into seven happy years as head of Union Congregational Church in Upper Montclair, New Jersey, from 1895 to 1902.

Howard enjoyed his life in Upper Montclair and hesitated to leave it for Beirut. But Daniel and Abby, Stuart Dodge, the SPC Board of Trustees—all urged him to take up his father's reins.[13] Howard seemed the logical choice: he was Daniel Bliss's son; he was a minister who had made his own mark; he would have the benefit of his father's presence and experience; and he felt a loyal son's duty to continue his father's work. Yet Howard felt ambivalence, self-doubt, and even sadness, as he confessed to his parents and siblings:

> I am frank in saying that I do not expect again to have the same kind of exultation that has often come to me during these past seven years. As yet there is no *leap* in my blood, no verve in my soul, not much enthusiasm even in my heart. Perhaps the best I can honestly say is this: I cannot undertake the responsibility of declining an appointment for which others seem to think I am far better fitted than I can bring myself one moment to believe myself to be. I am leaving a certainty for an uncertainty.[14]

His wife, Amy, encouraged him to trust the judgment of his family and friends. His younger brother, Willie, told him it was the right thing to do. His older brother, Fred—eager to be reunited with him in Beirut—congratulated Howard and tried to cheer him up. "Your decision will bring relief to many an anxious mind," he wrote. "It is a strong case of *vox populi*. As for us we are all overjoyed. After your nomination a faculty member said to papa, 'The College is now safe for the next forty years.' 'What about Dan?' said papa!"[15]

In the end, Howard agreed to return to Beirut. He kept his feelings about this decision to himself for many years, until he wrote to a young man struggling with a similar choice. "You would find a lot of hard work, and the time might come when you would regret having come out," Bliss wrote in what amounted to a self-confession, "but on the whole you would, I believe, 'find yourself' here. Not that you need to come here to 'find yourself' so long as you have the desire to be a lifter and not a leaner in the world, for God will show you in the course of time where you can do that best."[16]

* * *

Handsome in looks and modern in dress, with deep-set eyes and a bushy, Edwardian mustache, forty-two-year-old Howard Bliss seemed, to Lyman Abbott, "neither a physical nor an intellectual athlete,"[17] but he had an open mind and communicated in a quietly forceful way that commanded respect. He epitomized a new breed of American missionary less stern in appearance and more tolerant in outlook. "Christ gives us certain definite values for the unknown situations in our life; Mohammed gives us others; Buddha others; Confucius others. Take those values and substitute them in the equation of your life and those values will be true in proportion as you find that peace enters into your heart, which means that the equation is satisfied and the balance made clear," he wrote.[18]

Howard Bliss's generation of missionaries sought to uplift the downtrodden rather than convert the heathen. This shift reflected the energetic and compelling spirit of Progressivism popular in America at the time. Progressivism combined a strong streak of utopian optimism and a positive view of change with an abiding belief that the world could be made a much better place. It sought to improve society—not save souls—by mitigating the fundamental evils of poverty, ignorance, and disease. Progressives believed the laws of society could be deduced and understood. Having understood these laws, they could act to shape and build the future. The techniques, powers, and insights gained through the study of society gave them both the opportunity and the duty to solve the problems of the human condition. Prominent Progressives like Jane Addams, John Dewey, and Woodrow Wilson saw education as one of the most effective ways of doing so.

Howard Bliss's generation also sought to exercise the growing weight of American power in world affairs. This reflected an optimism rooted in American culture and strengthened by recent economic successes. Europe still reigned as the great power at the dawn of the twentieth century, but the United States was rapidly closing the gap. The United States had surpassed Europe in manufacturing output and energy consumption, and it was rapidly gaining on Europe in volume of foreign trade. The surging American population exceeded every European nation's except Russia, while its steel production topped that of Britain and Germany combined. The United States was becoming a great power in its own right.

Howard Bliss's generation prided itself on the superiority of American civilization and felt a strong sense of Manifest Destiny and self-confidence. It did not see the United States as just another country (that merely happened to be bigger and richer than most). They believed the torch of Western civilization had made its way from classical Greece and Rome to imperial Britain and now, in 1900, to America. The United States exercised leadership for the world. Its moral values must not be selfishly hoarded; they must be shared. America had an obligation to spread the principles that a higher power had vouchsafed to it. The statesman, the businessman, and the missionary worked together overseas for the advancement of the United States *and* for the betterment of the world. Alfred Thayer Mahan, the naval officer and strategic theorist who popularized the term "Middle East," spoke for this generation. Mahan praised the work of American missionaries because he believed change came "not by fetters and bonds imposed from without, but by regeneration promoted from within."[19] This conviction drove Mahan and other Americans to champion the export of their ideology and way of life to those they considered less fortunate.

In Americans' minds, "less fortunate" included inhabitants of the Middle East. Most Americans in 1900 had little knowledge and made simplistic assumptions about what seemed a remote and turbulent part of the world. Their eyes had traditionally been on Europe and the Western Hemisphere—not the Middle East. On maps, lands to the east of Europe were labeled "the Orient," all of it strange and exotic. Washington occasionally dispatched warships to the eastern Mediterranean to protect American citizens abroad. But US policy remained one of studied indifference toward the "Eastern Question"; the great powers of Europe—not the United States—sparred in the Middle East. The popular image of Arabs in the American mind came from a few scattered sources: Bible stories told in Sunday school, tales in *The Arabian Nights*, sketches of ancient Mesopotamia and Egypt in schoolbooks. Americans caricatured Arabs as desert nomads who lived in an exotic and far-away world of sand dunes, camels, and harems, stuck in a backward existence perpetuated by the Ottoman Turks. American perceptions of the Middle East combined warped stereotypes and disparaging epithets with simplistic and romanticized images. This unfortunate combination would dominate, and dog, American attitudes toward the Middle East for decades to come.

Few Arabs traveled to the United States or read books about it. As a result, most Arabs acquired their knowledge of America from missionaries in their midst or from the growing number of Middle Easterners—particularly Armenians and Lebanese—who had immigrated to the United States. Most of these immigrants depicted America in glowing terms to their wide-eyed relatives and friends back home. One described America as a bustling "land of cities and civilization" defined by its people "from all tribes and races."[20] Another wrote that in America,

> you will feel as though you have arrived in a country whose inhabitants are giants among men. When you enter the city and walk among the people, you will be struck by how eager Americans are to go to their work, how quick their pace is, and how active and energetic they are. You will then realize that you are not in a country like others, and you are not among a people like others, but rather among a people superior in their qualities,

distinguished in their vitality, and unique in their abundance of energy. The matchless skyscrapers, the quick pace of life, the ability to focus on one's work, are none other than manifestations of the dynamism of a nation that is full of youth and pulsating with tremendous energy.[21]

As a result, most Arabs had a benevolent vision of the United States. It seemed a distant and wonderful land of opportunity. Arabs felt drawn to "gold-swept shores of distant lands, to the generous cities and bounteous fields of the West, to the Paradise of the World—to America."[22] Arab nationalists saw America as a former colony that had broken free and established a government based on the principle of self-determination. An Egyptian journalist introduced George Washington to his readership as "one of the geniuses of the eighteenth century and one of the greatest men of freedom."[23] Life, liberty, and the pursuit of happiness enchanted Arabs who yearned to become their own masters.

Ottoman officials in Istanbul felt more ambivalent about America. They admired the United States' rising prosperity and power and saw America as a relatively disinterested nation compared to rapacious European empires. They also looked to it for help in economic and technological development. But Ottoman officials remained wary of American missionaries for their work in a polyglot empire that had begun to erode along the edges.

Howard Bliss and other Americans in the Middle East believed in the greatness of their own culture, distinguished by economic strength and an enduring Protestant religion and form of government. Bliss saw it as his duty, and destiny, to bridge the gap between America and the Arab world. He wanted Americans to understand the Middle East and to help reform the long-standing institutions and customs that governed its society. Stability and prosperity were impossible without justice and economic development. Real change must come. The moment had arrived for the Ottoman Empire to reform itself—or perish. The SPC would play a great role in this drama by reshaping the Middle East through the education of native leaders who would spearhead political, economic, social, and cultural reform in the Arab world. Daniel Bliss's generation had sought to convert individual Arabs. Howard Bliss's generation sought to transform the entire Arab world.

Another American who shared these beliefs was Howard Bliss's longtime friend Theodore Roosevelt, who enthusiastically supported the college. The two had first met as teenagers when the Roosevelt family toured the Middle East in the 1870s. The Roosevelts were New York Brahmins who socialized with the Dodges and supported humanitarian philanthropy, including missionary work. Theodore Roosevelt's father, known as Thee, heavily influenced his son. He taught TR that social privilege must be balanced by social service, and Thee lived the creed. He devoted considerable time to work with the poor, organizing clubs for street boys in slum neighborhoods. Every Sunday he taught a class at Madison Square Presbyterian Church. He was also an active father who took his family on extended trips overseas.[24] In November 1872, the Roosevelts visited Egypt, Syria, and Palestine. The holy places that TR saw—not only Christian sites, but also those of great significance to Judaism and Islam—stirred his young imagination. In Beirut, his father, Thee, spoke to the mission Sunday school about his work among the poor of New York, while the Roosevelt and Bliss boys (TR, Howard, and Fred) rode a donkey together across the cactus-covered hills of Rās Beirut. They formed a lasting friendship yet scarcely imagined what the future held in store for them.

TR inherited the *noblesse oblige* that led his father to organize Bible classes in the slums and transformed it, as US president from 1901 to 1909, into the conviction that America should be an active force for good throughout the world. This conviction included the Middle East, where the Sunday school teacher's son took a special interest in the work of missionaries. In November 1905, while on a visit to the States, Howard called on his friend from Beirut donkey-riding days who now occupied the White House. It was a crisp autumn day in Washington, and TR—fresh from his Nobel Peace Prize–winning mediation of the Russo-Japanese War at the Portsmouth Conference—felt as buoyantly confident as the American people themselves. Howard described their meeting in a letter to Amy:

> He [TR] was full of interesting questions and keen interest; showed a remarkable knowledge of the racial, linguistic and religious and political phases of the affairs of the nearer East. I spoke of the Philippines[25] and the problems of dealing with slowly developing peoples. I told him to his evident pleasure of his popularity in Syria. We spoke of many things: the

Maronites; the unifying influences of College athletics; my two books as my missionary equipment; and Rudyard Kipling's Poem of the man who tried to hustle the East.[26] It was very delightful.[27]

Roosevelt invited Bliss back to the White House the next day for lunch. Howard described the occasion in another letter to Amy:

> Promptly at one o'clock I presented myself at the main entrance of the White House. The Porter or Butler inspected our cards which evidently corresponded with the list of guests which he had on a slip of paper in his hand and we were given a cordial welcome. We were ushered from the magnificent Hallway into a small room where coats, hats and gloves were left and hair was brushed and were then taken into a sort of Reception Room where there were a number of people. The man-in-waiting (he hardly looked like a butler) announced our names to a man who undertook to introduce us to those who were present. Sometime later Secretary [of War William Howard] Taft[28] came in looking brown and hearty. Presently the President came in looking so fresh, alert, hearty, clean and vital. He greeted us all most heartily with a personal and cordial word for each one. He was very charming. Soon after we had been introduced lunch was announced and we went into the large and really superb Dining Room[29]— very large, beautifully paneled and decorated with the triumphs of the chase. The President indicated where we were to sit about the large square table. We had soup in cups, broiled oysters, chops and potato, salad, and dessert and fruit. Mrs. Roosevelt poured the tea. Some of the conversation at table was general. I talked more or less about the College and the President seemed most interested as I spoke of Ramadan and the Muslims. He spoke most warmly of his interest in yesterday's conversation and said that he simply *had* to invite us to lunch! It was all very charming. He is a *remarkable* man![30]

* * *

Like Theodore Roosevelt, Howard Bliss saw America—and, by extension, the SPC—as a force for good in the Middle East. He believed deeply in the college's purpose and mission. He emulated his father's style, involving himself in student life, handling disciplinary issues with forbearance, and stressing the practical dimension of education. But when another crisis erupted on campus in 1909 when Muslim and Jewish students refused to attend chapel and Bible classes, he did not clamp down as his father had during the Darwin controversy of 1882. He adopted a conciliatory approach instead, stressing the requirement of religious education for all students but not insisting that non-Christians attend worship. "The first task is the task of putting ourselves in the place of our non-Christian students, our Moslems, our Tartars, our Jews, our Druses, our Behais," he said.[31] Bliss modernized the curriculum, including introducing electives and graduate study leading to a master's degree. The college became a university. Within a few years, locals began calling it the American University of Beirut—the name it goes by to this day.

The American University of Beirut (AUB) had become an integral part of the life of Lebanon and the entire Arab world. AUB students, who numbered nearly one thousand by 1910, came from all classes and countries throughout the region. The campus atmosphere created by faculty and students reflected a diversity of backgrounds and cultures at the same time that it encouraged a mixing of viewpoints. Young people from very different traditions studied together, made coffee and tea together, and played soccer and ran track together. In the process, they got to know one another in a way and to a degree that they never had before. In a very real sense, AUB became a melting pot for the Middle East. All of this reflected how radically the SPC had changed and grown in the half-century since the school's creation in 1866. However, these progressive innovations barely hinted at the momentous changes in store for AUB and the Middle East during the First World War.

Chapter 5:

AMERICA CONFRONTS GREAT POWER POLITICS IN THE MIDDLE EAST

The first decade of the twentieth century represented the calm before the storm in the Middle East. The region prospered, and nowhere did this prosperity stand out more than in Beirut. By 1900, Beirut had become a major commercial and cultural center of the Ottoman Empire. It had a modern, bustling harbor; a thriving community of merchants, intellectuals, and professionals; and top-notch schools that attracted students from afar. The American University of Beirut (AUB) had become the most important university in the Ottoman Empire. People across Lebanon and throughout the Middle East flocked to Beirut for the opportunity it afforded them to build a better life.

The Middle East seemed content, but, beneath the surface, its people grew restless. The Ottoman Empire, which had been losing ground to Europe since the eighteenth century, had entered a downward spiral. Central authority from Istanbul had become more myth than reality; beyond urban areas, Ottoman administration had practically vanished. Most of the Balkans and all of North Africa had been lost to European powers, which prowled at the periphery of Ottoman domains. These once vast domains had shrunk in Europe to a small area around Istanbul, and in Asia to Anatolia, the Levant, Mesopotamia, and western Arabia. Political and military leaders in Istanbul known as Young Turks tried to bring the decaying empire into the twentieth century through a program of sweeping reforms (*tanzimat*) before the modern world overwhelmed it, but little progress had been made.

Arabs throughout the empire had begun to forge a sense of separate identity. Arabism originated in the nationalism of the West and spread throughout the Middle East from places like AUB. "I know why the Turks are hated in this country," the Ottoman governor of Syria complained. "The Syrian Protestant College breeds contempt for the Turk and the books used in the institution breathe this spirit."[1] Nationalism took root slowly at first among Arabs, a conservative people who traditionally identified themselves as Muslims. But Arabs increasingly saw themselves in a new light. They had been a great people with a splendid civilization that had stretched from Baghdad to Cordoba. In 1517, they had fallen under the domination of the Ottomans. Arabs longed to reassert themselves and to restore their former glory. Their demands—first for reform, then for autonomy—met stiff Ottoman resistance. Mutual suspicion between Arabs and Turks exacerbated tensions. Arab nationalism had become a smoldering fire as World War I approached.[2]

At the same time, the drive for a Jewish homeland in the ancient land of Israel gathered momentum under the banner of Zionism, a Jewish movement founded by Austrian Theodore Herzl in the late nineteenth century. Jews had lived in exile since the Romans had driven them from Judaea in the second century CE. They had suffered centuries of persecutions, massacres, and expulsions, mostly in Europe, while holding fast to their religious customs and sense of special destiny. Zionists came to believe anti-Semitism throughout the world could only be solved by establishing a homeland for Jews in Palestine. Only there, and then, would Jews be able to forge a society free from tyranny based on the religion and culture of Judaism. Jews began immigrating to Palestine, where they settled in towns like Jerusalem and Jaffa (today called Tel Aviv), and in the countryside, where they established communal (*kibbutz*) and cooperative (*moshav*) farms.

By 1914, an unsettled atmosphere gripped the Middle East. This made the region a prime target for European powers that viewed it as a pivotal arena in their geopolitical rivalry known as the Great Game. Americans unpracticed at the Great Game (at least in the Middle East) barely perceived the force of the gathering storm. Elderly Daniel Bliss remarked confidently just before the war, "I believe that the world is getting better every day."[3] But the war that was about to explode would draw his son Howard Bliss more deeply into the whirlpool of Middle East politics than he or his father could ever have imagined.

* * *

News of the war's outbreak in August 1914 shocked and unsettled Western residents of Beirut. "The clouds seem to be gathering around in this land and we do not know what may happen next," an American residing in the city wrote shortly after the war began. "Day by day, the tension increases in Beirut."[4] They did not know what to expect. Ottoman officials looked suspiciously on all Western institutions, including the AUB. To Ottoman eyes, AUB was a school supported by Western money, controlled by Western authorities, and which promoted Western interests. After Turkey entered the war on Germany's side in November 1914, the Ottoman governor imposed martial law, closing the harbor, quartering troops in private homes, and confiscating provisions. Turkish soldiers dug trenches along the sea road, placed guns on the only landing beach near the city, and covered the hills above Beirut with barbed-wire entanglements and artillery batteries. Germany established a submarine port in the harbor.

Britain responded by taking direct control of Egypt and by joining France in blockading the Lebanese coast. British and French expatriates in Beirut sought refuge at AUB because the United States remained neutral in the conflict. America did so because it still had only limited interests in the Middle East. Europe, Latin America, and the Far East all drew more attention from the United States. America had traditionally avoided involvement in the "Eastern Question," steering clear of the rivalries that made the Middle East a cockpit of conflict among European empires. The United States maintained its neutrality until eventually entering the war on Britain and France's side in April 1917. But it never declared war against Germany's Ottoman ally.

The decision to abstain from declaring war on the Ottoman government resulted, in large part, from the lobbying efforts of industrialist Cleveland Dodge, nephew of Stuart Dodge and father of Bayard Dodge (Howard Bliss's son-in-law and successor as AUB president), whom President Woodrow Wilson counted among his closest friends since their days as college roommates at Princeton University. After Wilson became president, Cleveland Dodge occasionally stayed at the White House, and Wilson often visited Dodge's Hudson River estate, Riverdale, a few miles north of Manhattan. They had many discussions about the Middle East. Dodge persuaded Wilson not to declare war on the Ottoman Empire in order to safeguard American schools in the region. Wilson, the son and grandson of Presbyterian ministers, saw these schools as exemplars of the values he cherished. He also knew the United States could not protect the schools, and that thousands of people throughout the region now depended on American relief for food and medical care—relief that would be jeopardized if the United States went to war with the Ottoman Empire.[5]

Howard Bliss resolved to keep AUB open and functioning no matter what. He held fast to this goal despite many pressures and risks. Mobilization depleted student ranks. Turkish officials censored textbooks and conscripted medical students into the Ottoman army. The university had to find a way to feed thousands of students, faculty, staff, and hospital patients as the Allied naval blockade dwindled food and medical supplies. Clothing materials became so limited that women used curtains to make dresses. Conditions only worsened as the Allied blockade tightened. "Day by day the consequences of the war became more visible, and people were overcome by fear," wrote an Iranian student attending AUB during the war.[6]

Starvation constantly loomed around the corner. Food became scarce and unbelievably expensive. Hundreds of thousands of undernourished Lebanese succumbed to typhus in winter and malaria in summer. Half-naked people, hopeless and hungry, roamed the streets of Beirut, begging for scraps of food and digging through garbage. An AUB faculty member who witnessed the spreading misery lamented to his diary, "Did you ever see a starving person? I hope you never may. No matter how emaciated a person may be from disease, he never looks exactly like the person suffering from pangs of hunger. It is indefinable but when you have once seen it, you can never mistake it, nor ever forget it."[7]

Americans in Beirut faced confinement to the campus and the constant threat of sudden deportation. (Hundreds of British expatriates had been herded into boxcars and imprisoned in unknown villages.) Lebanon became one of the most isolated regions of the world during the war. Cut off from Western news sources—these were the days before radio, television, or the Internet—they had no idea what was happening in America or on Europe's battlefields, no sense of what the future might bring. Feeling themselves alone, they lived in a state of anxious suspense. "The clouds hang low," Howard Bliss wrote. "The distress and cruelty and inhumanity and stupidity and suffering involved weigh heavily upon us."[8]

During these years of crisis, Howard Bliss found himself. Out of adversity he seemed to draw greater energy and determination. He overcame his self-doubt and learned to project a steady confidence that bolstered others' fragile morale. He dealt so tactfully with Ottoman officials that they came to trust and even support him, eventually selling him army supplies at cost. He organized soup kitchens for starving mountain villagers and dispatched teams of AUB medical students to southern Palestine to treat wounded combatants of all sides brought in from the front on camels. His religious Progressivism won the confidence of Beirut's powerful Mufti, despite the *jihad* (holy war) decreed by Istanbul against all Allied Christians.[9] By doing all of these things and more, Howard saved AUB from closing—a fate from which it might never have recovered. But guiding AUB through the war also took its toll. The constant pressure and responsibility strained him physically. Before the war, Howard Bliss had looked young and vigorous. By war's end, he had aged far beyond his years and neared the point of exhaustion. And the conundrum of how to deal with the powers that be in Beirut during wartime would plague the college from then on.

* * *

Wars are potent crucibles. The Great War changed Beirut as well as many other things.[10] It irrevocably transformed the Middle East. Britain and France seized the opportunity created by the war (and the fall of the Ottoman Empire hastened by it) to realize their ambitions in the region. But British and French leaders knew little, and cared less, about the wishes of the people who lived there. Their arrogance reflected a deep-seated attitude of superiority toward non-Europeans. Europeans saw themselves as all-important, all-knowing, all-powerful—in other words, naturally entitled to run the world. This ideology affected how they perceived Middle Easterners and made decisions relating to them. Europeans based decisions more on ill-informed stereotypes than on in-depth knowledge of political, social, and cultural institutions. They treated Middle Easterners' aspirations with little sensitivity, sympathy, or concern. They worried, instead, about how the Middle East fit into the Great Game. How would the region's boundaries be drawn after the fall of the Ottomans—and by whom? Such an outlook is typical of empires. But Europeans' willful neglect of local aspirations would have profound consequences in years to come.

During the winter of 1915–1916, Britain and France negotiated the Middle East's future between themselves, without consulting or even informing the region's inhabitants. They chose as interlocutors British parliamentarian Mark Sykes and former French consul in Beirut François Georges Picot. Sykes, a young Conservative Party MP (Member of Parliament) and aristocratic dilettante of Ottoman affairs, had traveled widely from Cairo to Baghdad and had close ties to Lord Kitchener of the War Office. He epitomized the arrogance of Britain's ruling class: imperious, patronizing, and smug. While he was a Cambridge undergraduate, Sykes had described Arabs as "insolent yet despicable," "vicious as far as their feeble bodies will admit," and "rapacious, greedy . . . animals."[11] During the war, he wrote to a friend:

Turkey must cease to be. Smyrna shall be Greek. Adalia Italian, Southern Taurus and North Syria French, Filistin [Palestine] British, Mesopotamia British and everything else Russian—including Constantinople . . . and I shall sing a *Te Deum* in St. Sophia and a *Nunc Dimittis* in the Mosque of Omar. We will sing it in Welsh, Polish, Keltic, and Armenian in honour of all the gallant little nations. . . .

To the Censor

This is a brilliant letter from one genius to another. Men of base clay cannot be expected to understand. Pray pass on without fear.

Mark Sykes, Lt. Col. FRGS, MP, CC, JP.[12]

Picot shared Sykes's convictions, prejudices, and ignorance. Spokesman for the powerful colonial lobby in the French Foreign Office and the Chamber of Deputies, Picot favored French control of Syria and Lebanon—whatever might be the wishes of their inhabitants. Proudly Gallic, politically conservative, and devoutly Catholic, Picot believed Syria and Lebanon comprised the "France of the Near East," dating back one thousand years to the establishment of Latin Crusader kingdoms. Intoxicated with the glory of imperial France, Picot and the government in Paris had convinced themselves that Syria and Lebanon's inhabitants overwhelmingly desired to be ruled by France. France intended to assert direct rule over coastal Lebanon and to control the rest of Syria through local puppets, imposing French language and culture on native Arab society in the name of its "civilizing mission."

Talks between Sykes and Picot resulted in May 1916 in a notorious secret agreement spelling out the future division of Ottoman spoils in the Middle East. It covertly recognized French predominance in Lebanon and Syria and British predominance in Egypt, Palestine, Transjordan, and Mesopotamia. London and Paris could establish any government they wished in their respective spheres of influence. They did not think to share the agreement with the people of the Middle East, whose fate it directly affected.

Britain and France also did not inform the United States of the agreement until May 1917—one month *after* Washington entered the war on their side, and even then only when pressed for details by President Wilson and his national security adviser, Edward House. House expressed disapproval: "It is all bad and I told [Foreign Secretary] Balfour so. They are making it a breeding place for future war."[13] Wilson likewise suspected British and French motives in the Middle East and refused to commit the United States to the terms of the secret agreement.[14] In his famous Fourteen Points address of February 11, 1918, in which he outlined his vision for the postwar world, Wilson declared: "The Turkish portions of the present Ottoman Empire should be assured a secure sovereignty, but the other nationalities which are now under Turkish rule should be assured an undoubted security of life and an absolutely unmolested opportunity of autonomous development." "Every territorial settlement," he added, "must be made in the interest and for the benefit of the populations concerned."[15] A postwar showdown loomed among the three Allies on this issue.

Before excluding Arabs and Jews from secret talks determining the Middle East's future, Britain had cultivated them as military allies against the Ottomans while making expedient, but conflicting, promises to each. Turkey's entrance into the war had made the Arabs an important element in British strategy and policy. Britain recognized the advantage of detaching the Arabs from the Turks and encouraging Arab nationalism. It would relieve pressure on the Suez Canal, remove the danger of Germany establishing a submarine base in the Red Sea, weaken Turkey's position in Mesopotamia and Palestine, and save British lives.

At the time, British prospects in the Middle East looked dark. The Gallipoli expedition to force the Dardanelles Straits, capture Istanbul, and force Turkey's surrender had been a tragic fiasco, and London sought a way to turn the tide of the war. From July 1915 through January 1916, Britain's high commissioner in Egypt, Arthur Henry McMahon, secretly corresponded with Sharif Hussein Ibn 'Ali, a descendant of the Prophet Mohammed and guardian of Islam's Holy Places in western Arabia (known as the Hejaz), encouraging Hussein to launch an Arab revolt against Ottoman rule. In return, Britain promised to support the creation of a sovereign Arab state in the Middle East under the Sharif. McMahon and Hussein disagreed over the status of Lebanon and coastal Syria after the Ottomans. (The Sykes-Picot Agreement bound Britain to support France there.) But McMahon and Hussein needed each other's support, so they agreed to collaborate without settling their differences on this issue. It would come back haunt both sides.[16]

At the same time, Britain approached Zionists, seeking the support of Jews in Palestine against the Turks. Many (though not all) members of Britain's governing class believed a Jewish homeland should be established in Palestine under British auspices. This would coincide with biblical prophecy and bolster the Allied effort by appealing to Jewish communities in America and Russia. It offered a new lease on Britain's empire weakened by the war's destruction in Europe. Foreign Secretary Arthur Balfour issued a letter to Baron Edmund Rothschild, a prominent British Zionist and wartime financier, on November 2, 1917. The Balfour Declaration pledged Britain's support for a Jewish homeland in Palestine, provided this did not "prejudice the civil and religious rights of existing non-Jewish communities in Palestine." Balfour's letter to Rothschild revealed nothing about the Sykes-Picot Agreement or the McMahon-Hussein Correspondence. But the public announcement of the letter one week later gave the Balfour Declaration a life and a momentum of its own.

A month before ninety-two-year-old Daniel Bliss died, in June 1916, the Arab Revolt began. Aided by British naval control of the Red Sea, as well as British arms and money channeled through liaison officer T. E. Lawrence (later known as "Lawrence of Arabia"), Hussein's army of Hejazis, Bedouins, and Iraqis[17] and led by his third son, Faisal, captured one Turkish stronghold after another from Mecca to Aqaba. Hussein proclaimed himself King of the Hejaz in November 1916. His army reached Palestine the following summer, where it linked up with British general Edmund Allenby's Egyptian Expeditionary Force to advance on Jerusalem. Allenby entered the holy city on December 9, 1917. Allenby's and Hussein's armies defeated the remaining Ottoman forces at the Battle of Megiddo on September 18, 1918.

Two weeks later, on October 1, Faisal entered Damascus and proclaimed the establishment of an Arab kingdom in his father's name. Beirut soon came under the control of Hussein's army. Celebratory bonfires burned on the mountainsides of the Lebanon range. Ordinary people rejoiced and danced. On October 8, Beirut newspapers published Faisal's proclamation.[18] When Allenby learned of Faisal's proclamation, he rushed a British force from Haifa to Beirut to dam the Arab torrent and implement the Sykes-Picot Agreement. As a result, Arab rule in Beirut lasted barely one week. The black, white, green, and red chevron Arab flag came down from Beirut's Government House, replaced by the Union Jack. British and French officials assumed all the important administrative posts and distributed food throughout the city, ending the famine their blockade had created. Allenby gave Faisal "an official assurance" that Britain's occupation of Beirut was "purely provisional" and would not prejudice a final settlement at a postwar peace conference. "I reminded Faisal," Allenby reported to London, "that the Allies were in honour bound to endeavour to reach a settlement in accordance with the wishes of the peoples concerned, and urged him to place his trust wholeheartedly in their good faith."[19]

Turkey surrendered on October 31. The once vast, centuries-old Ottoman Empire was exhausted. When the Great War finally ended two weeks later, on November 11, Britain controlled Palestine, Transjordan, and Mesopotamia; Hussein's Arab army controlled the Hejaz and inland Syria; France and Britain jointly controlled coastal Syria and Lebanon. The end of the Great War left Americans in Beirut, like Howard Bliss, and policy-makers in Washington, like Woodrow Wilson, confronting a host of prob-lems. Among the thorniest of these concerned the postwar status of Lebanon and how America might help shape it.

* * *

Many of the most intractable and explosive issues in today's Middle East have roots in decisions made at the Paris Peace Conference after the end of the Great War. The peacemakers who met in Paris between January and June 1919 in an atmosphere of rivalry, maneuvering, and ambition failed to live up to their promises and professed ideals. The triumph of secret treaties over self-determination planted the seeds for problems that haunt the Middle East to this day. "Hypocrisy," wrote Harold Nicolson, a member of the British delegation at the conference looking back some years later, "was the predominant and unescapable result. . . . The falsity of our position led us into being false."[20] It was a cynical tragedy that undercut incipient Arab-Jewish understanding and bred abiding bitterness, suspicion, and resent-ment among people of the Middle East toward the West.

Woodrow Wilson arrived in Paris on December 12, 1918, the first American president to journey to Europe while in office. He came as head of the strongest country in the Allied coalition, bolstered by the lavish popu-larity of his person and principles. Yet Wilson represented only one power in a coalition of three powers, and America—unlike Britain and France—had no occupation troops on the ground in the Middle East. Wilson recognized these limitations and the thicket of power politics he faced. But he saw him-self as a modern-day prophet and savior of politically voiceless people. Wilson seemed, in many respects, like a preacher in politician's clothing. At once idealistic and naïve, sensitive and sanctimonious, he intended to per-suade his fellow peacemakers, French premier Georges Clemenceau and British prime minister David Lloyd George, to apply the principle of self-determination to the Middle East. Wilson did not believe populations should be "bartered about from sovereignty to sovereignty as if they were chattels or pawns in a game." He understood people's desire for freedom and believed in consent of the governed.

The leaders of Britain and France saw things very differently. If Wilson epitomized idealism, Lloyd George and Clemenceau epitomized imperialism and intrigue. They intended to manage their lofty American colleague and to curb what they considered his decidedly inconvenient vision for the Middle East. Unbeknownst to Wilson, Lloyd George and Clemenceau met in London in December 1918—just before Wilson arrived in Europe—and reconfirmed their two countries' division of Ottoman territories laid out in the Sykes-Picot Agreement. They promised to support one another against the Americans on this issue at the Paris Peace Conference.[21]

Only the month before, Britain and France had published a declaration to the people of the Middle East in the *Palestine News*, the official journal of the Egyptian Expeditionary Force, which conveyed a very different promise:

> The aim which France and Britain have in view of waging in the East the war let loose on the world by German ambition, is to ensure the complete and final emancipation of all those peoples so long oppressed by the Turks, and to establish national governments and administrations which shall derive their authority from the initiative and free will of the peoples themselves.
>
> To realize this, France and Great Britain are in agreement to encourage and assist the establishment of native governments in Syria and Mesopotamia, now liberated by the Allies, as also in those territories for whose liberation they are striving and to recognize those governments immediately after they are effectively established.
>
> Far from wishing to impose on the peoples of these regions this or that institution, they have no other care than to assure, by their support and practical aid, the normal workings of such governments and administrations as the peoples shall themselves have adopted.[22]

Wilson, meanwhile, made his own preparations for the upcoming talks. He had opinions about the Middle East but little knowledge; he needed to understand how his principles could be applied in the thicket of Middle

Eastern politics. At Cleveland Dodge's suggestion, Wilson wrote Howard Bliss from the American headquarters at the Hotel Crillon, inviting Bliss to advise him and the American delegation in Paris. Dodge told the president about Bliss's deep experience and knowledge of the region as well as his great esteem and respect in the eyes of Arabs. "I worship him," Faisal said of Bliss to a member of the American delegation, "as all Arabs do because he is a sage and a prophet. It was he who foretold the future of our race, and it was he who by educating our boys made that future possible. In my army there were some who had been educated by the French fathers and a few by the English doctors, but those who had studied at the American college in Beirut were the most reliable and efficient."[23] To a newspaperman in Paris, Faisal said:

> Dr. Daniel Bliss, the founder of the College at Beirut, was the grandfather of Syria; and his son Howard Bliss, the present President, is the father of Syria. Without the education that this college has given, the struggle for freedom would never have been won. The Arabs owe everything to these men.[24]

Howard Bliss received Wilson's invitation on January 8, 1919. Less than twenty-four hours later, he was on his way to Paris. Bliss arrived in the French capital on January 22, where he rendezvoused with his younger brother Will, a journalist covering the peace conference for a Chicago newspaper, at a borrowed apartment on the *Rue de la Bienfaisance*. Paris was very cold and dreary that winter. Falling snow froze and remained for days on the streets. The great influenza pandemic stalked the French capital. Howard wrote his wife, Amy:

> Paris is certainly not a gay place. Everyone is distracted—confused and full of a mixture of hopes and fears. I lead a most quiet life on the exterior—have seen no sights—but pass my time trying to see people—writing notes—trying to get things done—trying to see how problems can be disentangled.[25]

The biggest problem, in Bliss's mind, concerned Syria's future. "Having just come from Syria," he wrote Wilson at the Hotel Crillon, "I beg to state to you how earnestly and even passionately the people of Syria are depending upon your twelfth point and upon the Anglo-French Declaration of

November 1918." He loaded Wilson with ammunition. Syrians wanted their independence and looked to America to help them win it. He cautioned Wilson against trusting France, warning that it "would exploit [Syria] for her own material and political advantage." Syria should not be handed over before her people's wishes had been considered. Wilson replied by saying he wanted Bliss to appear before the conference.[26]

*   *   *

Amid a deluge of other pressing international issues, the peacemakers took up the Middle East on January 30. They met in the Clock Room of the Quai d'Orsay, the French Foreign Ministry Building overlooking the River Seine. At the top of a massive branching staircase, the long Clock Room was the largest of a series of reception rooms and offices on the second floor. It had huge windows framed by green silk curtains that reached up to a decorated ceiling illuminated by elaborate chandeliers. Elegant red and gold seventeenth-century tapestries covered wood-paneled walls. Exquisite Aubusson carpets covered most of the parquet floor. The peacemakers stayed warm during their deliberations in the big and drafty room with massive log fireplaces kept constantly going.

Wilson told his two colleagues seated with him on fat, gilt chairs at the heavy, ebony conference table that self-determination represented the best way forward. Clemenceau and Lloyd George listened respectfully, but beneath the tight smiles they smoldered at what they considered Wilson's presumptuous sermonizing. "The Almighty gave us Ten Commandments," the French leader commented acidly in private, "but Wilson has given us Fourteen." He believed Wilson thought himself "Jesus Christ come upon the earth to reform men."[27] Wilson's call for self-determination rankled Clemenceau and Lloyd George. The United States had not been at war with Ottoman Turkey. It had not suffered casualties in the Middle East. Their nations—unlike the United States—had *real* interests at stake in the region. They did not intend to sacrifice those interests to what they dismissed as pious American meddling. They intended to dispose of the former Ottoman territories to suit themselves.

But first, they would politely hear out the Arabs. Faisal traveled to Europe from Beirut aboard a British warship. Before he arrived, he submitted a memorandum to the peacemakers in which he affirmed Arab nationalist aspirations, noted the sacrifices Arabs had made at the Allies' request in their revolt against the Turks, cited Wilson's principle of self-determination, and expressed his naïve belief that "the Powers will attach more importance to the bodies and souls of the Arabic-speaking peoples than to their own material interests."[28]

Faisal presented his case in person before the peacemakers on February 12. Lawrence was his interpreter. Wearing a long-flowing white robe and gold Bedouin headdress with a scimitar and a revolver on either hip, Faisal cut a dramatic figure. He came not as a suppliant but to demand political rights for his people. Faisal told the peacemakers that Arabs wanted freedom. He recognized his people needed help from outside, but not at the price of their independence. He wanted a unified Arab state with religious liberty for all sects and faiths.

He excluded Palestine from his claims. Seeking to improve his position by reaching an understanding with Jews, Faisal had met with Zionist leader Chaim Weizmann in June 1918 near Aqaba and in January 1919 in London. At these two meetings, Faisal had agreed that Palestine would not be part of the Arab state and had accepted the right of Jews to immigrate to Palestine, acquire land there, and manage their own affairs. Weizmann, in turn, had promised to provide economic and technical support to the Arab state and to respect Palestinian Arab rights. There was a catch: Faisal conditioned his agreement with Weizmann on Britain fulfilling its promise of independence to the Arabs. (Palestine became a British mandate in 1920, and, thereafter, Britain began carrying out the Balfour Declaration.)[29]

Faisal ended his presentation by challenging the peacemakers to live up to the promises made to his father when the British wanted and needed the Arabs' military support. The Arabs, he noted, had kept all of their wartime promises. He read aloud from the McMahon-Hussein Correspondence. "And now we are told," he said, his voice rising, "that none of these promises can be fulfilled because of the Sykes-Picot pact, an agreement to divide many of the Arab lands between France and England, negotiated months before. . . .

We are told," continued Faisal with a bitter irony he made no attempt to conceal, "that this secret agreement cancels the promises that were made to us openly before all the world."[30] Wilson's closest advisor, Colonel Edward House, who sat in on the meeting, later cogently summarized Faisal's predicament: "He made the impression of a lovable and high-minded personality, too little ruthless to carry through to success against Western diplomacy, Western desires for commercial privilege, and Western arms the wishes of the Arab people for real independence."[31]

Howard Bliss addressed the peacemakers the next day. Late afternoon shadows filled the Clock Room of the Quai d'Orsay as he began. He was the only person, beside Faisal, to put the case for Arab independence before the Allied leaders. "Mr. President, Gentlemen," Bliss began, "I shall not detain you for long. My deep interest in the people of Syria, irrespective of race, creed or condition, bred from a long residence among them—in fact I was born on Mount Lebanon—is my only excuse for detaining you at all."[32]

Bliss made his case to the world's leaders in a quietly forceful and convincing manner. He told them the Fourteen Points and the British-French declaration of November 1918 obligated the West to respect popular aspirations. "I maintain that such an opportunity for self-expression has not as yet been given," he bluntly declared. The golden hour was passing away. He urged them to send out fact-finding commissioners as soon as possible to learn what the Arabs themselves wanted. "Their task will not be an easy one," he noted. "They must approach it, in my opinion, in the spirit of large sympathy, infinite patience, frankness and goodwill. In the hands of fair and open-minded men, very valuable results can be secured." If denied the opportunity to express their views, he predicted the outcome would be discontent, sullenness, resentment, and even bloodshed.[33]

Bliss's words, like Faisal's, registered. Shortly after their appearances at the Quai d'Orsay, Lloyd George urged Clemenceau to accept Arab rule of Syria—in effect, prioritizing the McMahon-Hussein Correspondence over the Sykes-Picot Agreement. Lloyd George did so, in part because Britain faced growing financial and domestic pressure to demobilize its troops in the Middle East, and General Allenby had cautioned him that Lebanon and Syria would violently oppose French occupation and this might spill over into

British-controlled Egypt, Palestine, and Mesopotamia. But in the end, Lloyd George feared alienating the French more than he feared alienating the Arabs—he needed France's help to prevent the resurgence of Germany—so he did not press Clemenceau on the issue. As Lloyd George candidly put it, "For us, the friendship of France is worth ten Syrias."[34]

Clemenceau refused to budge. He looked upon Faisal as a British puppet. He would not release Britain from the Sykes-Picot Agreement merely because it conflicted with a promise Britain had made (and had not shared with France at the time it was tendered) in the McMahon-Hussein Correspondence. Irritated, Clemenceau resented the mess he believed British bad faith and double-dealing had made. If Britain claimed territory in the Middle East, why shouldn't France? Compounding this frustration, he faced intense domestic pressure. Clemenceau told one of Lloyd George's advisers that "he personally was not particularly concerned with the Near East," but France "always had played a great part there, and French public opinion expected a settlement which was consonant with France's position. He could not make any settlement which did not comply with this condition."[35] There seemed to be no way of reconciling the divergence of views.

Wilson, growing disgusted with the whole business, tried to turn the tide by pushing Bliss's proposed fact-finding mission. Bliss, he said, had lived among the Arabs for years and had assured him such a mission would be well received. Lloyd George and Clemenceau reluctantly agreed on March 25. But they undercut and stalled the mission by steadfastly refusing to name representatives to it. Exasperated, Wilson finally decided to act on his own. In late May, he sent out two American commissioners—Henry King, a Congregationalist clergyman and president of Oberlin College, and Charles Crane, a Chicago businessman and Democratic Party activist—along with a small staff of regional experts before more time was lost. Wilson hoped the commission's findings would strengthen his bargaining position against the Sykes-Picot Agreement with Lloyd George and Clemenceau.

The King-Crane Commission, as the inquiry came to be known, arrived at Haifa on June 10, 1919, and spent the next six weeks canvassing popular opinion in the Middle East. A faculty member of the AUB Medical School, Dr. Sami Haddad, served as the commission's translator. Using eight "mechanical camels" (Ford® Model-Ts®) and General Allenby's own yacht *Maid of Honor*, the commission jostled over miles of road and sand to meet hundreds of delegations and visit nearly forty cities, from Haifa, Jaffa, and Jerusalem in the south to Adana, Mersina, and Tarsus in the north, from Aleppo, Damascus, and Homs in the east to Acre, Alexandretta, and Beirut in the west. They interviewed people of all religious and political persuasions, who greeted the commission warmly and enthusiastically. Most Middle Easterners trusted America because of the AUB, reports from immigrants in the United States, and Wilson's idealistic pronouncements. They also viewed the commission as the only way to make their aspirations known to the peacemakers.

The commissioners ended their grueling tour on July 21, when they boarded the American destroyer *Hazelwood* at Mersina and returned to Istanbul. Five weeks later, on August 28, 1919, they submitted their findings and recommendations to the Allied leaders still gathered in Paris. The King-Crane Commission reported that an overwhelming majority of inhabitants in Lebanon and Syria preferred independence to a French mandate. Frustrating this legitimate aspiration, the commissioners noted, courted trouble in the future. "Dangers," they wrote, "may readily arise from unwise and unfaithful dealings with this people, but there is great hope of peace and progress if they be handled frankly and loyally." They also recommended a limited Zionist program for Palestine.[36]

The King-Crane Commission's report made little impact, however. Britain and France suppressed its findings by blocking its publication. British foreign secretary Arthur Balfour candidly stated that "in Palestine we do not propose even to go through the form of consulting the wishes of the present inhabitants of the country, though the American Commission has been going through the form of asking what they are. The four Great Powers are committed to Zionism. And Zionism, be it right or wrong, good or bad, is rooted in age-long traditions, in present needs, in future hopes, of far profounder import than the desires and prejudices of the 700,000 Arabs who now inhabit that ancient land."[37]

The following month, September 1919, Lloyd George pulled British troops out of Lebanon and Syria and allowed French forces to replace them, in effect, creating a French mandate through military occupation. France quickly jailed many locals who had testified before the commission. By then, Faisal had returned to the Middle East with his hopes dashed, and an exhausted Wilson had returned to the United States. "I gained impressions in Paris," the president told Secretary of State Robert Lansing, "which I must frankly say were altogether unfavorable to the methods of both the French and the English in dealing with that part of the world."[38] Lansing privately wrote, "The President has undoubtedly found himself in a most difficult position . . . on a level with politicians experienced in intrigue, whom he will find a pretty difficult lot. . . . What will be still more disastrous will be the loss of confidence among the peoples of the nations represented here. A grievous blunder has been made."[39]

One month later, Wilson suffered a massive, incapacitating stroke while on a national speaking tour to win Senate confirmation of US participation in the League of Nations. Washington protested the transfer of control in Lebanon and Syria to the French, but by then it was too late. America had begun to turn inward by the fall of 1919. Its power in the region was simply no match for Britain and France—it had no troops in the Middle East, while Britain and France had thousands. In the last analysis, Britain and France could ignore America's advice and do what they wished in the Middle East. And they did just that, with fateful consequences.

* * *

Howard Bliss's experience at the Paris Peace Conference dismayed and dispirited him. His idealistic hopes for the Middle East had been smashed on the anvil of imperialism. The realization of promises made and broken crushed his confidence in the future. This strain, added to what Bliss had endured in Beirut during the war, carried him to the brink of exhaustion. He felt spent, emotionally and physically. He left France for the United States aboard an American troopship on March 13, 1919. When he reached New York on March 24, he immediately checked into Presbyterian Hospital for recuperation. He was a very sick man.

Acquaintances could see physical evidence of the anguish he had endured. Deep lines furrowed his face. He had lost weight and strength, and his hair had turned from brown to gray. He struggled on for another year, a broken man fighting his pessimism about the Middle East while his body fought against tuberculosis complicated by diabetes and a weakened heart. As his body failed, he penned a testament for publication in the widely read *Atlantic Monthly* titled "The Modern Missionary." The modern missionary, he wrote, accepts "ungrudgingly and gratefully" that Christianity is not "the sole channel through which divine and saving truth has been conveyed." Indeed, confessed Bliss, such a missionary "prays for all men with a new sympathy—for all mosques and temples and synagogues as well as for all churches."[40]

On May 2, 1920—the last day of his life—he talked at length in Arabic. That evening, he died, surrounded by members of his family. He had asked to be buried in the Old Burial Ground behind the Meeting House in Jaffrey, New Hampshire,[41] near Mount Monadnock, where he had hiked as an Amherst student and courted the love of his life, Amy Blatchford. Its cool, pine-spiced air, he told family and friends, reminded him of Mount Lebanon.

Chapter 6:

BAYARD DODGE AND AMERICAN IDEALISM

Six feet tall and slender, with light-blue eyes, fair hair, and an ascetic appearance, Bayard Dodge grew up in the milieu of upper-class, turn-of-the-century Manhattan vividly brought to life in the novels and short stories of Edith Wharton. Born in New York City in 1888, he came of age in a privileged world of quiet confidence, social certainty, and patrician restraint. His father, Cleveland Dodge, who headed the family's immensely lucrative copper business called Phelps, Dodge & Company, gave Bayard and his siblings a strong sense of identity, security, and *noblesse oblige*. "To whom much is given, much is expected" was a mantra often repeated in the family mansion at Riverdale-on-the-Hudson, in church, and at school. Bayard's father taught him to value honesty and charity more than theology.[1] From his parents, Bayard inherited a clear-eyed, firm expression that hinted at his drive to pursue a life of purposeful activity in a field devoted to the service of others.

As a boy, Bayard attended the exclusive Browning School, a few blocks up leafy Park Avenue from the Dodges' spacious brownstone townhouse at 26 East Thirty-Ninth Street. When Bayard entered Princeton University, his father, a wealthy alumnus and trustee, bought a house near campus where Bayard entertained his '09 classmates on weekends. After Princeton, he enrolled at Union Theological Seminary on Manhattan's Upper West Side, where he studied Oriental religion and civilization under the great Hebrew scholar Richard Gottheil and filled his free time doing social work in the teeming immigrant ghettos of Manhattan's Lower East Side (as had his father-in-law, Howard Bliss). Union "was a radical place in those days," Bayard later recalled, "and a good place to compare religions. It was easy to see we had a great deal to share with the Muslims—much more than we had to differ with them on."[2] He earned a divinity degree, but chose not to be ordained—a significant and revealing departure from Daniel and Howard Bliss. "Protestantism," he said, "means religious freedom."[3]

Bayard first visited the Middle East in the summer of 1910, during an around-the-world trip with his twin brother, Cleveland Jr., and a mutual friend. Howard Bliss met the three young travelers in Egypt and escorted them to Beirut. When their boat reached Rās Beirut and rounded the light-house into St. George's Bay, Bayard caught sight of the tawny buildings of the American University of Beirut (AUB) nestled among spires of pencil-thin, dark-green cypresses set against the snow-capped Lebanon Mountains. Before him lay the Lebanon of which he had dreamed. The rumblings of war in far-away Europe seemed a remote possibility in this idyllic and optimistic world.

Howard Bliss escorted Bayard in an *arabiyeh* (open carriage) up a winding driveway bordered by flowers and flagstone paths to Marquand House, the AUB president's spacious residence built of creamy sandstone and covered in creeping ivy. From its second-floor balcony trimmed in delicate iron railing, Bayard looked to the east and saw 8,500-foot Mount Sannin, and to the west he saw the beautiful Mediterranean Sea stretching almost like infinity to the horizon. He found Marquand House a welcoming sanctuary, though it was a good deal less grandiose than most of the hotels he had stayed in around the world.

Everything Bayard saw and heard seemed mesmerizingly different from the world he knew. He found Howard Bliss impressively forward-thinking and Beirut itself "a very free, delightful place." The experience left him over-whelmed, astonished, and quite understandably fascinated. An idealistic and ambitious young man bent on improving the world, AUB seemed a place where he could fulfill his sense of adventure and the ethos of service imparted to him since childhood. "My idea was to see whether I couldn't contribute to producing a better feeling with the Muslims," he later recalled. This brief sojourn to the Middle East left him smitten.[4]

During this visit Bayard met Howard Bliss's oldest daughter, Mary, home from college for the summer. Bayard and Mary hit it off and continued their courtship after they both returned to America in the fall—he to theological studies at Union, she to undergraduate studies at Vassar. Bayard returned to Beirut in 1913 as director of student activities at AUB and wed Mary early the following year in the college chapel. White-haired Daniel Bliss, her grandfather, sat in the front pew, beaming. AUB president Howard Bliss, her father, gave away the bride. Bayard and Mary's wedding united the Bliss and Dodge families at last.

When Bayard became AUB president in 1923, he had just turned thirty-five and had never headed a university. But he charged ahead boldly nevertheless, with great poise and authority, armed with a clear vision of where he wanted to lead AUB and the Middle East. "Sometimes the Orient has been on top, with a stream of cultural influence flowing into the Occident," he told an interviewer. "Today, the West is on top, with social, political, and scientific ideas pouring into the East. The future is full of opportunity, but it is also full of danger."[5]

A cultural tide of modernity was flooding into the Middle East. Middle Easterners experienced this tide as invasive, disturbing, and alien. A modernizing process that had taken Europe four centuries to absorb, from the Renaissance through the Industrial Revolution, crashed upon the Middle East at a ferocious speed and had a dizzying, almost vertiginous effect. Peoples' lives were profoundly disrupted by this process. They watched their region and way of life become utterly strange and unrecognizable. Middle Easterners felt adrift in their own land, forced to comply with the West's modernization program. Above all, they resented the fact that they no longer controlled their own destiny. They felt disconnected from their roots and experienced a sinking loss of identity.

Dodge wanted to help Middle Easterners cope with this cultural tsunami, for the alternative was radicalization of alienated Arab masses. Dodge sounded this prescient theme in his inaugural address in June 1923. "Tremendous forces have been let loose which may become a menace, unless they are properly controlled," he announced to Christian, Muslim, and Jewish listeners. "Patience and moderation are imperative; each man must learn to cherish the rights of his neighbor, as well as those of himself. . . . This ideal of being a good neighbor in one's own community is so essential at the present time," he hastened to note, "that we do not desire to Americanize the young men of the Levant, but rather to make them good citizens of their own lands."[6]

To this end, the new president greatly expanded AUB's curriculum in Arabic language and history, modernized the medical school and hospital through generous grants from the Rockefeller Foundation, and established open appointments and equal salaries and academic rights for faculty, regardless of nationality or faith.[7] With that, Middle Easterners began to occupy important administrative positions. Dodge also put more emphasis on research and graduate study, making AUB more than just a fine teaching college.

Perhaps most importantly when viewed in hindsight, Dodge brought together Arabs and Jews in common efforts that broke down barriers. AUB did what many thought impossible: It enabled Arabs and Jews to work together, depend on one another, and grow to like one another. Athletics became one way that young men of differing religions and backgrounds made daily discoveries of friendship and common purpose. In April 1930, the AUB soccer team boarded a train to Cairo to play an Egyptian team. Most members of the AUB team were Arabs, but the star right-wing forward was a young man from Tel Aviv named Cohen. To the Arab players, Cohen was not a Jew—he was their teammate and they needed him. On the train ride to Cairo, Cohen shared a bunk with a Muslim and meals with a Druse. Sometimes the team spent weekends together outside Beirut on a beach by the Mediterranean, in the shadow of the Lebanon Mountains. No one cared about another's religious background; such labels didn't matter at such moments. The Tel Aviv Symphony, comprising some of the world's finest Jewish musicians, performed regularly on the AUB campus. The chapel featured the organ playing of a Russian Jew. The Grand Rabbi of Baghdad heard about an AUB education and sent many Iraqi Jewish teens to the school.

AUB also educated future leaders of Israel. Eliahu Elath, Israel's first ambassador to the United States and later president of Hebrew University, was an AUB student from 1931 through 1934. Elath studied the life of Bedouins while at AUB, conducting field research in neighboring Arab countries as part of his studies. He also worked part-time as a reporter for the *Palestine Post* and the Reuters News Agency while in Beirut. In 1937, Elath became the Jewish Agency's representative in Beirut, where he worked with

Lebanese officials on behalf of the Jewish Agency headquartered in Jerusalem. Lebanese Arabs and Palestinian Jews discussed the creation of a joint Litani River water project to provide irrigation and hydroelectric power generation. Elath even arranged a meeting between Chaim Weizmann and Lebanese president Emile Eddé in Paris in June 1937 to explore the idea. The Litani River water project never materialized, but such a collaborative endeavor remains a tantalizing dream to many in the arid region to this day.[8]

Quarrels among AUB students over nationality or religion seldom occurred. In a region of the world where group loyalty reigned and social interaction across religious and tribal lines rarely happened, AUB became a place where Arabs and Jews could meet on neutral ground and fraternize. (Fanatics on both sides prohibited fraternization. A young Palestinian confessed, "Some of my best friends on the campus are Jews; in fact I prefer them to some of my Arab friends. But as soon as we get back to Jerusalem, I can't allow myself to be seen speaking with them."[9]) AUB allowed young Arabs and Jews to argue, laugh, play, and tackle problems together. The AUB motto became "The realm in which we share is vastly greater than that in which we differ."[10] There was only one rule: "Respect the religion and nationality of others." Dodge observed this rule himself. Whenever he invited a Christian to speak on campus, he gently admonished his guest to forego referencing the divinity of Jesus, in deference to Jews and Muslims in the audience.[11]

Bayard Dodge's most revolutionary and far-reaching change involved the admission of women to AUB—a radical step in the Muslim world with profound effects on the status of women in the region. Traditionally, Arab men and women had been strictly segregated. Arab women's opportunities remained limited throughout their lives by their inability to read and write. Bayard Dodge became an outspoken advocate of enhanced social and political rights for women. In 1924, his second year as president, AUB admitted a young Egyptian woman named Ihsan Ahmad. She wore two veils and her husband accompanied her to every class, where she sat apart from her male peers, listening attentively to her teacher.[12] Her presence broke an invisible but powerful barrier. A few years later, the AUB pharmacy school graduated its first female student, a young Jewish woman from Palestine named Sara

Levy. A vast world had opened up to Middle Eastern women, with incalculable consequences that persist to the present day—and beyond.

Four years after the first female attended AUB, in 1928, the daughter of a prominent Beirut family, Nazira Zayn al-Din, published a sensational book, *al-Sufur wa al-Hijab* (*Unveiling and the Veil*), boldly proclaiming women's right to shed the veil, yet remain good Muslims.[13] It took many more years to break down old habits of domination rooted in long-standing customs and prejudices against female education. But today, women comprise a crucial part of the workforce in business, education, and government throughout the Middle East, thanks in no small part to the pioneering trend in women's rights introduced at AUB by Dodge.

His influence on the issue of women's rights in the Middle East demonstrates how Dodge immersed himself in Islam to a degree Daniel and Howard Bliss never did. Every Thursday, this scion of New England Puritanism closely studied a passage from the Qur'an with Sheikh Ahmed Omar al-Mahmassani, a distinguished Islamic scholar from Cairo's famed al-Azhar Mosque. The two discussed the Qur'an's wording and meaning together in classical Arabic; Al-Mahmassani did most of the talking, but Bayard listened intently. "You young Americans are here to give," Bayard would tell new AUB instructors, sounding very reminiscent of Daniel Bliss—then would add, very unlike Bliss: "You must also remember that you can take into your own lives a great deal of value from this great culture of the Near East."[14] "We do not propose to proselytize," he had declared in his presidential inaugural address. "God forbid that our University should carry on a new crusade in eastern lands."[15] When preaching to students, Dodge quoted from the Qur'an as well as the Bible.

Not only did he appreciate and learn from the teachings of Islam, but he also fell in love with the aesthetics of Arab culture. This passion revealed itself in a scholarly project he pursued for decades during precious moments of free time. Whenever he had a few hours—at his office desk, in his sitting room at home, even under a tent at summer camp—he surrounded himself with dictionaries and reference books, lost in the translation of a rare tenth-century Abbasid encyclopedia by an Arab scholar of Baghdad. The two-volume *Fihrist of Al-Nadim: A Tenth-Century Survey of Islamic Culture*, translated and edited by Bayard Dodge, was eventually published by Columbia University Press in 1970.[16]

Mr. Dodge the AUB president sometimes obscured Bayard the man, but certain occasions cleared away the fog, and he could reveal elements of his true character. Early in his presidency, he traipsed the muddy cactus lanes of Rās Beirut to attend a musical performance by poor Armenian students, using an old crate as his chair. When the dining hall got a new manager in 1938, the president unexpectedly poked his head in the manager's office and invited him to go for a noon swim in the Mediterranean. When he walked around campus, he greeted nearly every student by name. He never accepted a salary, secretly covered needy students' tuition costs, and donated large sums of money to the school anonymously, as his great uncle Stuart Dodge had done. The Lebanese fondly said of him, "He has millions but he wears hob-nailed shoes." Bayard, wrote someone who knew him well, was "experienced in the wisdom of reticence."[17] "A little modesty and humility," he liked to say, "increases a person's size rather than diminishing it."[18]

People who knew Bayard liked him. When he felt comfortable, a dry sense of humor emerged—a willingness to laugh at himself. Yet he always smiled nervously, and people sensed a restlessness in him. "He had an inner dynamo that drove him," recalled his daughter Grace, "he was almost never still."[19] He would tap his fingers while talking or even reading. On summer hikes in the mountains, while his companions walked the well-worn parts of paths, he kept to one side, where the walking was more difficult and exhausting. Hidden behind wire-rimmed glasses, his eyes cast a mild-mannered but inquisitive gaze at the world around him. Yet he rarely let his feelings show—and almost never in public. In response to personal questions, he often replied with a hurried, "Yes, yes, yes," or "Oh, no, no," as if he were physically brushing the query away. His aloof benevolence and restrained demeanor struck many people who understood his background and upbringing as quintessential WASP (white, Anglo-Saxon Protestant) reserve. Still even his own wife and children sometimes wondered whether he feared to expose and share his emotional vulnerability with the world at large.

A tragedy during World War II revealed how Bayard Dodge dealt with matters that cut to the heart. Shortly after Pearl Harbor, his youngest child and namesake, Bayard Jr. (known in the family as "B. D."), rejected his privileged connections and enlisted in the United States Army as a private. He served as an infantry scout with the Seventh Army in France all the way from D-Day in June 1944 until he was killed in action near Saulcy on November 22, 1944, while making himself a target for German fire as other members of his squad captured a machine gun emplacement. He posthumously received the Silver Star for gallantry.[20] B. D. was buried in the Épinal American Cemetery on a quiet foothill of the Vosges Mountains, alongside thousands of fellow US servicemen who sacrificed their lives in the struggle against Nazi evil that included the Holocaust of European Jews. He was just twenty years old.

When the official telegram bearing the awful news reached Marquand House, Bayard stoically returned to the reception he and his wife were hosting without saying a word. He waited until the next morning to tell Mary what had happened. Then he took her up to the mountain village of Brummana, where the family had spent many happy summers, so they could mourn together privately and tenderly. The emotional dam finally broke several months later, during a brief visit Bayard made back to the States. At a picnic with his daughters Grace and Margaret in the hills above Harper's Ferry, West Virginia, in June 1945, he wandered over to the edge of a cliff, pulled from his pocket the few personal belongings B. D. had left at home in Beirut, and hurled them as far as he could into the distance. When he returned to the picnic table, his daughters saw tears in his eyes. He had last seen his youngest son the day sixteen-year-old B. D. sailed for boarding school at Deerfield Academy in Massachusetts in the summer of 1940. He never knew the gentle, unassuming, and quietly humorous young man B. D. became.[21] His wife, Mary, never really recovered from the devastating loss.

* * *

Bayard Dodge's stewardship of AUB coincided with the era of the French Mandate over Lebanon and Syria after the conclusion of World War I. During this period, Beirut became the showcase of France's *mission civilisatrice* in the region (the French Colonial Exposition was held there in 1921) and became the leading commercial and financial center of the Middle East.

French-built roads and bridges, an expanded railway system, an enlarged and modernized harbor, and a new airport all sharply increased commerce. Beirut's foreign population tripled from 5 to 15 percent. The city's cosmopolitan population owed its growing wealth to trade with Europe and other cities around the Mediterranean. Urban planning launched during the late Ottoman period was expanded and filled the city with elegant new buildings and wide boulevards. Beirut emerged as a modern, vibrant city, "the Paris of the Orient." Arabs driving donkey wagons loaded with firewood passed a cabaret that featured "The Arab Al Jolson." Beirut's openness and sophistication lured young people from all over the Middle East to study there. The universities, in turn, enriched the life of the city.

Bayard Dodge managed relations with the French as effectively and tactfully as his late father-in-law Howard Bliss had with the Ottoman Turks, avoiding the friction and jealousy many expected between colonial officials and a private institution. "His mind saw possibilities for dreams," an acquaintance wrote of him, "yet he recognized the times when reconciliation had to be made to the constraints."[22] He diplomatically courted the goodwill of French officials, wisely and steadfastly refusing to let AUB be drawn into the vortex of politics.

Despite austerities triggered by the Great Depression that gripped the world for a decade beginning in 1929, the university grew during the 1930s into an eighty-acre campus with more than three thousand alumni. Most AUB alumni remained in the Middle East, where they assumed leading roles in their communities, armed with a secure sense of place, purpose, and public service. Many doctors—widely admired by the general Arab public—owed their talents to an AUB education, which became a mark of distinction in Middle Eastern society.

AUB became a magnet for young people of all classes and faiths, regardless of color, at a time when most colleges and universities in the United States only educated the offspring of America's elite and systematically barred minorities. Lebanese, Syrians, Palestinians, and Egyptians still comprised the majority of students, but AUB also enrolled young people from Aden, Albania, America, Argentina, Armenia, Brazil, Bulgaria, Canada, Colombia, Cuba, Czechoslovakia, Ecuador, Ethiopia, France, Germany, Great

Britain, Greece, Honduras, India, Iran, Iraq, Italy, Lithuania, Malaysia, Mexico, Panama, Poland, Romania, Russia, Spain, Sudan, Switzerland, Turkey, Venezuela, and Zanzibar. Religions represented at AUB included Armenian Catholics, Assyrian Orthodox, Bahai, Chaldean Catholics, Coptic Catholics, Coptic Orthodox, Druse, Greek Catholics, Greek Orthodox, Jews, Maronites, Nestorians, Protestants, Roman Catholics, Sunni Muslims, Shiite Muslims, Syriac Catholics, Syrian Orthodox, and Zoroastrians. Nowhere else in the world could one find such an array of race and religion on one campus.

Word about the university's reputation spread quickly. Many governments sent their brightest students to AUB to be educated as accountants, doctors, nurses, pharmacists, secretaries, and other professionals. The opening of roads across the deserts brought isolated villagers and nomadic Bedouins by automobile to Beirut. Influential Middle Eastern families flocked to send their children to the school. King Faisal of Iraq sent his son, Crown Prince Ghazi, to the university in 1925.[23] AUB under Bayard Dodge became widely and affectionately known among Arabs and Jews alike as "the great Oriental queen."[24] The university's already considerable prestige skyrocketed. Between 1920 and 1940, enrollment doubled to nearly two thousand, making it the largest overseas American university in the world.[25] Its network of influential alumni read like a virtual *Who's Who* in the Middle East. They included the prime minister of Lebanon, the president of the Syrian parliament, the Arab mayor of Jerusalem, the owner and publisher of the largest Egyptian newspaper in Cairo, the secretary of Palestine's Supreme Muslim Council, the head of the Jewish Labor Bureau in Palestine, the foreign ministers of Iraq and Saudi Arabia, and the Crown Prince of Kuwait.[26] AUB's influence ran far and wide across the region and, indeed, the world. The modest, self-effacing Bayard Dodge had become the most respected foreigner in all the Middle East.[27]

AUB's stately buildings amid cypress and palm trees and lush gardens of honeysuckle and poppies tangibly symbolized the growing power of the United States and the growing emphasis on education in Middle Eastern society. Increasingly, ability and education—rather than social background and patronage—began to shape career prospects. Governments, professions, and businesses increased their demand for university graduates. The accomplishments of graduates accelerated the trend. AUB reinforced this trend by encouraging its eager, ambitious students to apply textbook knowledge to everyday problems and inculcating a strong sense of civic responsibility. It also instilled a respect for democracy and modernism as well as a crucial dose of self-confidence that reflected the American sense of mission and the school's elite status in the Arab world.

* * *

Everything seemed pleasant. Yet beneath the surface, the contrast between the idyll of the AUB campus and the political turmoil simmering beyond its walls jarred many students. The era of the French mandate marked a tense and tumultuous period in Middle East history. After defeating armed Arab resistance under Iraq's King Faisal at the Battle of Maysalun Pass outside Damascus in July 1920, France ended Arab dreams of unity and independence—and split off Lebanon from Syria. France made little effort to fulfill its custodial obligations under the mandate. Instead, France set out to divide and rule, deepening divisions already inherent in a multiethnic and multireligious society. It deliberately incited sectarian loyalties in order to suppress the rise of nationalism. It stationed an army of occupation, stifled free speech, censored media, monopolized the bureaucracy and economy, imposed heavy taxes, and jailed and exiled dissidents. Meanwhile, it continued to contend with an Arab nationalism centered in Damascus that remained hostile to French rule. Skirmishes and uprisings known as the Great Revolt claimed thousands of Arab and French lives in the 1920s. France's authority, as a leading scholar of this period has written, "was illegitimate and thus was unstable."[28]

Some Lebanese—especially the Maronites and Greek Catholics—viewed France as a friendly power protecting their interests and guiding them toward independence. (The mercantile-financial Maronite elite aspired to be a Lebanese state distinct from Muslim Syria and closely linked to France.) But the much larger number of Sunni and Shiite Lebanese, and almost all Syrians, viewed France as an uninvited and unwelcome colonial power that denied citizens' national aspirations and treated them as inferior people incapable of ruling themselves. Lebanese and Syrians resented their subordination; they reluctantly reconciled themselves to French rule while openly chafing at their condition. Lebanon struggled to become a stable political entity in which diverse communities of Christians and Muslims coexisted peacefully. Sectarianism, fueled by the traditional divisions of clan, family, and faith, remained a troubling current beneath the surface. Volatility plagued Lebanese political life. This instability remains powerful and frighteningly present today.

AUB students keenly felt the contradiction between the French colonialism they experienced and the American egalitarianism they learned in the classroom. Many developed a deep ambivalence toward the West. One version of the West (France) symbolized their oppression; another version of the West (America) symbolized what they most admired: a democratic political process, the rule of law, economic opportunity, and social mobility. AUB became a bastion of anticolonialism and fertile ground for Middle Eastern nationalists resentful of the British and inherently distrustful of the French.[29] Always discreet and diplomatic in public, Bayard Dodge severely criticized European imperialism in private. Writing to his parents in 1920, he confided, "The British have commenced their regime in Palestine in a most disgraceful and unfair way, as they promised it to the Arabs and Jews at the same time and have not made either promise good."[30]

The egalitarianism and republicanism taught in AUB classrooms inspired a generation of Arab and Jewish students who had grown discontented under European imperialism to imagine the day when they would lead their peoples to freedom. AUB became the cradle of anti-French and anti-British nationalism. In fact, many of the intellectuals and political activists who led independence movements in the Middle East after World War II attended AUB during these prewar years.

Others began to view Westernization and the modernization it brought as a threat to long-standing values. Western ways were pouring in upon Muslim culture with relentless and overwhelming force, straining a traditional social fabric to the limit. Arabs felt fatally caught between worlds. Bayard Dodge witnessed an event that symbolized this disorienting process. One day, while on a cream-and-brown Beirut streetcar, he watched an elderly Muslim man trying to say his prayers. Each time the devout old Muslim got himself faced toward Mecca, the streetcar would round a corner, swaying the passengers and forcing the old man to rearrange himself. He looked at the other passengers, bewildered and lost.[31]

Middle Easterners wanted much of what the West had to offer, but they nonetheless feared the onset of materialism and unbelief. Some reacted by equating Western education, symbolized by the AUB, with cultural imperialism—in seeking to dominate and control minds as well as territory and resources. This, therefore, posed a challenge to Arab identity and interests, which indirectly strengthened the capacity of the West to dominate the East. Those who felt this way began to perceive AUB much as American students might perceive a New England college founded by Muslim missionaries to educate young Americans in the ways of the Orient: they smelled a wisp of paternalism. They felt Americans in the Middle East meant well but still harbored deeply rooted—if wholly unconscious—prejudices.

They pointed to the way Americans in Beirut lived and thought to make their point. Instead of residing among the local population, Americans usually lived in their own isolated (and privileged) communities. During the twenty-five years of his presidency, Bayard Dodge and his family always lived in the protective cocoon of Marquand House inside the AUB campus. He and his wife, Mary, sent their four children, Grace, Margaret, David, and B. D., to the American Community School next to campus, where they studied French—not Arabic—as their second language.[32] The Dodges' oldest daughter, Grace, remembered her parents' (and, to be fair, their generation of Americans') opposition to interethnic and interfaith marriage.[33] It was hard for Lebanese and other Middle Easterners to miss the assumptions and priorities implicit in such judgments.

* * *

France's economic and political fragility during the interwar years made its control over Lebanon and Syria constantly tenuous. France's military defeat and occupation by Nazi Germany in the summer of 1940 weakened its colonial position even further. Paris tried to maintain influence in Lebanon through the Maronite elite, but even before 1940, Christian and Muslim leaders yearning for autonomy began to work together to end French rule. A common desire for independence overrode sectarian competition—at least temporarily. Adopting an evolutionary approach to the goals of unity and independence, local political leaders resigned themselves to working within the framework established by the Mandate. A multiparty and multifaith alliance known as the National Bloc negotiated a gradual power-sharing agreement with the French High Commission.[34]

After the fall of France in World War II, Vichy collaboration with Hitler in the Middle East became possible.[35] Britain feared the Vichy French would allow Nazi Germany to use Lebanon and Syria to attack oil-rich Iraq, Palestine, and Egypt, home of the Suez Canal and headquarters of its campaign against Axis forces in North Africa. German propaganda agents and military officers, trumpeting recent Nazi victories in the Balkans, Crete, and Greece, openly walked the streets of Beirut. There was a feeling that war was near.

When the Vichy high commissioner, General Henri Dentz, seized the British oil pipeline in northern Lebanon and granted the German *Luftwaffe* access to airbases at Aleppo and Palmyra in support of an anti-British uprising in Iraq in May 1941, Britain imposed a blockade (as it had during World War I), stopped pumping oil from Kirkuk to the Mediterranean, and invaded Lebanon and Syria. British/Australian, Free French, and Palmach forces drove toward Beirut and Damascus from Haifa on June 8.[36] Vichy French forces put up fierce resistance. After five weeks of intense fighting, during which British planes and warships bombarded Beirut, General Dentz surrendered on July 12, when the German help he had expected never materialized.[37] Eight days later, Free French leader General Charles de Gaulle stopped by Marquand House and joined the Dodges for tea.

Beirut during World War II experienced many of the same hardships it had experienced during World War I. Martial law and rationing went into effect. Authorities imposed strict censorship and requisitioned whatever supplies they needed, sending prices soaring. Lebanon's borders closed and Beirut became isolated. Air-raid shelters, slit trenches, and blackout curtains appeared on campus, with people expecting the Nazis to drop from the skies any day. This prospect especially frightened the German Jewish refugee professors to whom Bayard Dodge had given desperately needed jobs after their hasty flight from Hitler's regime. The AUB hospital treated the wounded from all sides. This practice, which had begun during the First World War, would continue during Lebanon's bloody civil war from 1975 to 1990, and on through today.

Feeling the pressure of events, many Western faculty members took temporary refuge in neighboring British-controlled Palestine and Egypt, although classes continued to be held. Bayard Dodge and his wife, Mary, remained in Marquand House, where they witnessed the growing conflict at close hand during June and July 1941. One evening a British cruiser attacked a Vichy French destroyer right offshore from their second-floor balcony. Nighttime anti-aircraft barrages were deafening and shrapnel landed all over campus. Bayard and Mary secretly made plans to escape through Turkey and Iran should Nazi paratroopers descend on Lebanon, as they had on Crete and Greece.

World War II brought difficulties to Beirut and the region, but it also brought sweeping social changes. Large numbers of Western soldiers—every Muslim country in the Middle East except Saudi Arabia, Turkey, and Yemen was occupied by foreign troops—brought a flood of money into the region. Middle Eastern families became richer and, therefore, increasingly able to afford higher education. Since their sons did not face conscription (as they had under the Ottomans during World War I), they enrolled in record numbers at AUB. Tradition gave way to modernization. Women's enrollment increased substantially and male and female students studied and socialized together. Women stopped wearing the veil, played tennis in shorts on AUB's courts, and wore modern bathing suits on the seashore at the foot of the campus. These years marked the increasing secularization of Middle Eastern society that gathered momentum in later decades—and eventually precipitated a sharp reaction among conservative religious elements of Muslim society.

The Lebanese during World War II harbored bitter memories of the promises Europeans had made during World War I—promises the Arabs had trusted and then seen broken. This humiliating experience made them extremely sensitive and anxious to liberate themselves from foreign interference and condescension. They viewed Britain's ouster of the Vichy French skeptically at first, as merely the replacement of one self-interested European power by another. But this time Britain encouraged Arab nationalists while pressuring the High Commission, now in the hands of the Free French, to grant independence. The Free French proved much like their Vichy predecessors. Intent on restoring France's prestige by revitalizing France's empire, they balked at first. But Britain reminded the Free French they were in Lebanon to fight the Germans, not the Lebanese, and impatient nationalists became more eager than ever to rid themselves at last of the French. Lebanon and Syria became formally independent in late 1943 and early 1944, respectively.[38]

The United States quickly recognized both countries' independence. President Franklin Roosevelt sympathized with Woodrow Wilson's self-determination principle more than he did with his cousin Theodore Roosevelt's pro-imperialist policies. In July 1941, FDR and British prime minister Winston Churchill signed the Atlantic Charter, pledging self-government to all peoples liberated from Axis conquest. Churchill, an inveterate imperialist (he had served as Britain's Colonial Secretary in the early 1920s and helped draw the borders of Iraq and Jordan), conveniently interpreted this pledge to apply only to Nazi-occupied Europe.

FDR had no intention of rescuing Britain's and France's colonies in the Middle East or anywhere else. He insisted the Atlantic Charter applied to all nations. To that end, in March 1943, Roosevelt asked Patrick Hurley, a bipartisan Republican from the southwestern United States who had served as secretary of war under President Herbert Hoover from 1929 to 1933 and as an occasional roving envoy for FDR, to survey opinion throughout the Middle East. Roosevelt thought the State Department incapable of providing an objective assessment—he considered most Foreign Service officers too Euro-centric—so he decided to use Hurley as his eyes and ears in the region. Like most Americans in the 1940s, Hurley had never been to the Middle East and began his mission there woefully ignorant of its peoples and cultures. As he traveled, Hurley tried to view the existing situation from the point of view of the local population. He found widespread nationalist sentiment throughout the region and a growing chorus of popular demands for the European colonial powers to leave. At the end of 1943, the Roosevelt administration announced that the people of Lebanon and Syria were "prepared to make a good attempt at running their own show if given a chance."[39]

The end of the French Mandate came reluctantly and violently. France formally ceded sovereignty to Lebanon and Syria, but feelings still ran high among French officials in Beirut and Damascus, who intended to retain France's preeminent position in the region. Lebanese and Syrians, fearing a repetition of 1918, would have none of it. Anti-French riots erupted in Beirut, Damascus, and other towns during the spring of 1945 and reached a climax in late May. France reacted by sending more troops, shooting demonstrators, bombing Damascus, and firing artillery point-blank into the Syrian Parliament House. Hundreds of Arab civilians and French troops died in bloody street fighting. It was virtually a war between the civilian population of Syria and the armed forces of Free France.[40]

Bayard Dodge's oldest son, David, witnessed the chaos as a young US Army intelligence officer stationed in Damascus during the spring of 1945. He was the only American military officer in all of Syria at the time, filing intelligence reports on the turmoil to US Army regional headquarters in Cairo. When the French attacked Damascus on May 29, he found himself in the city's Orient Palace Hotel. Bullets whizzed through the hotel. A British intelligence officer was killed, but David survived unharmed, despite twenty bullet holes in the walls of his room.[41] Eventually the British High Command, with American backing, forced the French to return to their barracks and give up their lingering imperial ambitions. France withdrew the last of its troops from Lebanon and Syria the following year.

Lebanon's occupiers, dating back to the Egyptian pharaohs, had left inscriptions commemorating their occupation at Nahr el-Kelb, a narrow pass where the Dog River runs through a gorge from the mountains to the sea just north of Beirut. Long ago, chariots had worn deep ruts into the rock—traces of an ancient Roman road. Every conqueror from Pharaoh Ramses II onward had marked his victory on the face of the cliff: Nebuchadnezzar, Darius, Rome's III Legion, Richard the Lionheart, and on down to Napoleon and Allenby. De Gaulle had etched the most recent inscription. Lebanon's new president unveiled a plaque at Nahr el-Kelb that commemorated the withdrawal of the last foreign occupiers of Lebanon, in a way asserting the nation's independence from foreign rule. Lebanon and other newly independent Arab states sent representatives to the founding conference of the United Nations at San Francisco in April 1945. There were more AUB graduates at this conference than from any other college or university in the world.

* * *

Lebanon's independence at the end of World War II brought the precarious balance of its sectarian differences to the forefront, where it has remained ever since. The vast majority of Lebanese—then and now—hoped Lebanon would occupy a special place in the Middle East, where Muslims and Christians could live together in mutual tolerance and respect; a haven where Sunnis, Shia, Druse, Maronite, and Orthodox Christians could feel safe with one another; a country that could maintain a window to Western ideas and influences, as well as intimate links to the Arab and larger Muslim worlds. It would be a bridge between two civilizations. This vision of Lebanon has remained a persistent but elusive dream ever since.

The end of World War II also fundamentally transformed US involvement in the Middle East. For more than a century, commerce and education had defined most American activity in the region. After 1945, however, the nature and range of US interests changed utterly. The collapse of Europe's empires, the rise of America's Cold War with the Soviet Union, and the West's growing dependence on foreign oil (the United States became a net importer of oil for the first time in its history in 1943) combined to revolutionize America's role in the region. For the first time in its history, the United States plunged headlong into the Middle Eastern arena of great power politics, religious and national rivalries, and competition over oil. Most Americans—inside and outside of the government—found this transition abrupt, jarring, and fraught with unanticipated and thorny consequences.

AUB and the Middle East stood at the dawn of a new era. Dodge and other American expatriates expected and welcomed a more active and visible US role in the region. Until now a distant and benign force, Washington, they believed, would make its presence felt in the Middle East in immediate and beneficial ways. They barely predicted the storm about to break.

Chapter 7:

AMERICA IN THE POSTWAR MIDDLE EAST

F or outside powers like the United States—and just as much as for the Arabs and Jews who lived there—1945 marked a turning point in the history of the Middle East. The era of European imperialism was ending, and nationalism was emerging as the dominant impetus in the area. The United States was now one of two great world powers deeply interested in the Middle East, a region of rapidly growing economic and strategic significance close to the southern frontier of America's new rival, the Soviet Union. What had mattered to the Blisses and the Dodges now mattered to all Americans, though this realization would take some time to sink in.

It had not always been so. Shortly before World War II, an article in the widely read *Harper's* magazine surveyed US relations with the rest of the world. When its author got to the Middle East, he declared that this area "is not often marked by excitement. . . . Our relations with these peoples," he hastily added without the least irony, "are not important."[1] Several months later, an American diplomat drew an assignment to the Middle East. He felt devastated, his promising career suddenly and cruelly sidetracked. One of his ambitious foreign service colleagues commiserated, saying of the area, "Nothing ever happens there."[2]

World War II changed all that. The United States in 1945 emerged from the Second World War and the mortal weakening of European empires the war produced as *the* rapidly rising power in the Middle East. For the United States, the Middle East suddenly represented an area of vital geostrategic importance. The developing Cold War between America and the Soviet Union—at a time when Britain, which had traditionally served as a bulwark against Russian ambitions in the Middle East, had begun to pull back from its traditional commitments in the region—and the rising significance of oil to Western economies made the Middle East a foreign policy priority for the first time in American diplomatic history. The United States enjoyed immense prestige throughout the whole region. Arabs and Jews alike viewed America as a wealthy, friendly, impartial, freedom-loving giant.

Washington, however, neither anticipated nor adequately prepared for its new role in the Middle East after World War II. American policymakers in 1945 recognized the potential collision between Arab and Jewish nationalisms in Palestine, but they failed to grasp both the growing Jewish determination for an independent state and the increasing population, social dislocation, and political radicalization of Arab societies triggered by the forces of Zionism and modernization. Washington sought (and expected) political and economic influence in the Middle East, without considering how much this would involve the nation politically or militarily in the region, or planning intelligently for its new responsibilities.[3]

The Arab world in 1945 was also entering a new age. Systems and values rooted in the conservative and communitarian Islamic tradition were giving way to secularism, individualism, and materialism, which created rising expectations among urban, middle-class Arabs and creeping frustration among the larger number of *fellaheen* (peasant farmers) who benefited less from these modernizing changes. National rivalries—rather than pan-Islamic unity—dominated politics as Arab countries gained their independence. The dream of Arab unity symbolized by Faisal's short-lived regime in 1918 foundered on both the competing ambitions of nationalists in Jordan, Lebanon, Palestine, and Syria, and the disagreement between secularists who sought statehood for all citizens of all religions and Islamists who equated secularism with atheism and materialism. This fundamental division would plague Arab politics for decades to come, down to the present day. But the dream of Arab unity did not die; it would live on in the politics of Egyptian leader Gamal Abdel Nasser during the 1950s and 1960s.

Frustrated by years of foreign condescension, domination, and exploitation, Arabs sought autonomy and strength. They struggled to define themselves in increasingly turbulent times that produced uprooted, urbanizing populations struggling to find their bearings in a rapidly changing Middle

East. They also intensified their opposition to a Zionist state as European Jewish immigration to Palestine increased in the aftermath of the Holocaust. "It is difficult to exaggerate the feeling that exists on this subject throughout the Muslim nations," a US official in the Middle East observed after the war.[4] Many Arabs felt little emotional connection to the horrors of the Holocaust and its victims. They viewed Zionism not in the context of its impact on European Jewry, but its impact on Palestinian Arabs.

For Jews, 1945 brought adversity—and hope. Nazi Germany's ghastly anti-Semitic genocide known as the Final Solution had led to the deaths of more than six million European Jews. Hitler's dreadful and unprecedented crime seemed to powerfully confirm the basic argument of Zionism: Jews could only be safe as a majority in a Jewish state. Holocaust survivors began immigrating to Palestine, many settling on farms in Galilee or in the new Jewish city of Tel Aviv on the Mediterranean coast. Britain, which had controlled Palestine as a mandatory power since the end of World War I, tried to stem the increasing tide of Jewish immigration as Arab resistance increased. But Britain's imperial days were running out, and British control of Palestine was being overtaken by events on the ground.

* * *

In 1948, at the age of sixty, Bayard Dodge retired as AUB president after twenty-five years. He had accomplished quite a lot. *Time* magazine wrote: "Bayard Dodge has done more than any other single American to win and keep good will for the U.S. in the Near East."[5] He and Mary returned to the United States and settled in Princeton, New Jersey. It was a homecoming of sorts; he had spent four happy years there as a college student. They purchased a modest nineteenth-century federal-style house at 19 Alexander Street, within walking distance of Princeton's Firestone Library, which housed one of the best Middle Eastern collections in the United States.

Bayard found occasion, at last, to reflect on the Middle East's past, present, and future. He had seen and learned plenty along the way. Life had sensitized him to the Arab perspective. It coincided with his experiences, aesthetic values, intellectual fascinations, and—not least—institutional interests. He did not know or understand the Zionist perspective nearly as well. He personally abhorred the Holocaust and had sacrificed his youngest son in the fight against it, but he did not feel its searing psychological impact on European Jewish refugees now making their way to Palestine. He did not realize, as a perceptive writer noted, "that the death-camp-haunted Jews of Palestine read the Old Testament with different eyes from those of a Protestant missionary."[5] He failed to grasp the visceral appeal of a Jewish state to Jews after the Holocaust. He was not anti-Semitic, but he was anti-Zionist, because Zionism threatened the Middle Eastern political order he had known and in which AUB had operated so successfully for so many years. Dodge had spent the greater part of his life watching Arabs and Jews teaching, studying, and working together. The prospect of Arabs and Jews opposing and killing one another over Palestine dismayed and distressed him. It threatened to undo all he had done.

Dodge began to make his views widely known. He informed American news reporters that he opposed partition as unwise and unjust to the Arabs. The following month, Dodge traveled to Washington, DC, to brief American government officials about the situation in Palestine, including Secretary of Defense James Forrestal, a fellow Princeton alumnus; Deputy Secretary of State Robert Lovett; and leading Republican senator Robert Taft of Ohio.[7] What Dodge told these officials privately he expressed publicly two months later in a personally signed article in the popular magazine *Reader's Digest*, titled "Must There Be War in the Middle East?"[8]

The *Digest* introduced Dodge as a "distinguished friend of the Arabs and Jews." Dodge began by noting that the lack of a national home for Jews represented the "emotional root" of Zionism and stressed that "not all Jews are Zionists and not all Zionists are extremists." He even chided fellow Christians for acting in ways that made the Jewish sense of vulnerability "more acute."[9]

Dodge then laid out his central argument: Most Arabs opposed the creation of a Jewish state. He quoted the leader of an Arab state, who said:

> We shall struggle without end to eject the Jewish state from Palestine. When we die, we shall pass the torch to our sons. Years and years which could have been devoted to building up our Arab peoples will be spent in a bitter and unending struggle against Zionism.[10]

Demographic changes made such remarks seem more than just ominous blustering. Thirty-eight million Arabs lived in the Middle East, compared to only 750,000 Jews. How would Zionism survive, let alone prosper, in the face of hostility from so many Arabs, with their overwhelming numerical superiority? The odds would be heavily against a Jewish state from the start.

Dodge pointed out other problems and dangers. He cautioned that US support for Zionism threatened to trigger widespread anger among Arabs, potentially undermining American relations with the larger Muslim world as well. He acknowledged both Jews and Arabs had legitimate and long-standing claims, but he believed splitting tiny Palestine—all of ten thousand square miles, about the size of Sicily or Vermont—between Jews and Arabs would fragment already scarce natural resources and public infrastructure, creating two perpetual economic mendicants. He feared protecting a Jewish state against a coalition of numerically superior Arab neighbors might one day require the deployment of American troops that could appear like a new Christian crusade against Islam. And Dodge fretted Arab leaders might retaliate against US support for a Jewish state by denying Washington and its allies access to Middle Eastern oil and siding with the Soviet Union, America's Cold War rival in the Persian Gulf.[11] All of this, he warned, would lead to the tragic deaths of Jews and Arabs, two Semitic peoples, "blood brothers" in Dodge's words; hurt US moral influence and material interests; and turn America from the favorite foreign country in the Middle East to one of the most resented and hated.[12] He did not, however, propose a solution to the growing Arab-Jewish rivalry in Palestine.

Today, Dodge's viewpoint seems controversial at best and polemical at worst. But it was not extreme—many eminent American Jews shared his view at the time. According to British Zionist Isaiah Berlin, as many as half of American Jews in 1948 preferred the assimilation of displaced Jews into Western countries to the creation of a Zionist state in Palestine.[13] Prominent Jewish anti-Zionists included legendary physicist and Nobel laureate Albert Einstein, industrialist and philanthropist Lessing Rosenwald, *New York Times* publisher Arthur Sulzberger, *Washington Post* publisher Eugene Meyer, and Hebrew University president Judah Magnes, former rabbi of New York City's premier Reform synagogue, Temple Emanu-El, who envisioned a very different future for Palestine and the people who lived there.

Magnes proposed negotiation and reconciliation with Arabs leading to a binational Palestinian state, where Jews and Arabs would share equal rights and opportunities. "The Jews have more than a claim upon the world for justice," he declared, but "I am not ready to try to achieve justice to the Jew through injustice to the Arab."[14] He added, "Palestine is not just a Jewish land or an Arab land." "It is an international interreligious land of Jew, Moslem and Christian. . . . Do not estrange Jews and Arabs from one another. Make Jewish-Arab cooperation the chief objective of a generous bi-national policy. The response by Jews and Arabs will be increasingly constructive."[15]

* * *

The future of Palestine forced US president Harry Truman to confront a decision his predecessor, Franklin Roosevelt, had finessed. FDR had expressed sympathy for Zionist aspirations, but he felt defeating Nazi Germany first best served Jewish interests. This remained Roosevelt's position until his death in 1945, when Truman suddenly became president. Two years later, in 1947, Britain announced its intention to quit Palestine—its days as an imperial power were running out—and turn Palestine over to the trusteeship of the United Nations. The situation on the ground in Palestine, however, made the idea of a UN trusteeship moot. Jewish immigration to Palestine (the overwhelming destination of choice for Holocaust survivors in Europe) had increased dramatically, leading to escalating conflict with local Arabs, who felt they were unjustly being made to pay for the crimes of Hitler. By the spring of 1948, a *de facto* partition of Palestine between Arabs and Jews had begun.

Like most Americans, Truman sympathized with the Zionist cause. Instinctively, "his sympathies were naturally with the underdog," wrote his foremost biographer.[16] Horrified by the disclosures of the Holocaust and the plight of homeless Jews after the war, he saw a Jewish homeland in Palestine as a sanctuary for a historically persecuted people pushed to the edge of extinction by fathomless Nazi evil. At the same time, he understood that supporting Zionism served his own political interests in a presidential election year. Sixty-five percent of American Jews lived in the three large states of New York, Pennsylvania, and Illinois, which together held 110 of the 270 electoral votes necessary to be elected president. Jewish-American political and financial support could help him win in 1948.[17]

Humanitarian concern and political expediency reinforced Truman's basic impulse to acknowledge events on the ground in Palestine and recognize an emerging Jewish state. Zionists were not asking the United States to create a state for them but to grant American recognition to what *they* were creating through their own blood, sweat, and tears. They hoped this would bring President Truman and the US government to recognize a *fait accompli*. Polls showed this position coincided with American public opinion. When asked in the spring of 1948, "If Jews independently set up a Jewish state," should the United States support them? Fifty percent of Protestants and 44 percent of Catholics said yes; only 10 percent of Protestants and 14 percent of Catholics said no.[18]

In the end, Truman decided to support creation of the new Jewish state, making the United States the first foreign country to recognize the State of Israel. Truman's extension of US diplomatic support was not unconditional, however. He expected Israel to behave responsibly in return for American recognition. "The Jews must now display tolerance and consideration for the other people in Palestine with whom they will necessarily have to be neighbors," he had written former treasury secretary Henry Morgenthau Jr. a few months earlier.[19] President Truman and his advisers acted as they did "not because they were anti-Arab," historian Ussama Makdisi rightly observed, "but because they made a basic calculation that the balance of domestic and foreign interests suggested one course of action. They hoped that Arab disillusionment would be short-lived, or at any rate, contained or mollified."[20] The events of subsequent decades suggest they miscalculated badly.

* * *

On May 15, 1948, the day after Zionists announced the creation of the State of Israel, the combined armies of Egypt, Iraq, Jordan, Lebanon, and Syria invaded to crush Jewish nationalism and establish an Arab state in Palestine.[21] The British-officered Arab Legion rapidly occupied the West Bank of the Jordan River and the area south of the Sea of Galilee.[22] The much smaller

Israeli army—then known as the *Haganah* and now known as the Israeli Defense Force (IDF)—fought back from interior lines of communication, capturing Jaffa on the Mediterranean coast from Arab militias and reopening the roads between Tel Aviv and Jerusalem and between Haifa and the western Galilee. Large numbers of Arab refugees, fleeing out of fear or evicted by Jewish forces, streamed out of Palestine.

Numerically superior Arab armies suffered from conflicting aims and lack of coordination. Outnumbered *Haganah* forces, fighting for their very survival in the face of great danger, resisted fiercely on all fronts, particularly against the Egyptian invasion up the coast, which threatened the new Israeli capital of Tel Aviv, and the Arab's Legion's siege of Jerusalem, which threatened to close the highway to Tel Aviv and thereby sever Israel in two. The *Haganah*'s speed, surprise, and interior lines of communication and supply offset the Arab armies' superior tactical training, mobility, and firepower.

As the war raged, occasionally interrupted by fragile, UN-brokered truces, Israel occupied more of Palestine and strengthened its military position while more than one-half million Arabs (two-thirds of the Arab population), unwilling to live under Israeli rule or expelled under threat by the *Haganah*, sought refuge in Arab countries, where their descendants live to this day. (A majority of Jordan's population since 1948 has been Palestinian.) The refugee problem remains potent today. "After the war," wrote one historian, "the refugees ultimately would fulfill as useful a political purpose for the Arab states as the Jewish displaced persons had served initially for the Zionists."[23] The Israeli government has steadfastly opposed the right of Palestinian Arabs to return to their pre-1948 homes ever since.

Both sides committed atrocities amidst the bitter fighting, deepening the widening emotional divide between Arabs and Jews. The leader of the Arab League proclaimed on the eve of the Arab invasion that "this will be a war of extermination and a momentous massacre which will be spoken of like the Mongolian massacre and the Crusades." Arab guerrillas stripped and mutilated Jewish civilians. At the village of Deir Yassin, Jewish forces massacred more than 250 Arab old men, women, and children, mutilated their bodies, and then threw the corpses down a well.[24] It was becoming a ruthless and brutal war of hate.

Portrait of the young Daniel Bliss, circa 1855. The frontiersman-turned-missionary exuded determination and optimism. *(Photo courtesy of the Bliss Family Papers, Amherst College Archives and Special Collections, Amherst College Library.)*

Abby Wood Bliss at the time of her marriage to Daniel. She possessed intelligence and sensitivity like her close hometown friend Emily Dickinson. *(Photo courtesy of the Bliss Family Papers, Amherst College Archives and Special Collections, Amherst College Library.)*

The *Sultana*, the fast bark that transported Daniel and Abby Bliss from New England to their new home—Lebanon—in 1856. *(Photo courtesy of the Henry Jessup Papers, Special Collections, Yale Divinity School Library.)*

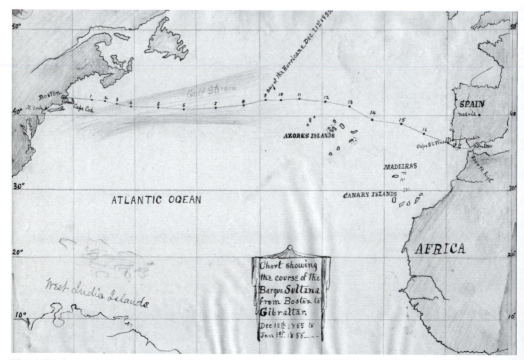

The Atlantic crossing of the *Sultana*, December 1855–January 1856. The ship and its passengers weathered perilously rough seas. *(Photo courtesy of the Henry Jessup Papers, Special Collections, Yale Divinity School Library.)*

Beirut in the 1850s. A booming seaport in the eastern Mediterranean, the ancient city lay at the base of the beautiful Lebanon range. *(Photo courtesy of the Library of Congress.)*

William E. Dodge. A Puritan merchant, his money—together with Daniel Bliss's leadership—created and sustained AUB during its formative years. *(Photo used with permission from the Cleveland H. Dodge Foundation, Inc./The Frick Art Reference Library, New York City.)*

Stuart Dodge. As a representative in Beirut for his father, William, Stuart Dodge helped Daniel Bliss build AUB into a distinguished university during the period 1870–1900. *(Photo courtesy of the American University of Beirut/Library Archives.)*

The first generation of AUB faculty and students, circa 1875. East met West in classrooms of cultural interchange. *(Photo used with permission from the Cleveland H. Dodge Foundation, Inc./The Frick Art Reference Library, New York City.)*

Daniel Bliss as AUB president, circa 1875. The realities—and limits—of America's mission to the Middle East had sobered but not deterred him. *(Photo courtesy of the Bliss Family Papers, Amherst College Archives and Special Collections, Amherst College Library.)*

Daniel and Abby Bliss in retirement, early twentieth century. The decades they had spent in the Middle East had tempered their initial arrogance but not their determination and resilience. *(Photo courtesy of the Bliss Family Papers, Amherst College Archives and Special Collections, Amherst College Library.)*

Howard Bliss *(top row, second from left)* as a graduate student at Mansfield College, Oxford, 1880s. His father, Daniel, groomed his second son to succeed him as AUB president—a destiny Howard initially resisted. *(Photo courtesy of the Bliss Family Papers, Amherst College Archives and Special Collections, Amherst College Library.)*

Howard Bliss as AUB president, 1902–1920. He led AUB during a period of profound transformation in the Middle East before, during, and immediately after World War I. *(Photo courtesy of the Bliss Family Papers, Amherst College Archives and Special Collections, Amherst College Library.)*

Bayard Dodge, circa 1945. A great-nephew of Stuart Dodge, he succeeded Howard Bliss as AUB president in 1923 and guided it for the next twenty-five years. Patrician and progressive, he understood modernity's challenge to Muslim traditionalism—but not the emotional resonance of Zionism triggered by the Holocaust. *(Photo courtesy of the American University of Beirut/Library Archives.)*

David Dodge, circa 1980. Son of Bayard Dodge and grandson of Howard Bliss, David continued his families' tradition of service to AUB and the larger Middle East. As AUB's interim president during the tumultuous Lebanese Civil War and Israeli incursion of 1982, he fell victim to Shiite extremist kidnappers and was held hostage for one year in Lebanon, Syria, and Iran before being released in 1983. *(Photo courtesy of the American University of Beirut/Library Archives.)*

The son of AUB faculty, Malcolm Kerr grew up on campus and loved the school, even as he made his academic career in the United States. He returned to AUB to lead the school in 1983 and gave his life for it, felled by assassins' bullets the following year. *(Photo courtesy of Ann Kerr.)*

The main entrance into AUB from Bliss Street, Beirut. The school's credo, in English and in Arabic on either side, reads: "That they may have life and have it more abundantly." *(Photo courtesy of the author.)*

College Hall. *(Photo courtesy of the author.)*

Daniel Bliss Hall. *(Photo courtesy of the author.)*

Marquand House. Home to AUB presidents and their families since 1879. *(Photo courtesy of the author.)*

After more months of fighting, UN mediator Ralph Bunche convened a series of negotiations at the Hotel des Roses on the island of Rhodes.[25] Initially, Arab negotiators refused to speak with their Israeli counterparts led by Moshe Dayan. But, gradually, the two sides began communicating—first arguing with each other, then talking with each other, and finally staking out common ground with each other. By the end, the unexpected and seemingly impossible happened: Arab and Israeli representatives sat down together and shared family photographs. The first Arab-Israeli War ended in the summer of 1949. Bunche earned the Nobel Peace Prize for successfully ending the war, the first African American so honored.[26]

People hoped an enduring modus vivendi would emerge between Israel and its Arab neighbors. But the end of hostilities brought no end to the antagonism. "The European Jews who built Israel came out of a culture of sharp edges and had to rely on their own deep tribal sense of solidarity," explained Jewish American journalist Thomas Friedman. "They were never part of a Middle Eastern kaleidoscope, like Lebanon, where today's enemy could be tomorrow's friend. For the Jews coming out of Europe, today's enemy was tomorrow's enemy."[27] Many convinced themselves there was no legitimate Palestinian nation with whom they had to share the land of Palestine. The Arabs, in turn, continued to see Israel as an illegitimate Zionist creation that had unjustly displaced Palestinians and therefore must be rejected and resisted. Each side viewed the other as a physical and existential challenge. The year 1948 marked the first conflict between Arabs and Jews over Palestine. It would not be the last.

* * *

The first Arab-Israeli War had widespread effects. Most Arabs rightfully regarded the war as a decisive military defeat. This triggered political upheaval in Arab nations for years to come. Most Arab states perceived the United States as too pro-Israel, but they remained preoccupied with internal problems, such as rapid population growth and the social and economic pressures it generated. Meanwhile, Jews throughout the Middle East and the Maghreb (known as Sephardim) immigrated in increasing numbers to Israel in the face of rising local antipathy, swelling the Jewish state's population from 750,000 in 1948 to 1.9 million by 1960.[28]

The first Arab-Israeli War also affected Lebanon and AUB, as Bayard Dodge had feared and warned. A flood of more than 100,000 Palestinians streamed into refugee camps south of Beirut, upsetting the country's delicate balance between Christians and Muslims.[29] The AUB student body split into Arab and Jewish camps, creating a bitter and hostile division. Arab students vocally sympathized with the Palestinian diaspora; many of them were a part of it. Jewish students encountered resentment, threats of violence, and visa denials from the Lebanese government. They reacted by leaving AUB and enrolling in Israeli institutions like Hebrew and Tel Aviv Universities instead. In 1946, 10 percent of AUB students had been Jewish. By 1948, the percentage had fallen to 4 percent. A decade later, the number fell to zero.[30] This postwar exodus of AUB's Jewish students represented the loss of something vitally important. AUB as a meeting place and common ground for young Arabs and Jews of the Middle East—so rare and yet so indispensable to building a shared future together—had ended for an indeterminate period.

The creation of Israel also affected Arab students' attitudes and perceptions of the United States. America had traditionally been viewed as a beacon of hope for those aspiring to democracy and freedom from foreign control and as an anticolonial power having no imperialistic designs in the Middle East. Unlike Britain and France, America had never tried to impose its will on the region, either directly or through local proxies. Arab students saw AUB as a symbol of these qualities. They trusted it as an institution that had no political or religious ax to grind, no economic or chauvinistic philosophy to sell.

Those perceptions changed after 1948. The United States went from being viewed as a benevolent, disinterested outsider to a biased and increasingly overbearing presence in the Middle East. For the first time, Lebanese crowds protested against American policy and attacked the US Information Center in downtown Beirut. Students gave speeches and chanted their causes. The campus resounded with tirades against Israel and its "creator" the United States during the 1950s. One year during that decade, 40 percent of AUB sophomores used a history examination question on imperial Rome as a springboard to attack American imperialism.[31] Demonstrations erupted over the Baghdad Pact, a US-sponsored alliance created in 1955 aimed against Communist expansion in the Middle East that many in the region believed to be actually aimed against Arab nationalism and unity. Beirut riot police entered the university grounds that year and fired shots to restore order—something that had never happened before. One AUB student was severely wounded. Another accused the administration of "moral terrorism" in its efforts to suppress "the Arab spirit among its students."[32] The campus seethed with muted rebellion. The politicization of AUB that Daniel Bliss, Howard Bliss, and Bayard Dodge had always feared and strived to avoid had begun. They could no longer keep the politics around them at bay. AUB came face-to-face with the external realities of Middle East politics.

The life of George Habash, with its broken dreams and angry wounds, dramatically illustrated this change. Born in 1926 in Lydda[33] in the British mandate of Palestine into an Arab Christian merchant family, Habash grew up an introverted, hard-working, serious student. He entered AUB at the end of World War II on a merit scholarship to study medicine. When the first Arab-Israeli War broke out, he rushed home to serve as a medical orderly. He witnessed the deepening violence between Arabs and Jews. *Haganah* forces attacked Lydda from the air, strafing neighborhoods and dropping bombs and leaflets demanding the Arabs' surrender. After the Israelis captured Lydda on July 12, 1948, they ordered the expulsion of every Palestinian man, woman, and child, including Habash and his family, from their homes in order to relieve the pressure from a sullen population. "The inhabitants of Lydda must be expelled quickly without attention to age," ordered Lieutenant Colonel Yitzhak Rabin, a future Israeli Prime Minister assassinated by a right-wing Jewish extremist in 1995 after signing a peace accord with Palestinians.[34]

Haganah soldiers went house to house, in some cases pounding on doors with the butts of their guns, yelling at Palestinians to leave at once. They forced the Arab refugees to march at gunpoint for three days under the cloudless, extremely hot July sun to the front line at Beit Nabala. This Israeli strategy not only depopulated Lydda of Palestinians but also clogged the road, preventing the Arab Legion from mounting an offensive to retake the town.[35]

The Habash family joined thousands of other families moving east on foot, a long line of refugees walking slowly in the waves of heat. The temperature in mid-July on Palestine's central plain soared to one hundred degrees Fahrenheit in the shade. The Palestinians bent forward under the sun, stumbling along unpaved roads over stones, thorns, and sharp wheat stalks cut short from the recent harvest. They looked constantly for water but found little. They carried suitcases, bundles of clothes, and valuables strapped to their bodies. Their donkeys were loaded with hastily gathered belongings. They had planned for a short trip. They were certain they would be coming back soon, once the Arab Legion recaptured Lydda.

A *Haganah* officer later described the forced march from Lydda to Beit Nabala:

> A multitude of inhabitants walked one after another. Women walked burdened with packages and sacks on their heads. Mothers dragged children after them. . . . Occasionally, warning shots were heard. . . . Occasionally, you encountered a piercing look from one of the youngsters in the column, and the look said, "We have not yet surrendered. We shall return to fight you."[36]

Some *Haganah* soldiers stripped the displaced Arabs of rings, watches, and other gold jewelry as they left Lydda and at checkpoints along the march. Personal belongings fell by the wayside as they staggered along. In the end, bodies of men, women, and children dotted the dusty, sun-baked road from Lydda to Beit Nabala. Several hundred died from exhaustion, dehydration, and disease.[37]

The Lydda march changed George Habash from a quiet medical student into a disaffected, militant Palestinian activist. Habash returned to Beirut in the fall of 1948, where he resumed his medical studies at AUB. But Habash saw the university, and everything else for that matter, differently now. He remembered Bayard Dodge "telling us about an America that stood for justice, freedom, and humanitarian principles. . . . But now," Habash said with great bitterness, "I saw the contradictions between what he said about America and what the U.S. was doing to support Israel—and Zionism."[38] Habash had come to see AUB not as an oasis of opportunity and hope, but as a symbol of imperialism and hypocrisy.

Habash graduated first in his AUB medical school class in 1951. He could have tended to private matters and accumulated a fortune like other members of his profession in the Middle East. Instead, Habash moved to Amman, where he worked as a pediatrician in Palestinian refugee camps caring for undernourished and sickly children. Within a few years, he quit medicine and took up the cause of Palestinian resistance for the rest of his life. Known popularly as "Dr. George," he became one of the most charismatic leaders of the Palestinian resistance movement. In 1967, Habash founded the Marxist Popular Front for the Liberation of Palestine (PFLP), the main rival to Yasser Arafat's *al-Fatah* organization for political leadership of the Palestinian movement. The PFLP organized many terrorist attacks during the 1970s, including the hijacking of a Western airliner to Entebbe, Uganda, in 1976, which led to a dramatic rescue mission by Israeli commandos. Habash eventually lost his rivalry with Arafat and died in Amman in 2008.

As George Habash and other students began attacking AUB as an agent of US imperialism, the American government began viewing the school as a valuable asset in the Cold War. Lebanon lay near the southern border of the Soviet Union, Beirut had close ties with oil-rich Arab nations, and AUB represented a prestigious outpost of American culture. For all of these reasons, Washington began to support AUB financially. It financed a massive, state-of-the-art medical center and hundreds of scholarships for students from as far away as Nepal and Pakistan. Bayard Dodge's successor, Stephen Penrose (the first nonfamily president of AUB) welcomed this new flow of federal money. But AUB's growing reliance on US government funding—first through the Point Four Program of foreign aid, then through funding from the US Agency for International Development—came at an increasing, if subtle, cost. AUB's financial autonomy and independent reputation, carefully cultivated by the Blisses and the Dodges, slowly began to erode. Critics argued that AUB's financial dependency on the American government made it unwilling or unable to publicly criticize American policy in the Middle East.[39] Some feared this meant AUB would lose its political independence as well.

Then came the 1958 crisis. On July 14 of that year, four decades after the British had put Faisal on the throne of Iraq, anti-Western Iraqi army officers overthrew the Hashemite dynasty, killing the king and the prime minister. Lebanese president Camille Chamoun, an AUB graduate and pro-Western Maronite, felt threatened because he had publicly opposed Egypt's President Nasser, the charismatic hero-leader of Arab nationalism and vocal critic of Western imperialism in the Middle East. Lebanon had been the only Arab state not to break relations with Britain and France after the 1956 Suez Crisis. Chamoun had further antagonized his country's Muslims by refusing to merge Lebanon with Egypt and Syria as part of the newly created United Arab Republic and by scheming to change the national constitution—originally based on a "national pact" that divided political power between Christians and Muslims[40]—to permit him to serve a second, consecutive presidential term.[41]

Invoking the Eisenhower Doctrine, which allowed the United States to deploy troops to defend friendly regimes in the Middle East, Chamoun urged President Eisenhower to quell a potential civil war. On July 16, 1958, fourteen thousand American marines—more than the entire Lebanese army—landed on beaches near the Beirut airport, startling sunbathers and boys selling chewing gum and Coca-Cola® at highly inflated prices.[42] Warships of the US Sixth Fleet anchored in Beirut harbor. US tanks took up positions outside AUB's main gates. One evening, a group of marines attended a social gathering at the local USO (United Service Organization). "They look so young and so innocent," an AUB faculty spouse said to her husband, "far too young to understand the complications of war."[43] The US military presence quieted things down, and Chamoun abandoned his bid for a second presidential term. The marines withdrew three months later without suffering a single casualty.

The fateful precedent of putting American troops on the ground in the Middle East had been established—a precedent that would become easier with each successive intervention in the 1980s, 1990s, and 2000s. The Lebanese had bent with the wind, but their historic resentment at the presence of foreign troops had not diminished. Many Lebanese had regarded the US intervention as a return of foreign domination. Most importantly, the sectarian tensions and factional strife among Lebanese had not gone away. They had merely gone underground, where they continued to fester—ready to explode one day.

The Cold War had made Washington suspicious of any potentially destabilizing force in the Middle East, such as radical Arab nationalism, which it reflexively associated with Soviet expansionism. This changed the meaning of America for Arabs. Arabs had felt American military power firsthand for the first time. They now saw the United States less as a force for liberal, democratic change and more as a force for reaction and even repression through support of conservative, autocratic regimes. This shift of US policy toward preservation of the status quo sparked a wave of anti-American sentiment in the Arab world that would grow larger and stronger. In time, the wave would become a tsunami.

* * *

But for a time after the 1958 crisis, Beirut and AUB enjoyed an Indian summer of peace and prosperity. This stemmed in large measure from Lebanon's part in the Middle East oil boom of the 1960s and early 1970s. Oil had been discovered in Arabia in the 1930s, transforming it from an isolated desert peninsula into a world economic player. Abd al-Aziz ibn Saud had wrested control of Arabia a decade earlier from his rival, Sharif Hussein, and built the Kingdom of Saudi Arabia through the force of his personality. Ibn Saud was a Bedouin, but he was not a naïf; he understood well the tangible benefits and potential dangers of his country's newfound oil wealth. He had seen how Britain had used the Anglo-Iranian Oil Company to exploit and dominate Iran and wanted to avoid a similar fate.

A Saudi official visiting AUB in the early 1930s had told Bayard Dodge, "Ibn Saud intends to give a concession to [the Standard Oil Company of] California." Why an American company? Dodge had asked. Because "it is so far away that it can never send an army or a navy," the Saudi answered.[44] Ibn Saud could scarcely imagine the hundreds of thousands of US troops who would use Saudi Arabia as a staging area during the Gulf War of 1991 and the US invasion of Iraq in 2003.

Ibn Saud granted the Standard Oil Company of California (Socal) an exclusive concession in May 1933. The Socal concession eventually became the Arabian-American Oil Company (Aramco), a consortium of companies created to operate the vast Saudi oil fields, which had proved much larger than initially anticipated.[45] The United State's dependence on Saudi oil grew dramatically during World War II, when America's immense expansion of industrial output transformed it into an oil importer for the first time in history. The US-Saudi relationship based on oil began an American involvement with the Arab world far more strategic in conception and nationalistic in interest than the nineteenth- and early-twentieth-century missionary enterprise rooted in educational humanitarianism.

Saudi Arabia and the United States sealed their partnership at a famous meeting between King Ibn Saud and President Franklin Roosevelt aboard the US warship *Quincy* anchored in the Great Bitter Lake of the Suez Canal on February 14, 1945. Present at the meeting, helping to translate, was William Eddy, the son of early missionaries to Lebanon. Among other things, the two leaders agreed on the construction of a 1,400-mile pipeline to be built by Aramco's Trans-Arabian Pipeline Company (Tapline) linking the oil fields at Dhahran on the Persian Gulf across the Saudi desert, through Jordan's panhandle and Syria's Golan Heights, to a terminal at Sidon, Lebanon, just forty miles down the Mediterranean coast from Beirut.

Tapline took on added importance once the Cold War began. Western Europe looked vulnerable to Soviet expansion in the early days of the Cold War. A steady supply of Middle East oil would aid recovery of its war-ravaged economies and contribute to the success of the European Recovery Program while reducing the burden on American domestic oil production. The terminal at Sidon would facilitate oil shipments to America's European allies by substantially shortening the twenty-day, seven-thousand-mile journey by tankers down the Persian Gulf, through the Indian Ocean to the Red Sea, and then through the Suez Canal. US secretary of state George Marshall understood all of this. "The oil of the Middle East is an important factor in the success of the European Recovery Program," he said of the program that later became known as the Marshall Plan, and Tapline would "provide a vital transportation link in moving Saudi crude to western Europe.[46]

The Tapline project represented the biggest pipeline construction project in history up to that time. (It would remain so until the Trans-Alaska Pipeline in the 1970s). California-based Bechtel Corporation supervised the project, which involved twenty thousand Arab laborers working nonstop for two years, laying over 300,000 tons of steel pipe and constructing six gigantic pumping stations across more than one thousand miles of shifting desert sand. In some areas, engineers used gigantic trenching machines to hollow out beds for the huge pipe; in others, they used metal struts to hold the pipe in place above rolling dunes and rocky hills. When Tapline officially opened on December 2, 1950, tankers offloaded three-quarters of one million barrels of Saudi Arabian crude oil in less than twenty hours for the short journey to refineries in France and Italy.[47] Tapline soon pumped more than 300,000 barrels of Saudi crude through its thirty-inch pipes each day.[48] The six million barrels of oil in Tapline at all times was more than all the oil pumped daily from all the wells in the United States. It was a staggering engineering achievement.

Beirut and AUB benefited tremendously from the Tapline terminal at nearby Sidon, which complemented the older British-controlled Iraq Petroleum Company (IPC) pipeline that terminated at Tripoli, up the coast from Beirut. Lebanon had become the major transit point on the oil routes from Iraq and Saudi Arabia to western Europe. A huge supply storage facility also went up in Beirut. This, combined with the hefty transit fees Tapline and IPC paid on the oil carried through their pipelines and remittances sent by Lebanese working abroad in oil-producing countries, produced an economic boom in the city. Always multisectarian and multiethnic, Beirut's cosmopolitanism reflected the rollicking pluralism and prosperity of the growing city.

In the eastern part of Beirut, the Christian districts of Achrafiyeh and Gemmayzeh blossomed with affluent businesses and restaurants. In the western part of the city, Rās Beirut's old stone villas, with fragrant gardens of bougainvillea, honeysuckle, jasmine, and oleander fringed with cactus, gave way to beachfront hotels and Western embassies on the corniche road and multistory office and apartment buildings on Rues Abdul Aziz and Jeanne d'Arc built for Palestinian exiles who had money. (The 1948 war brought not just destitute refugees, but also Palestinian businessmen, bankers, lawyers, writers, teachers, civil servants, artists, and poets.) Rue Hamra, once a sleepy street of small shops, now pulsed with boutiques selling luxury goods from around the world. Busy thoroughfares encircled the AUB campus. AUB's tolerance, freedom of thought, and cultural diversity attracted intellectuals and dissidents from across the Islamic world as far away as Morocco in the west to Sudan in the south to Afghanistan in the east.

A world away, in the southern part of Beirut, the traditional working-class Muslim districts of Ramlet al-Bayda and Burj al-Barajneh teemed with small mosques and cafes where old men puffed on *narghiles* (waterpipes), clicked *tawleh* (backgammon) pieces on fine inlaid tables, and fingered their well-worn prayer beads between slow sips of thick, black coffee. While uptown Beirutis basked in increasing prosperity, the less fortunate Shia and the poor, uneducated Palestinians who occupied the crowded refugee camps in these southern districts lived in wooden lean-tos and cement-block hovels roofed with corrugated tin, held menial jobs as day-laborers and maids, and remained mired in hopeless poverty. In these squalid conditions, the resentment of the displaced Palestinians festered.

The contrast between rich and poor Beirut could not be sharper—or more potentially explosive. In rich Beirut lived the 4 percent of the population that held one-third of the wealth. In poor Beirut lived the bottom half of the population that held less than one-fifth.[49] Beirut was separated by subterranean currents of fear, envy, and tribalism. It was a bifurcated world of economic disparity, and historical animosity passed within families from one generation to the next. These dark currents would eventually erupt to the surface and envelop AUB.

But for now, the affluent part of Beirut became a mecca for the international "jet set" and rich Arabs of the oil-rich Gulf states, who enjoyed the Mediterranean on yachts during the day and clubs along fashionable Rue Monot at night. Beirut became a chic port of call for cruise ships, the one place in the region visited by Western tourists. In 1966, the popular magazine *Life* described Beirut as "an amalgam of the ancient Middle East with Western sophistication, a kind of Las Vegas-Riviera-St. Moritz flavored with spices of Araby."[50] Lebanese newspapers (the product of a free press) circulated throughout the Arab world. Capital flowed into the laissez-faire economy. Beirut had more banks than Manhattan and more newspapers than London. Beirut became the business world's New York in the Middle East.

Meanwhile, AUB continued to grow in size and sophistication while maintaining its status as the largest American university outside of the United States and the best university in the Middle East. Generously supported by funding from the US government, profitable American oil corporations, and philanthropies like the Ford and Rockefeller Foundations, its arabesque gates now enclosed eighty acres of fragrant pine and palm gardens and more than fifty ivy-covered buff stone buildings. Students crisscrossed campus in both traditional Middle Eastern dress and blue jeans. By the late 1960s, 70 percent of AUB faculty was Middle Eastern.[51] No longer just American missionaries, they felt a strong sense of mission nonetheless and eagerly educated students to think critically about what it meant to be Arab in the twentieth century. "The students," said one professor, "can't help but respect the United States because we give them the freedom to disagree."[52] Top academics from around the world came to AUB to work in an atmosphere of internationalism and intellectual freedom. Just off campus on Rue Bliss, the intelligentsia of the Middle East—artists, dissidents, poets, and writers— clustered in coffeehouses and sidewalk cafes, where they swapped ideas that appeared in avant-garde literary magazines, eccentric periodicals, art galleries, and experimental theaters. Plays, exhibits, concerts, and conferences made AUB the center of cultural and intellectual life in the Middle East.

Rās Beirut's mixed ethnic and religious composition and permissive political atmosphere offered a welcoming refuge for individuals and groups periodically out of favor with regimes in neighboring Arab states. The environment was one of mutual respect and deference to pluralism. There was room for everyone (except, apparently, Jews). Ideologies that influenced the lives and vision of millions of Arabs—Baathism, Marxist-Leninism, Palestinian nationalism, Pan-Arabism—all found expression here. These ideologies generated ripples that traveled far beyond west Beirut. It became, in important respects, the Greenwich Village of the Middle East. At its center stood AUB, which served as a laboratory for testing new ideas and ways of life. The university tolerated—indeed, encouraged—eclecticism and experimentation in both public and private spheres, ranging from serious political ideologies to trendy fashions. Freed from the yoke of oppressive political regimes at home, AUB students challenged and debunked conventional authority and orthodox doctrines.[53]

AUB and Beirut seemed ideal intermediaries between the Arab world and the West. In the words of one observer, they "lived in two worlds, which placed them in the ideal position to interpret one to the other: to articulate the Arab heritage and Arab causes in a manner that the West could understand; and to provide a screening mechanism for Western social and cultural influences reaching the Arab world. They alone could explain to the Arabs what was actually happening in the outside world, and explain to the outside world what the problems and aspirations of the Arabs were." AUB graduates articulated and popularized ideas and values that transformed the lives of millions of Arabs.[54]

Perhaps the best embodiment of AUB as a bridge between America and the Arab world was the life and works of distinguished scholar Philip Hitti, who pioneered Arab and Oriental studies in the United States as a professor at Princeton University from 1926 to 1954. Born in 1886 into a poor, Maronite Christian family in the picturesque mountain village of Shimlan in the Lebanon Mountains, Hitti broke his arm when he was eight. A compound fracture that village shepherds failed to cure, gangrene set in and Hitti would have died—had his arm and his life not been saved by two operations performed by AUB medical missionary George Post.[55]

Inspired to get an education, Hitti graduated from AUB in 1908 and stayed on at the school to teach Arabic. Then-president Howard Bliss encouraged Hitti to pursue graduate study at Columbia University and promised to pay his tuition. Hitti arrived in New York in the fall of 1913 with a letter of introduction from Howard Bliss to Stuart Dodge. The address on the sealed envelope read "99 John Street," but Hitti could find no "99" between "98" and "100" until a passerby directed him to the other side of the street.[56] Hitti performed brilliantly at Columbia, earning a doctorate in 1915 and becoming the first Arab to receive a PhD from the university. He returned to AUB to teach Oriental history until he moved to Princeton, New Jersey, in 1926.

At the time, even educated Americans knew virtually nothing about Arabs. The best US colleges and universities, such as Harvard, Princeton, and Yale, offered no Arabic language courses. Hitti set out to change all that. Within a generation, he and his Princeton colleagues established the finest

Arab and Islamic studies program in the United States and one of the best in the entire world. Hitti's magnum opus, *A History of the Arabs*, became the standard treatment of the subject (and it is still in print today). When he retired in 1954, Hitti was widely recognized as the preeminent scholar in the West of Islam and the Arabs.

* * *

Lebanon seemed to be the Switzerland of the Middle East, free from the fanaticism and chauvinism plaguing other countries in the region. Diverse and yet sophisticated, Lebanese society seemed to prove that groups with conflicting interests could live and work together peacefully. The ability of Lebanon's Christians and Muslims to live in apparent tranquility while Israel and its other Arab neighbors exchanged threats, Egypt's Nasser railed against Western imperialism, the Baathist regimes in Iraq and Syria insulted each other, and Palestinians took up arms struck most observers as remarkable and commendable. It seemed to be a country that could build a democracy out of diversity. Even cynics thought the Lebanese love of making money would hold things together indefinitely.

Perceptive observers, however, noticed the mounting tension beneath the surface glitter. Noted British travel writer James Morris sketched this dark prediction in 1956:

> Beirut feels a transitory place . . . such a way of life, you feel, cannot be permanent: it is all too fickle, too fast, too make-believe and never-never. Beirut feels a rootless city, virile but infertile. A breath of wind, it seems, a shift of fortune, and all this bright-painted fabric would be whisked away into oblivion, like the countless predecessor cities of this Phoenician shore.[57]

Few people at the time recognized—or wanted to recognize—the inconsistency between Beirut's alluring image and its underlying reality. But twenty years later, in 1975, Beirut would change from a luxurious, tolerant, and culturally diverse city into an ugly cauldron of hatred, civil war, and terrorism. Then, AUB would find itself not a haven but a battleground.

* * *

When Bayard Dodge returned to the States and to Princeton in 1948, he was shocked to learn the university offered no courses on the contemporary Middle East. Princeton asked him to conduct a seminar for students hungry to learn something about the Middle East. When not teaching, he continued his research at the Firestone Library. He worked at his study carrel throughout the morning, took a short break for lunch, and returned to work through the late afternoon. In winter, he walked to campus wearing a black astrakhan cap that sharply contrasted with his thinning white hair. His desk at home, arranged efficiently and neatly with paper, envelopes, legal-sized notepads, and clips in separate drawers, reflected his lifelong discipline and drive.

He and Mary took under their wings many foreign graduate students studying at Princeton. They knew how lonely it felt to be young and part of an academic community in a foreign land far from home, learning to balance cultures and to make sacrifices in pursuit of personal ambitions and dreams. Bayard also gave speeches, hosted conferences, and entertained house-guests—sheikhs, princes, and prime ministers from all over the Middle East. In a very real sense, Dodge never stopped being a college president.

In 1955 he accepted an offer from the State Department to serve as a freelance cultural attaché in Egypt. He and Mary returned again to the Middle East. They settled in Cairo, where they rented an apartment over-looking the Nile River. Across town was al-Azhar Mosque, the great center of Islamic learning for almost one thousand years. Dodge initially worked with the American Embassy, but Nasser's relationship with the West was strained—it was the era of triumphal Arab nationalism—so Dodge decided to operate on his own in order to be an effective sounding board of Arab opinion at the time of the Suez Crisis.[58] He learned a lot by inviting al-Azhar's distinguished imams to his apartment for tea and simply listening to them talk. Bayard Dodge's personal austerity and mild manner must have facilitated easy communication. Dodge also occasionally taught seminars at the American University of Cairo and continued his scholarly research on Muslim medievalism.[59] For him, retirement meant no break from the past but rather a continuation of his life's pursuit, an expression of his aesthetic values and intellectual fascinations.

Bayard and Mary spent their other days traveling widely throughout the Middle East, visiting places they had been before and places they had somehow missed. Dodge personally knew many movers and shakers in the region because they had been educated at AUB. He proudly wrote his twin brother, Cleveland, from Khartoum in November 1956 of his pride in "living to see a Beirut graduate receiving guests in Lord Kitchener's former palace and going about in the Governor General's bright red Rolls-Royce®, with the new flag of the Sudanese Republic on the hood."[60] Such moments validated his life's work.

He and Mary returned home to Princeton in 1959. During the following years, Bayard, ever restless, continued to travel—this time, to places that had particular meaning to him. Nineteen years after B. D.'s death, in 1963, he and Mary finally visited their youngest son's grave in the Épinal American Cemetery. The simple white cross marking B. D.'s burial site lay in a vast field among five thousand other young American GIs who had given their lives in the struggle against Nazi evil. It was a somber occasion. They also visited Andalusia in Spain, where the historic drama between Christianity and Islam—two of his greatest passions—had played out for centuries during the Middle Ages. And they returned to Beirut, where their son David and his family—and so many vivid memories—still lived. These years represented the calm before the storm that broke in June 1967.

* * *

During the month of June 1967, the second Arab-Israeli War—commonly known as the Six-Day War—began. The Six-Day War represented a watershed in the history of the Middle East. It demonstrated the tremendous military superiority of the IDF and redrew the map of the region as Israel made sweeping territorial gains in a lightning preemptive war intended to secure its borders. Egypt's Nasser provoked Israel's attack by ordering UN peacekeeping troops from the Sinai Peninsula, moving Egyptian troops east of the Suez Canal toward the Israeli frontier, and closing the Gulf of Aqaba to Israeli shipping. From June 5 until June 11, 1967, the Israeli air force and army decisively defeated Egyptian, Jordanian, and Syrian forces, capturing the Sinai Peninsula and Gaza Strip from Egypt, the old city of Jerusalem and the West Bank from Jordan, and the Golan Heights from Syria. It was a stunning victory for Israel and a crushing defeat for its Arab neighbors. Israel exulted in its success, but in some ways it was a Pyrrhic victory: by annexing the Gaza Strip and the West Bank, Israel now occupied territory inhabited by more than one million Palestinian Arabs, many of them hostile to Israel and longing for an independent homeland of their own.

The Six-Day War destroyed Nasser's dreams of presiding over the creation of a pan-Arab state. It also sounded the death-knell of the secular Arab nationalism that Nasser had championed. Israel's crushing defeat of the Arabs galvanized the emerging Islamist alternative. The Arab military humiliation of June 1967 touched something deep in Muslims' souls. The Six-Day War was a sign that something had gone gravely awry in Islamic history. The Qur'an had promised that a society that surrendered to God's revealed will could not fail. Before, when misfortune had struck, Muslims had turned to religion, and the *umma* (community of believers) had not only been revived but had usually gone on to greater achievements. How could the forces of Islam fall to the Israelis and their secular, Western allies? Throughout the Middle East, a fusion of politics and religion began to permeate the Muslim world as Arab leaders sought to justify their failed campaigns and Palestinians in the occupied territories sought to incite support for their cause and justify their struggle with religion. A defensive interest in roots, in the past, and in the Islamic cultural heritage took hold. The Iranian Revolution of 1979 would carry this Islamist alternative to new heights, with fateful consequences for the Middle East and the United States.

Although Lebanon sat out the Six-Day War, unlike the first Arab-Israeli War, the war deeply affected the country. It brought another wave of Palestinian refugees that destabilized and polarized Lebanese society because most Palestinians lacked opportunities. Lebanese laws prohibited them from entering professions governed by a professional syndicate, such as engineering; largely barred them from owning property; and granted them only limited access to public health care, education, and social welfare benefits. The severely understaffed United Nations Relief and Works Agency (UNRWA) ran the refugee camps' schools, hospitals, women's centers, and vocational training programs.

Palestinians lost faith in others' capacity to champion their cause. So

Palestinians began to arm themselves to regain their homeland. Refugee camps became centers of guerrilla resistance, launching raids into Israel from southern Lebanon. Israel swiftly retaliated. In May 1968, the IDF struck across the border, targeting Lebanese villages harboring guerrillas. Seven months later, Palestinian militants based in Beirut machine-gunned an El Al plane at the Athens airport, killing one passenger.[61] Within forty-eight hours, Israeli commandos landed at Beirut Airport and destroyed thirteen jetliners of Lebanon's Middle East Airlines as punishment for the government's failure to curb guerrilla operations against Israel. The Lebanese army clashed with Palestinians militants but remained too weak to suppress them completely and lacked the power to dislodge them.

In September 1970, Jordan's King Hussein found himself in a civil war with Palestinians in his country, which had been the center of the Palestinian movement since 1948. Hussein had already lost the West Bank of the Jordan River to Israel; he determined to keep control of what remained of his kingdom on the East Bank. Using loyal Bedouins of the Jordanian army, Hussein ruthlessly suppressed the Palestinians, whom he saw as a threat to his power, and expelled their leadership (including the PFLP's George Habash and Fatah's Yasser Arafat) during what came to be known among Palestinians as Black September.

This triggered another wave of Palestinian refugees into Lebanon. The PFLP and *al-Fatah* sought refuge in south Beirut among the Palestinian refugees there and joined together under an umbrella organization, the Palestinian Liberation Organization (PLO). Palestinians working in the Gulf oil states provided ample financing. Serious fighting broke out between armed commandos in the Palestinian refugee camps that surrounded the city and the Maronite-controlled Lebanese army. The PLO soon became a power to be reckoned with. Much like Hamas in the Gaza Strip several decades later, the PLO organized guerrilla raids against Israel and welfare relief for the Palestinian poor. The PLO also effectively took control of Lebanon's southern border with Israel. Israeli-Palestinian tensions now played out on Lebanese soil, which became the setting for the wider Arab-Israeli conflict. This destabilized Lebanon's already precarious sectarian balance and presaged a dangerous future for this most fragile of Middle Eastern countries.

The Six-Day War greatly affected AUB. Israel's overwhelming victory and the widespread feeling among Middle Easterners that Washington had leaned toward Israel in the brief but decisive struggle inflamed anti-American feeling among Arabs, whose wounded pride intensified their reaction. Arab governments and individuals, in turn, expressed their displeasure with what they saw as American support for Zionist expansionism by curtailing or ceasing donations to the school. A new wave of Palestinian refugees in Beirut launched anti-American demonstrations, some aimed against AUB. Arab students at AUB—many of whom were Palestinians—interpreted US policy in the Middle East through the prism of Vietnam. These students saw the government of Israel the same way they saw the government of South Vietnam: as an agent of American imperialism. They questioned AUB's mission of service to the Arab world. Radical Palestinians like Leila Khaled, who attended AUB for one year in the early 1960s, attacked it as "a 'finishing' school for the rich children of the Middle East and a social club for the colonial elite of the Arab world."[62] Other AUB students adopted a Che Guevara–style Arab nationalism fashionable in the 1960s, complete with student strikes, protest marches, and revolutionary slogans.

AUB had always been viewed as an outpost of America in the Middle East. But now America was under siege in the Middle East. Tension and mistrust grew between students and administrators. When an administrator told a group of protesting Palestinian students that their cause would be better served by studying than striking, one of the Palestinians shot back: "Don't get logical with me!" rejecting the tradition of rational thought and reasoned debate AUB stood for.[63] In April 1970, the situation intensified as students hurled stones at the US embassy adjacent to the university and burned an American flag on campus. AUB could not escape its identity as a visible and accessible symbol of the American presence in the Middle East nor its fate as a target of growing anti-American sentiment in the Arab world.[64]

In the United States, the Six-Day War generated pro-Israeli and anti-Arab sentiment that worked against AUB. This sentiment, combined with the radicalization of Palestinian AUB students after 1967, changed the school's image in the minds of many Americans. Newsweek's October 1970 article titled "Guerrilla U." illustrated the change. "For the better part of a century," the article began, "the American University of Beirut has been supplying Middle Eastern countries with a steady stream of presidents, prime ministers, ambassadors, doctors, lawyers, and businessmen. To that imposing list of professional elites can now be added two striking new categories: aerial hijackers and guerrillas." *Newsweek* went on to note that some AUB students spent weekends and summers in commando training camps; a few were even accused of stealing chemicals from university laboratories to use in making explosives. Americans no longer saw AUB as the best university in the Arab world but as a hotbed of Arab radicalism.[65] AUB administrators knew this all too well and understood its implications. "I don't think a college like ours could possibly be founded now," said Dean of the Faculty Terry Prothro in March 1971. "Only because we have existed for so long can we continue to exist in the present climate."[66] AUB found itself trapped in a vice between Arab anger and American resentment.

* * *

Bayard Dodge suffered his own hardships in the late 1960s. A rare malignant blood disease began to slowly ravage his body. Always ramrod straight, osteoporosis now painfully bent his spare frame. Still vigorous in mind and spirit, Dodge continued to lead a weekly Bible study group in the elegant wood-paneled, book-lined living room of his home on Alexander Street in Princeton. He tacked a *National Geographic* "Lands of the Bible Today" map over the fireplace, arranged a few chairs in a semicircle, and made the Old and New Testaments come alive for his weekly audience. He remained an educator at heart.

Bayard Dodge died at Princeton Hospital on May 30, 1972, at the age of eighty-four. AUB held a memorial service for him one week later, on June 8. Family, friends, and former students in Beirut and across the region gathered in Assembly Hall that day to say farewell and to honor his leadership and service to the Middle East. It was a beautiful spring day in the eastern Mediterranean and the chapel was filled to capacity with many people standing outside to hear the service through open doors. Lebanon's Muslim prime minister, Saeb Salam, compared Dodge favorably to Daniel and Howard Bliss. "He and his predecessors were a magnificent example in this country of the relation of man to man which is not spoilt by egoism or politics."[67] Lebanon's Christian president, Suleiman Franjieh, posthumously awarded him the Order of the Cedars, the country's highest honor.[68]

A more personal and touching tribute came in a letter to his widow, Mary, from their nephew Samuel Rea, serving as a Peace Corps volunteer in Africa with his wife Nickie:

> June 15, 1972
> Gaborone, Botswana
>
> Dearest Aunt Mary,
>
> Uncle Bayard will always be a special touchstone for me, as (I know) many others. I think of one man, a Lebanese doctor who treated Nickie in Beirut late in 1966. We had flown from Dar es Salaam to AUB for special care, when no doctor in Dar or Nairobi could cure Nickie after six months of trying. When we arrived in this man's office, I must confess I namedropped, and I mentioned that Bayard Dodge was my uncle. A graduate of AUB, this man stared in disbelief, then bowed very low, then poured out his praise and respect. True to his AUB medical training, he proceeded to diagnose, then cure, Nickie of what had ailed her for six straight months.
>
> So much love, Aunt Mary. How we missed the service in the chapel! But, then, the two of you have helped to show us (including our Lebanese doctor) service of another kind.
>
> All our love,
> Sam[69]

In one of his final reflections on AUB, Bayard Dodge had declared, "The peoples of the Middle East must be educated to solve the problem of entering into cooperation with their neighbors, at the same time that they uphold their own independence and national sovereignty. . . . The Golden Rule," he added with equal conviction, "is more far-reaching than the atomic bomb." He believed AUB should continue to do what it had always done best: "play a leading part in helping the peoples of the Middle East to avoid the dangers and to enjoy the benefits of their independence and renaissance. The responsibility is a great one. It is truer than ever before that history is 'a race between education and catastrophe.'"[70]

* * *

Dodge's warning seemed powerfully relevant as Lebanon entered the fateful decade of the 1970s. The country's sovereignty diminished in the escalating fight between Israelis and Palestinians. Wealth piled up in the hands of Maronite bankers and Sunni merchants in Beirut, while Palestinian refugees grew radicalized, and poverty spread among underprivileged Shia. The 1970s also witnessed growing disillusionment with secularism among Arabs in Lebanon and throughout the Middle East, who turned to Islamic fundamentalism as an ideological alternative to secularism's failure to rectify material inequalities and improve living conditions for ordinary people. Fundamentalism became an escape into tradition for those whom modernity had benefited very little, if at all. It became a refuge when secular nationalist politics failed to deliver concrete solutions to foreign weakness and domestic breakdown. Islamic fundamentalism also provided consolation for the shock of military defeat in the Six-Day War. The Israelis had shown what a people fighting for religion could do. The Arabs had turned away from God, so the thinking went, and God had turned away from them. Modernity had been a false prophet. Lebanon's Maronite Christians looked on this new Arab sensibility, and the emerging Palestinian state within a state, with fright and took up arms to defend their privileged place in a rapidly changing and factionalizing society. Finally, fighting between Maronites and Palestinians erupted on Beirut's streets.

Maintaining peace in Lebanon amidst all these pressures became a desperate trapeze act. Toleration gave way to sectarian tribalism and escalating disorder. The drift of events was clear: Lebanon was becoming a country of armed camps, a society on the threshold of crisis. A violent storm of warlords, militias, checkpoints, and massacres would soon break, and AUB would be caught right in the middle of it.

Chapter 8:

DAVID DODGE AND AMERICAN FRUSTRATION

Born in Beirut on November 17, 1922, David Dodge absorbed the Arab and French cultures around him while growing up, but at heart he remained an American and felt very patriotic. He played with other American youngsters on the AUB campus, attended Cub Scout meetings overlooking Beirut harbor, and picked mountain thistles to throw into bonfires on July Fourth. He hiked and skied in the Lebanon range, where the legendary cedar trees had stood since antiquity. And in summers, David pitched tents with his family for weeks on end in the mountains. "The Lebanon I knew as a boy was such a peaceful place," he remembered.[1] It was a wonderful life of privilege, intimacy, and familiarity. Like earlier generations of Blisses and Dodges, David came to love Lebanon and its people.

In 1938, as war clouds gathered over Europe and the Middle East, David's Beirut idyll ended. His parents sent him across the Atlantic to Deerfield Academy in western Massachusetts in preparation for entering his father's alma mater, Princeton University. Set amid the pastoral charms of the Berkshire Hills, Deerfield prepped the progeny of some of America's most prominent families for college. Its headmaster, Frank Boyden, a Congregationalist and Amherst College graduate like Daniel and Howard Bliss, built a great school by developing students' character, making Deerfield boys high-minded and well-mannered, almost to a fault. Boyden mixed Deerfield's well-born with a good number of needy scholarship students. Every boy, regardless of background, slept in a farmhouse dormitory and waited tables at mealtimes. Deerfield was not an academic pressure-cooker. Boyden thought it more important to teach the boys to do good deeds in order to improve the world and to help the less fortunate. He constantly urged each

Deerfield boy to become part of something greater than just himself. Above all, Boyden taught Deerfield boys to be disciplined and stoic. Every boy played on a sports team. No matter how good he was, if he showed arrogance or anger, he would be benched. Lanky and bespectacled, David Dodge absorbed the lessons imparted to him at Deerfield and made them guideposts for his life.

A member of the Princeton class of 1945, David left early to join the legendary Office of Strategic Services, the forerunner of the CIA, which prized the Arabic language skills and Middle Eastern expertise of missionary offspring like him. During the latter part of World War II he served in Damascus, where he witnessed the end of the European imperial order in the Middle East created after World War I. After the war, he landed a job with Aramco's government relations organization in Saudi Arabia, then, in 1954, he was employed with Tapline in Beirut, where he worked quietly and effectively for the next twenty-one years.

During these years, David traveled widely, cultivating contacts with AUB graduates who occupied influential positions in government and business across the Middle East. He got to know the marginalized Shia communities of southern Lebanon at a time when most foreigners rarely strayed beyond the cosmopolitan confines of Beirut. (One of Tapline's main routes ran from Saudi Arabia through southern Lebanon.) He mediated rivalries among Lebanese Shia factions that threatened to sabotage the oil consortium's pipeline through the region. He would travel to the south of Lebanon, drink interminable cups of coffee with village elders, and help smooth out frictions before they exploded into destabilizing violence.

On the surface, David Dodge the businessman seemed to break with the Bliss and Dodge tradition of educational leadership in the Middle East. Quiet and reserved, he lacked the outgoing charm of Daniel and Howard Bliss and the forcefulness of his father, Bayard. Yet he was "totally unselfish and driven by duty," noted a close friend.[2] He was also intensely devoted to the American University of Beirut (AUB), which he served quietly in many ways during his Tapline career. Like his father and great-great uncle Stuart Dodge before him, David anonymously paid the tuitions of several AUB scholarship students, a philanthropic gesture he continued even as he put his

own children through college in the United States. When David retired from
Tapline in 1975, he and his first wife, Doris, moved to Princeton, New
Jersey, where he commuted to work at the Near East Foundation in New
York City. But the couple deeply missed Beirut, so they returned there—
returned home—just two years later when the last of their four children,
Bayard, Nina, Simon, and Melissa, moved away to college.

Back in Beirut, David went to work as AUB's vice president for administration and development, using his extensive and influential contacts in the
Arab world to raise considerable sums of money for the school. He was
capable and "very well-versed in the nitty-gritty of running the business end
of AUB," said a university associate.[3] David later became a trustee and then
the university's acting president, temporarily following in the footsteps of
his great-grandfather, grandfather, and father. David and Doris were living
on the AUB campus when Lebanon's bloody civil war broke out in 1975.

* * *

The civil war that tore apart Lebanon and nearly sundered AUB began on
April 13, 1975, when members of the Maronite Phalangist militia attacked
and killed twenty-seven Palestinians aboard a bus passing through a Christian suburb of east Beirut. The Phalangist attack reflected the aggressiveness
of a self-superior minority feeling endangered. The Maronites feared
Lebanon's shift away from a Christian-dominated government and abhorred
the growing influence of the Palestine Liberation Organization (PLO) in
Lebanon, which Lebanese Muslims and Druse used to bring pressure on the
Maronites to share more power.[4] The Phalangist attack triggered a volcanic
explosion. Like in 1860, the delicate social fabric and balance of power in
Lebanon succumbed to sectarian strife. Tolerance gave way to paranoia as
tribal passions reignited with brutal intensity. Coexistence and harmony
between various groups went out the figurative window.

Beirut became a writhing vipers' nest of rival militias, and ethnic
cleansing became a bloody neighborhood sport. Young militiamen sporting
cowboy hats, fatigue pants, and T-shirts emblazoned with American college
logos and images of Snoopy® cruised Beirut's litter-strewn streets in jeeps

mounted with recoilless rifles, their passengers armed to the teeth with pistols, hand grenades, and Kalashnikov rifles, shooting up neighborhoods with reckless, nihilistic abandon. The once-vibrant city center degenerated into a nightmarish, surreal battleground. The city's modern beachfront hotels and old stone houses, with their red-tiled roofs and decorated balconies, crumbled into gutted piles of rubble amid the crossfire. Before the war, the palm-lined Place des Martyrs (known locally as the Bourj) had been the beating heart of cosmopolitan Beirut, where graceful stone churches and mosques had stood side-by-side and specialty *souks* (markets) had hosted shoppers of all faiths for generations. Now the Bourj became a burned out no-man's-land. Along it ran the notoriously dangerous Green Line, a swath of gutted buildings and weed-covered streets running north to south from the harbor through downtown that formed the no-man's-land between Christian enclaves to the east and Muslim enclaves (including AUB) to the west. The Green Line would remain an ugly scar running through the beleaguered city for fifteen long years. An eyewitness to the escalating violence and chaos described Beirut's self-destruction:

> The sight takes our breath away. Eleven hours of direct artillery shelling has left its mark. The street is lined with burned cars, all of them now the same shade of mustard yellow, some of them still smoking—one of them, indeed, still burning. Some of them lie upside down, some at crazy angles to one another. We remember the sound they had made as, one by one, they blew up: not a great roar, as you would have thought, but a gentle *pouf, pouf.* . . . The shops next door to us—or rather what is left of the shops, which isn't much—are still ablaze. The trees that had lined the street have been blown all over, their dismembered bodies strewn around, mingling with the glass and stones and burning cars, adding a strange, wintry look to the devastation. Electric wires and street lamps hang in disorderly lines and arcs, like a sloppy schoolboy's geometry exercise. Every building in sight stands gaping, shutters askew, glass hanging dangerously jagged from twisted aluminum frames, great and small holes everywhere. The atmosphere is thick with smoke and the smell of gasoline and fire. The streets are covered with a kind of ooze, not unlike the slushy combination of dirt and melting snow. But there is no snow. It is as though the streets are bleeding.[5]

At first, Beirutis found it hard to believe what was happening. Then they began recalling their city before the civil war with a faraway look. Once the cosmopolitan center of the Arab world, it had gone from being a vision of heaven to a vision of hell. Satirists caustically lampooned the pathology of sectarian violence. Lebanese novelist Ghada al-Samman, in his novel *Beirut:'75*, includes an escapee from an insane asylum who says: "The first thing I did was to steal the placard that read 'the asylum of the insane.' I carried the placard to the entrance of Beirut and I removed the sign that carried Beirut's name and in its place I put the other placard."[6]

New York Times reporter Tom Friedman, who spent five years in Beirut, came to think of it "as a huge abyss, the darkest corner of human behavior, an urban jungle where not even the law of the jungle applied."[7] The violence would eventually claim the lives of nearly 150,000 people in a nation of 2.6 million.

Syria intervened in its former province amid the growing anarchy. In June 1976, Syrian dictator Hafez al-Asad, manifesting traditional Syrian ambitions in Lebanon, which Damascus has historically viewed within its sphere of influence, sent twenty thousand Syrian troops into the fractured country as a policing force, occupying most of Lebanon except the Shiite region near the southern border with Israel. Asad did not want a PLO-dominated Lebanon to provoke the Israelis into a war with Syria. Despite Syrian policing, PLO guerrilla attacks on northern Israel continued, killing Israeli civilians and leading Israel to retaliate in March 1978 by occupying southern Lebanon. In the ensuing conflict, 200,000 Lebanese Shia lost their homes.[8] Many of them sought shelter in squalid refugee camps south of Beirut. Three months later, Israeli forces withdrew to a "security zone" south of the Litani River and installed the Maronite South Lebanon Army (SLA), a dependent mercenary force, as a proxy to protect its security interests in the volatile area.

As PLO rocket and guerrilla attacks into Israel resumed, tensions escalated. In 1982, hard-line Israeli prime minister Menachem Begin and Israeli defense minister Ariel Sharon decided on a full-scale invasion of Lebanon to put an end (they hoped) to PLO attacks on northern Israel. Israel's 1979 peace treaty with Egypt's Anwar Sadat, part of the Camp David Accords negotiated by President Jimmy Carter, meant Begin and Sharon would not run the risk of a two-front war. On June 6, the Israeli Defense Forces (IDF) crossed the Lebanese border in large numbers with tanks and heavy artillery.[9] The Israelis quickly pushed Syrian forces up the Bekaa Valley and, on June 13, reached the outskirts of west Beirut, inhabited by Muslims and dominated by the PLO.

The Israeli siege of west Beirut lasted through the summer of 1982. Television networks broadcast scenes around the world of physical devastation and human suffering inflicted by Israeli naval, aerial, and artillery fire.[10] American-made IDF jets screamed over west Beirut, bombing targets at will. One round smashed into the roof of the AUB hospital. (Ironically, the IDF later delivered fuel oil to the AUB hospital's generator without charge or publicity.) Israel tightened its noose around the city, surrounding refugee camps in Beirut's southern suburbs and seizing control of the airport. By the end of August, twenty thousand Lebanese civilians and Palestinian refugees had been killed, and much of west Beirut lay in ruins, looking "like a plaster-and-cement version of a forest after a fire: just a vast wasteland of fragments of walls, obliterated by thousands of exploding shells," lamented an eyewitness.[11]

Sunnis in west Beirut had used the PLO as their muscle in Lebanon's civil war; the PLO, in turn, had used the Sunnis to stay in Beirut. This bargain broke down under the pressure of the Israeli siege. West Beirut's Sunni elders asked Yasser Arafat's PLO to leave in order to spare the city further carnage. In late August, eleven thousand PLO fighters, guaranteed safe passage by a US-brokered agreement, boarded ships for exile in Tunisia and other parts of the Arab world. Another part of the agreement guaranteed the safety of Palestinian civilians remaining behind in Beirut. Less than one month later, on September 14, 1982, assassins killed Maronite leader Bashir Gemayel.[12] Four days later, Phalangists entered Beirut's Sabra and Shatila refugee camps and slaughtered more than one thousand Palestinian and Lebanese Shiite women and children. Photos of the butchered bodies sent shockwaves around the world. Although Israeli defense minister Sharon denied any knowledge of the Sabra and Shatila massacres, a subsequent Israeli government inquiry headed by Israel's Supreme Court president Yitzhak Kahan, known as the Kahan Commission, concluded the IDF not

only knew about the massacre as it occurred, but also had even escorted Phalangists to the refugee camps, watched through binoculars from nearby
rooftops as the massacre took place, dropped flares to illuminate the camps
at night, and lent bulldozers to the Phalangists to dig mass graves to cover
up the bloody crime.[13] All of this directly contradicted the Israeli government's oral promise to the United States government not to enter west
Beirut after the PLO evacuated. Sharon resigned as defense minister a short
time later.[14]

* * *

The siege of west Beirut upended AUB and David Dodge's life. Long a cultural and intellectual sanctuary above the turmoil of the streets, AUB now
found itself trapped in the midst of a vicious civil war that exposed just how
vulnerable the university had become. AUB's open and cosmopolitan atmosphere vanished and, with it, the tranquil search for knowledge and devotion
to free inquiry that had helped students transcend their parochial differences.
The trunks of excavated Roman columns still stood in front of the archaeo-
logical museum at the top of campus along Rue Bliss, but on the athletic
field at the bottom of campus, along the corniche road, the PLO installed an
antiaircraft battery, a symbol of all that had changed. A nearby resident
described the haunting scene one evening:

> From the balcony of my flat near the American University of Beirut, I
> watch the sun sink into the calm blue waters of the Mediterranean. The
> red-tiled roofs of the older buildings on campus, among the last left in this
> once beautiful city, and the dark green grace of the cypress trees gradually
> lose their distinctive contrast as the sun rays fade away and the city lights
> come on. . . . The clock on the tower above College Hall strikes, and the
> chimes die away into the quiet evening. I stand listening, thinking of how
> those same chimes have rung over the decades, when a clock was just a
> clock, not a bell tolling for a dying city and a dying time. Somehow the
> thought is comforting though infinitely sad. . . . With that sixth sense that
> Beirutis have developed, I go inside and turn on the radio. Martial music
> blares out, and my heart sinks. Another crisis. Where? Who is fighting

whom this time? I go out to the other balcony, the one facing the city, where the white stars fade in the light of red tracer bullets; the quiet of the evening is broken by the too-familiar sound of guns. They call to my mind drums in the jungle, a primitive, ritual warning of aggression and danger.[15]

The civil war sobered everyone at AUB. Students studied with rock 'n' roll turned up louder than the shelling and quickly moved to interior corridors or basement shelters when the shelling got close. Some listened to the radio, others recounted their latest experiences of the war. Most seemed accustomed to it—and yet not. Pitched gun battles erupted outside student eateries along Rue Bliss across from AUB's main gate. It made students sleep fitfully in their dormitory rooms at night, their ears perpetually cocked for the inevitable sound of renewed shooting.

Every student knew someone killed in the fighting. The AUB hospital overflowed with wounded of all sides, but lacked enough medicines to treat them adequately. "There was no politics anymore on campus," recalled Terry Prothro, a longtime AUB professor. "Staying alive was the only thing that mattered."[16] American faculty rarely ventured beyond campus after dark. Many wanted to stay in Beirut, determined that extremists would not drive them away. But they began having second thoughts. "We thought things would get better," said one. "Ask us how we feel now, and you'll get a different answer. It's time to go."[17] Arab faculty fared little better. "Once when I was walking home," recalled media professor Nabil Dajani, "a militiaman yelled, 'Grab him, he's a Palestinian!' I thought I was a goner. Then I heard another militiaman say, 'Leave him, he's my professor.' I just looked straight ahead and kept walking."[18]

An AUB student interviewed her classmates about their deepest anxiety: it was simply surviving the conflict—and being remembered if they did not. "In the United States if you die in a car accident, at least your name gets mentioned on television," the student numbly remarked. "Here they don't even mention your name anymore. They just say, 'Thirty people died.' They don't even bother to give their names." When asked her name and age by a journalist, the student wearily whispered, "We are all one hundred years old."[19]

Maronites and Israelis viewed AUB as a breeding ground for the Palestinian nationalism they feared and detested. Well-educated, affluent, and politically moderate Sunnis supported AUB, but their long-standing power in west Beirut collapsed during the civil war, especially after the PLO's evacuation. Shia refugees traumatized by fear and violence and raging with bitterness and pent-up frustrations now controlled west Beirut. They had been radicalized by two events: the 1979 Iranian Revolution and Israel's 1982 invasion of Lebanon, which had driven many Shia from their poor villages in the south to shantytowns on the outskirts of Beirut known, tellingly, as the Belt of Misery.

Lebanon's largest religious community and lowest economic class, the Shia farmed the hills and valleys of southern Lebanon and the Bekaa Valley as sharecroppers. Even the few who owned their own land struggled to eke out a living by selling fruits and vegetables. Known throughout Lebanon as *al-mahrumin* (the deprived), they earned one-fifth to one-sixth of the wages of urban Beirutis and enjoyed no safety net of state-provided social services. Life had traditionally been very hard for Lebanon's Shia. They had been socially excluded, economically deprived, and politically marginalized for generations. With a vivid awareness of second-class citizenship, they found Ayatollah Khomeini's message deeply resonant for it spoke to their bitterness, frustrations, and resentments. Revolutionary Iran became the rallying cry for underdogs in the Muslim world, and the Shia were Lebanon's underdogs.

Lebanese Shia flocked to join the secular Amal (Hope) and the more radical Hezbollah (Followers of God) militias, the latter a secretive organization[20] led by mullahs with close ties to Iran's clerical establishment, who preached fierce anti-Americanism in mosques and *husseiniyehs* (Shia social centers) to young Shia men to whom Lebanon's civil war had taught hatred and violence. Beginning as a cat's-paw of Iran, Hezbollah, in time, combined the functions of a militia, a social service and public works provider, and a political party, becoming a popular and potent force in Lebanon and the Middle East.

Many of Hezbollah's leading mullahs had studied at Shiite seminaries in Najaf and Karbala, where they imbibed radical Shiite ideology from prominent Iraqi and Iranian Shiite clerics—including Ayatollah Khomeini, who spent fourteen years in exile at Najaf.[21] The mullahs carried this network of personal contacts and relationships back with them to Lebanon. They received support from a contingent of eight hundred *Pasdaran* (Iranian Revolutionary Guards), who encamped at a former Lebanese army barracks in Baalbek after Israel's invasion in 1982. (Syria allowed the Revolutionary Guards' transit via the Beirut–Damascus Highway.) The Revolutionary Guards in Baalbek received support from Teheran via the Iranian embassies in Beirut and Damascus. Iranian diplomats provided Hezbollah with money and intelligence, while Revolutionary Guards provided weapons and training.[22]

Hezbollah and its Iranian allies held the United States responsible for supporting Israel economically and militarily to such a degree that it could invade Lebanon and hurt Lebanese Shia. Hezbollah and Teheran believed that religion and politics were inseparable, that the Islamic world must be liberated from exploitation by a "satanic" West dominated by aggressive materialism and unbelief, and, therefore, all Western influences must be purged from the region. Among its ranks were extremists who considered terrorism a noble, heroic campaign of *jihad* (holy struggle) against evil. Meanwhile, Hezbollah stepped up its verbal war against AUB as a cultural symbol of the United States.

Conditions worsened in the Hamra district of west Beirut, where David Dodge spent the summer of 1982 as acting AUB president. The neighborhood around AUB teamed with bullet-scarred buildings, rubble, and garbage. The sound of gunfire and militia checkpoints intensified. Hezbollah infiltrated the chaotic maze of west Beirut's poor Shiite suburbs. Armed gangs of bandits unleashed by the chaos began prowling Hamra at night. Looters also roamed the streets, pillaging shops and government buildings and ransacking the National Museum.

Dodge and AUB's administrative staff headquartered in College Hall kept the university going through it all. Dodge's job inspired a sense of historic responsibility in him, energizing him to confront a host of daunting problems. Electricity outages, water and gas shortages, and dwindling supplies of food and medicines became constant headaches. Dodge communicated with AUB's New York office by telex, reporting the number of wounded treated at the hospital and the number of artillery shells falling on campus. "God bless and keep thee safe and sane," AUB's board chairman, Najeeb Halaby, telexed back.[23]

A terrible wind was gathering force. AUB had always been an icon of the United States in the Middle East. Now that icon had become a target for those who hated America. Although most Americans in Beirut like David Dodge championed the Palestinian cause and criticized the Israeli invasion of Lebanon, radicalized Shia made no distinction between Americans and Israelis; they saw US citizens like Dodge as indirectly supporting what they considered Zionist aggression. "The hatred that has been generated," a Lebanese trustee of AUB lamentably predicted, "is going to overflow onto the campus."[24]

Hezbollah and its Iranian allies targeted David Dodge for kidnapping after Phalangist militiamen took four Iranians hostage on July 5, including the commander of the Revolutionary Guards contingent in Baalbek and the Iranian charge d'affaires to Lebanon.[25] The living embodiment of America's Middle Eastern aristocracy and acting president of its greatest university, Dodge would be a lucrative bargaining chip that Hezbollah could use to get the US government to pressure the Phalangists to release the four Iranians while maintaining the façade of Iranian noninvolvement, thus avoiding the risk of an open war with the United States, which Iran did not want. To Hezbollah, AUB was not an educational oasis to be valued and protected, but a hated symbol of the United States to be attacked and exploited. US diplomats fearing for Dodge's safety warned him to leave Beirut. Dodge recognized his and AUB's vulnerability. But he insisted AUB must remain open, and someone needed to lead and protect it.[26]

To implement their plan, Hezbollah sympathizers at the university surreptitiously accessed AUB personnel files to learn where high-profile Americans associated with the school lived. With this information, they reconnoitered Dodge's daily movements. Hezbollah moved on July 19, 1982.[27] No campus security protected him. At dusk that hot and humid summer day, just as a Mediterranean breeze began to cool the piercing heat, Dodge left his third-floor office in College Hall and walked across campus to a reception in Marquand House. As Dodge passed West Hall behind Marquand House, one-half dozen men in a red Renault® station wagon pulled up, jumped out, and ordered Dodge to get in. He refused. After a brief struggle, one of the men struck Dodge on the head with his pistol butt and shoved the semiconscious Dodge into the station wagon face down on the floor of the back seat, the kidnappers' feet pinning him to the floor. The station wagon sped off campus.

Then began a wild ride through the maze of streets and alleys of west Beirut to Dodge's first place of captivity in the Shiite slums a few miles south of AUB. Dodge could hear Israeli jets pounding the area from the dingy apartment where he was kept chained to a radiator for two weeks. "Meester David, these are your warplanes attacking us," his captors told him. The PLO, which controlled west Beirut at the time, ordered a house-to-house search for Dodge. They could not find him because he was soon blindfolded, bound, drugged, put under the false floor of a truck, and driven through militia lines over Mount Lebanon to Baalbek in the Bekaa Valley. Dodge spent eight months there and in the nearby Syrian border village of Zebdani in safe houses controlled by highly disciplined Iranian Revolutionary Guards wearing green battle fatigues. "If you try to escape, we will kill you," they often told him matter-of-factly in Farsi-accented English. In April 1983, his captors smuggled him to Teheran on a night flight via Damascus, bound, blindfolded, drugged, and hidden in a diplomatic crate immune from Syrian inspection. He knew where he had landed because he just glimpsed through his blindfold a sign on a brightly-lit airport terminal that read in English, "Welcome to Teheran International Airport."

Dodge spent one year in captivity. His Hezbollah and Iranian captors did not torture him physically, although one guard occasionally roughed him up. The guards fed and clothed him adequately. But Dodge suffered psychologically. He had very little human contact and only three books, two in English and one in French, and a deck of cards to alleviate his loneliness. "That was my life for many months," he recalled. Dodge asked for a Bible or a Quran to comfort him and to assuage his profound sense of isolation. His captors repeatedly refused.

His family also suffered. His wife, Doris, felt paralyzed by the uncertainty of not knowing his whereabouts or fate. "This has been a time when even the simplest acts can be quite formidably difficult," she confessed in a heart-wrenching letter to President Reagan. "The Dodge family has contributed greatly to the Middle East and David's role has been in the finest humanitarian traditions of which all Americans can be proud," replied Reagan. He promised his administration would do all it could to win her husband's release.[28]

After being moved to a small cell in the notorious Evin Prison—Iran's Lubyanka, where thousands of Shah and then Khomeini opponents had been tortured and executed—David underwent regular, intensive interrogations at the hands of senior Revolutionary Guard officers, who grilled him about the US government affiliations of various Middle Eastern figures whom he knew. Now and then, they slapped him hard across the face and screamed, "You're a spy! We know you. You work for the CIA! We will kill you, don't worry." They grilled him about the four abducted Iranians. Dodge had no idea what had happened to them, and said so. "Don't joke with us, they're dead," his interrogators replied, "and you will be too before long." Dodge sensed his interrogators knew he possessed no information of consequence, "they just wanted to scare me."

Dodge's ordeal ended when the Syrian president's brother Rifaat Asad responded to American entreaties and intervened with Teheran to win his release on July 21, 1983, in exchange for Lebanese Shia prisoners held by the Maronites. (Syria and Iran, ideological opposites but on-and-off allies-of-convenience, were cooperating at the time against Israel's presence in Lebanon and Saddam Hussein's Iraq, which had invaded Iran in September 1980.) A Revolutionary Guard escort took Dodge to Teheran's airport and put him aboard a Syrian Arab Airlines plane bound for Damascus—in first class. (Revolutionary Guards bound for Lebanon occupied all of the Economy Class seats, and the escort feared one of them might recognize Dodge and try to prevent his release.) He returned to the United States via Europe aboard an American military plane accompanied by government medical and security personnel, thus ending what he privately called a "long, agonizing ordeal."[29]

The ordeal did nothing to diminish his deep feeling for the region. "For four generations my family has been involved with educational and medical services in the Middle East," he told the Associated Press a few days after his release.[30] Dodge returned to Princeton and settled in to a long and quiet retirement. In 1990, the AUB Board of Trustees named him full president of the university—like his father, grandfather, and great-grandfather—for one year in honor of his service and sacrifice on behalf of the school. Dodge's oath of secrecy to the Syrians who had won his release and his concern about stoking anti-Iranian sentiment in the United States made him circumspect about publicly discussing the personal details of his captivity until he lost a long battle with cancer in January 2009.

* * *

Amid the crisis over David Dodge's kidnapping, President Ronald Reagan dispatched 1,200 marines to Beirut in September 1982 as part of a multinational peacekeeping force in the wake of the Sabra and Shatila massacres. Personally affable and staunchly conservative, Reagan approached the Middle East with a strong commitment to Israel and a decidedly Cold War perspective. He viewed the Middle East primarily as a battleground in that war, another arena in America's struggle with "the evil empire" of the Soviet Union. This perspective became fixed in Reagan's psyche. But much of Middle East politics had little to do with the US-Soviet rivalry. What is more, the taking of American hostages in Teheran in November 1979 blinded Washington to radical Islam's appeal to the Shia—Lebanon's largest single religious community—in the wake of Khomeini's triumph in Iran. Reagan and his advisers wanted to help the Lebanese rebuild their country, to find a solution that would end the civil war, and to help resolve the larger Arab-Israeli dispute, but they entered Lebanon with little knowledge and even less understanding of the complexity of its tribal politics, of the differences among Middle Eastern states, and of the instability in the region tied to the unresolved problem of a Palestinian homeland. Fundamentally, they overestimated the influence of American power and underestimated local rivalries and the intensity of resistance to an American military presence.

As a result, the Reagan administration sent marines to Beirut almost as an afterthought to help restore order. They believed the marines' presence would give the Lebanese a chance to resolve their differences and rebuild their nation behind the shield of a superpower—much like the Eisenhower administration's intervention in Lebanon in 1958. The marines deployed in 1982 in exactly the same area they had in 1958, amid the sand dunes and scrub on the city's southern outskirts, close to the airport. But this time, alienated and angry Palestinian and Shia refugees were their neighbors. The marines had been put in Lebanon to cool tensions, keep the peace, and show that the fractured country had begun to mend. Washington had little idea the marines had been dropped in the middle of a hornet's nest.

Lebanese politics had become a constantly changing kaleidoscope. The Maronites shifted alliances with dizzying speed: first with the Syrians against the Palestinians, then with the Israelis, and then with the Palestinians against the Shia and the Syrians. Next-door neighbor Syria and Khomeini's Iran—the pied piper of Lebanon's Shia and still embittered by the reign of the recently deposed American-backed Shah—wanted to drive the United States out of Lebanon and eliminate American influence in the region. A growing number of feuding warlords and nihilistic thugs added to the toxic mix. The Reagan administration had stepped into a situation it did not fully understand and could only marginally influence.

The nonpartisan US peacekeeping mission in time became a partisan commitment to Amin Gemayel, who had been chosen as Lebanon's president after his younger brother Bashir's assassination. Reagan wanted to help Gemayel build a strong coalition government in Lebanon. Gemayel wanted something else: to use American backing as a club against his Muslim, Druse, and Syrian opponents. US Marines began arming and training the Maronite-dominated Lebanese army. By the spring of 1983, the United States had openly taken sides in Lebanon's civil war.

Iran and its Shiite allies realized they could not keep America out of Lebanon. But while they did not have the ability to prevent US intervention, they knew how to retaliate against it with a vengeance. Iranian Revolutionary Guards moved from Baalbek into Beirut beginning in April 1983.[31] On the afternoon of April 18, a suicide bomber drove a Chevrolet® pickup truck laden with five hundred pounds of dynamite up the circular driveway of the US Embassy on the corniche road just below the AUB campus. Ryan Crocker, at the time a junior foreign service officer working on the fourth floor of the embassy, felt a tremendous force. "I heard no sound," he recalled, but it "slammed me into the wall."[32] When the windows blew in, the mylar glued to them turned the flying glass into projectiles. Many who survived the explosion had tiny shards of glass embedded in their skin; the shards slowly and painfully worked out of their skin over decades, so the survivors could never forget the trauma of that day. The tremendous blast sheared away the embassy's façade, dropping the building like a layer cake fallen on one side and enveloping the seven-story complex in black smoke. Sixty people died, including seventeen Americans. The embassy explosion was so powerful that it rattled windows seven miles away and caused a US naval vessel cruising five miles off Lebanon's coast to shudder.

In the fall of 1983, the Reagan administration began blocking arms shipments to Iran and extended two billion dollars in military credits to Iraq in its bloody war against Iran.[33] Just after dawn on October 23, 1983, a young Shiite terrorist-martyr steered a five-ton, yellow Mercedes® dump truck laden with sixteen thousand pounds of dynamite around concrete barriers, past a sentry post—smiling directly at the young marine on duty—and barreled at sixty miles per hour into the ground floor of marine headquarters. The ensuing blast—the largest nonnuclear explosion since World War II—left a thirty-foot-wide, ten-foot-deep crater and shook buildings ten miles away in the heart of west Beirut. It collapsed all four floors into a pile of twisted steel and crushed reinforced concrete, killing 241 American servicemen, many of them still asleep on their cots; dozens more were left maimed and crippled for life. Snipers in nearby refugee slums fired on rescue workers. The Beirut barracks bombing was and remains the bloodiest day in Marine Corps history.

Then came the tragedy of Malcolm Kerr, a lanky, gentle, and sardonic man with deep AUB roots. His father, Stanley, had been a longtime professor at the university; his mother, Elsa, had served as AUB's dean of women. Kerr grew up in Beirut in the 1930s and 1940s and attended the American Community School there. David Dodge had been a teenage friend of his; they had spent time together at the Kerr's small summer home in the mountain village of Ainab. Kerr went to college at Princeton and graduate school at Harvard and Johns Hopkins, eventually becoming a prominent professor of Middle Eastern politics at the University of California, Los Angeles (UCLA). He liked UCLA and taught there for twenty years, but his heart lay in Beirut and in the mountains above the city, where he had spent idyllic summers as a wide-eyed and sensitive boy. AUB was very special to him. "It was a place where Dad felt complete and where he and my mother felt a sense of overwhelming possibility," his daughter Susan remembered.[34] Revered figures like Daniel and Howard Bliss and Bayard Dodge had lived and worked there, men he had admired since childhood. The fifty-two-year-old Kerr gave up his tenured position at UCLA and returned to Beirut in 1982 to guide the university through the tempest and to help put his bleeding hometown back together again. For this son of Presbyterian educators, wrote an observer, "the AUB presidency had been the stuff of dreams."[35]

Kerr knew he faced personal danger; his predecessor, David Dodge, had been kidnapped. In August 1983, just before Kerr left for Beirut to begin his tenure as AUB president, he and his wife stopped in Princeton to visit Dodge, who had just returned to the United States after his release from captivity. Dodge and Kerr walked around the garden discussing what lay ahead. Dodge told Kerr his situation was very dangerous. "Watch out for the Iranians and Lebanese Shiites," warned Dodge, "they're very anti-American now."[36] He knew from personal experience. The Kerrs proceeded on to war-torn Lebanon.

Kerr walked a tightrope from the moment he arrived back at AUB. Anger toward the United States and its institutions ran very high in west Beirut in the fall of 1983. Kerr felt the fear and the danger, but he struggled to hide his fear and to insulate AUB from the danger. He wrote his eighty-seven-year-old mother: "I still cling to the belief in miracles, that the Lebanese government will somehow, with American help, get rid of its occupiers and gain full control over the whole country. Without optimism, there is little to be done, so we might as well think positively."[37]

His was a difficult—perhaps impossible—mission. "It's been pretty discouraging and there still is an atmosphere of gloom and apprehension," he wrote his daughter Susie in September. In this private moment, he made no effort to hide his doubts. "No one gives the country more than cautious odds now to pull itself out of the mess."[38] Kerr struck an equally frank tone in a letter to his parents-in-law a few weeks later:

> If we see during the next year or so that there's no chance of doing more than just limping along, and that Lebanon can't accommodate a real university anymore, then we'll call it quits and come back to the States. Ann and I have talked about this many times, of course. She has been understandably nervous these past few months—so have I—and sometimes wonders out loud what the hell we're doing here; I wonder the same thing

silently. . . . We're not here to be heroes or foolish romantics and we are not interested in getting ourselves killed, but simply to do something extremely challenging and exciting that we have always looked forward to, as long as it remains possible. We don't want to turn and run at the first sign of trouble, especially since part of the job for both of us is that other people depend on us to give a lead and set a good example.[39]

Kerr had devoted his life to the Middle East, but powerful elements there viewed him with suspicion. Phalangists considered AUB a hotbed of all they feared and disliked; Israelis distrusted his Arabist background; Syrians resented his ties to the United States; above all, radical Shia wanted to rid Lebanon of everything American—and nothing symbolized this more vividly than the president of AUB. Part of Kerr recognized this danger; he had written about "the unceasing orgy of killing and destruction in Lebanon."[40] But another part of him—the idealistic, nostalgic boy inside the educated, worldly man who cherished AUB and wanted to help save it— possessed stubborn American optimism and believed (or wanted to believe) his mission somehow insulated him from personal danger. He could not imagine that AUB, an independent institution devoted to humanitarian service, could ever be viewed with the same hatred as that directed toward American diplomatic and military power. Besides, because all sides in Lebanon's civil war had children studying at AUB, it seemed logical that all sides had a vested interest in keeping the school and those who ran it safe. Lebanon's vicious civil war would not last forever, and Kerr wanted to be there to help rebuild the country he loved. Looking back, his wife, Ann, later wrote, "It was easy to brush the dust under the carpet and listen to the optimists among our friends, who said that things were going to be better."[41] Still, in the back of Kerr's mind lurked a realization that he was indeed vulnerable. "I'll bet there's a fifty-fifty chance I'll get bumped off early on," he confided to his daughter Susie.[42]

Things deteriorated rapidly toward the end of the year. In late November, the Gemayel government severed diplomatic relations with Iran. In late December, the forty-five-thousand-ton battleship USS *New Jersey* off Rās Beirut lobbed Volkswagen®-sized shells over the AUB campus onto Druse and Shiite positions in the Chouf Mountains above Beirut in support of Gemayel's beleaguered government. (US government officials conceded the next day that the *New Jersey's* much-publicized and destructive shelling had in fact "hit nothing of military value."[43]) Shiite militia exchanged fire with marines posted on the corniche road just below campus. The danger grew closer. Anxious AUB officials arranged for a security team to guard Kerr around-the-clock beginning in late January. Vicious political posters vowing to extirpate the US presence in Lebanon appeared on the old stonewalls of AUB buildings. In Hamra, a bearded young man stopped an American woman on the sidewalk, pointed at her head with his finger, slowly said "Bang-bang," and walked away silently.[44] The incident seemed an omen of dark forces closing in.

Hezbollah zealots fired by Khomeini's anti-American ideology secretly labeled Kerr a "dangerous spy," and sent a female agent of its ruthless armed wing, Islamic Jihad, to smuggle a pistol equipped with a silencer hidden in her purse onto the AUB campus. She buried it in greenery beneath the banyan tree near College Hall that Kerr had climbed as a boy and where he had courted his future wife when both were AUB students in the 1950s. The silenced pistol remained hidden there until Hezbollah's central council of Shiite *mujtahids* (religious scholars) issued a *fatwa* (religious ruling) condemning Kerr to death.[45]

Malcolm Kerr left Marquand House on the drizzly morning of January 18, 1984. He went to the bank, visited the AUB museum director, and then headed toward his office on the third floor of College Hall. Two young men in black jackets carrying books asked to see the president. When Kerr's secretary told them he was not in yet, they waited by the elevator outside his office. The chimes of College Hall struck nine o'clock as the elevator carrying Kerr opened on the third floor. As Kerr exited the elevator, one of the assassins fired two bullets into the back of his head at point-blank range, killing him instantly. The assassins hurried down the adjacent stairwell, out of College Hall, and perhaps right past Kerr's unsuspecting wife, Ann, who was standing by the main gate beneath an umbrella reading a book as she waited for a friend. Her husband was pronounced dead a short time later in the AUB hospital, where he had been born in 1931. It was a tragically ironic fate for a man who had devoted his life to understanding the Middle East and advancing its welfare. President Reagan rightly declared that "his work strengthened the historical, cultural, and academic ties between the United States and Lebanon and other countries in the Middle East."[46] Islamic Jihad claimed responsibility for Kerr's assassination. His killers were never apprehended nor prosecuted.[47]

* * *

Kerr's death marked a turning point of sorts. President Reagan had talked bravely of "standing tall" against terrorism and not "walking away" from Lebanon and "allowing the forces of radicalism to prevail." He said a premature withdrawal of the marines from Beirut could "call into question the resolve of the West to carry out its responsibilities to help the free world defend itself." He told Lebanese prime minister Saeb Salam, a Sunni alumnus of AUB, that his administration had "no reverse gear" on Lebanon.[48] But opposition to a continued US presence in Lebanon grew very strong among the American public and lawmakers on Capitol Hill after the marines' barracks bombing of October 1983. When the Gemayel government splintered in February 1984 after Shiite and Druse militias in west Beirut launched a revolt against the Lebanese army, Reagan abandoned hope of rebuilding Lebanon and withdrew the US Marines, "redeploying" them to American naval vessels offshore. Meanwhile, the kidnapping of American journalists, priests, and professors, begun with David Dodge's abduction, became a regular occurrence making headlines. "The war in Lebanon grew even more violent," Reagan later observed, "and the Middle East continued to be a source of problems for me and our country."[49] Reagan was implicitly referring to the notorious Iran-Contra Affair, which grew out of his administration's effort during 1984–1986 to secretly trade arms for hostages with Iran, and then to divert the proceeds to fund contra rebels fighting the pro-Communist Sandinista regime in Nicaragua—in violation of congressional prohibitions on such funding. The spectacular political fallout from the Iran-Contra Affair, after it became publicly known in November 1986, severely damaged Reagan and his presidency.

Fear and chaos in west Beirut deepened through the rest of the 1980s. Bit by bit, the devastation of the civil war created a mood of sullenness and pervasive apprehension. In the past, the Muslim *tabal* of Hamra, a troop of men who walk the streets in the predawn darkness beating large drums to alert believers to eat a meal before the daytime fasting during Ramadan, muffled their calls in order not to disturb Christians in the neighborhood. Now, the *tabals'* drums got louder, while Christians in west Beirut became furtive about decorating their Christmas trees and stopped stringing their balconies with Christmas lights. Bars, clubs, and stores selling liquor and stereos—symbols of blasphemous and satanic decadence to Shiite fundamentalists—became targets of intense hostility and were often blown up.[50]

AUB, once a center of intercultural understanding between the Muslim world and the West, now became a place of danger, an isolated fortress in a sea of hatred and resentment directed toward the expulsion of Western influence and values. By the mid-1980s many AUB classrooms were empty. Most of its foreign students and American faculty—those who had not been kidnapped—had left, changing its international complexion into one predominantly Lebanese. (In February 1987, the US government ordered all remaining Americans to leave Lebanon, effectively sealing off Lebanon from the West for several years.) AUB and the city it called home seemed on the verge of utter collapse. Fortunately, things stabilized a bit when the Syrian army wrested control of west Beirut from Shiite militias later in 1987.

The problems of AUB mirrored the problems the United States faced throughout the Middle East during the 1970s and 1980s. Once driven by an expansive and optimistic view of its mission in the region, America pulled in its horns, at least temporarily, frustrated by the impotence and futility of its own actions. Frustrated, bloodied, and increasingly unpopular in the Middle East, the United States reacted by hardening its line against Khomeini's Iran and by drawing closer to Israel. In Israel, fear and concomitant distrust reinforced a bunker mentality that made Israelis reluctant to compromise with Palestinians and Syrians—thus widening the dangerous divide between Arabs and Jews even more. Meanwhile, the United States cultivated relationships with friendly Arab leaders in Egypt, Jordan, and Saudi Arabia but faced growing alienation from ordinary Arabs, who increasingly saw America as insensitive to the plight of Palestinians and more concerned with stabilizing Arab autocrats for strategic reasons than with championing the political rights and economic aspirations of the multitudes in the Arab street, whose numbers, disaffection, and therefore attraction to Islamic fundamentalism grew with each passing year.

AUB's final travail during Lebanon's civil war came on November 8, 1991. Early that morning, someone drove a Volkswagen bus laden with explosives through AUB's sea gate off the corniche, up the campus, and parked it on the north side of AUB's venerable College Hall, the oldest building on campus where Daniel Bliss had lived and worked as he oversaw the school's construction 128 years earlier. The ensuing explosion collapsed College Hall's bell tower and façade constructed in the classical, arched style of the Ottomans; it was so powerful it hurled the front axle and wheels of the bus onto a roof one hundred yards away. College Hall had been reduced to a heap of bricks, broken glass, and fallen plaster. A forty-nine-year-old university employee and father of four perished in the explosion. It would be nearly a decade before College Hall was rebuilt and even longer before AUB reclaimed a sense of normalcy.

AUB managed to survive during these years because Lebanese faculty and staff members, against all odds, held it together after the school's American leadership had been driven away. Deeply devoted to the university that had shaped their lives, they committed themselves—often at great personal risk—to keep AUB going amid all of the adversity. AUB hospital remained open through the darkest days of the civil war, even when its American administrators, David Jacobsen and Joseph Ciccippio, were kidnapped and bomb craters and dead bodies littered its parking lot and alleyways. Lebanese doctors and nurses took up residence in the bullet-marred hospital in order to serve patients and to signal that nothing—absolutely nothing—would close its doors. The Lebanese faculty and staff struggled and sacrificed mightily on behalf of a school they loved and had made their own. They kept alive the vision of AUB during dark years when it might otherwise have collapsed into oblivion.[51] In the crucible of the civil war, AUB had become a Lebanese institution as much as an American institution.

Chapter 9:

AMERICA IN THE CONTEMPORARY MIDDLE EAST

J ust as Lebanon's civil war ended, America's attention in the Middle East shifted to nearby Iraq, when Saddam Hussein invaded Kuwait in August 1990. Although Washington had supported Saddam during his war against Iran in the 1980s, providing him arms and intelligence, Saddam's takeover of Kuwait and the fear that he might keep pushing through Kuwait into Saudi Arabia, thereby gaining control of a large portion of the world's oil supply, triggered the largest ever American military intervention in the Middle East and the biggest single US military operation since World War II. When asked to explain the massive response, Secretary of State James Baker simply said, "Jobs."[1] His chillingly succinct reply underscored just how much America's economic health and national security had become dependent on a stable and abundant supply of cheap oil from the Middle East.

The threat of an Iraqi invasion compelled the Saudis to accept US protection in the form of American troops, who flooded into the Arabian Peninsula during the autumn of 1990. President George H. W. Bush continued the US military buildup as the United Nations imposed sanctions intended to pressure Saddam to leave Kuwait. Bush and his advisers doubted sanctions would work or that the disparate coalition Washington assembled against Iraq—including America's former adversary the Soviet Union,[2] Israel, and several Arab states—would hold together for long. Washington decided to eject Iraq from Kuwait by force. In late October, Bush doubled the number of US troops in Saudi Arabia to nearly one-half million. He also sought, and won, resolutions in the UN Security Council and the US Congress authorizing Washington to use force to expel Iraq from Kuwait.

The Gulf War began in mid-January 1991 with a monthlong American bombing campaign against Iraq and its positions in Kuwait. Then came a massive ground assault across the border from Saudi Arabia into Kuwait and Iraq. Iraqi resistance collapsed rapidly. Six weeks after the Gulf War began, US and coalition forces liberated Kuwait, pushed Saddam's forces back to Iraq, and ended the war.[3] The Gulf War confirmed that the region's flow of oil to the West was critical to American security, brought events in the Middle East into millions of American living rooms, and involved the United States in the region to a degree it had never been before—but would again later.

The American-led coalition during the Gulf War produced an odd and unexpected couple: Israel and Arab states in alliance against Saddam's Iraq. The Gulf War persuaded the Israelis that a strong air force and superior technology trumped the defensive value of territory. It left the Palestine Liberation Organization (PLO), which had supported Iraq during the war, cut off from financial assistance from the Arab Gulf states. Together, these factors generated momentum that eventually led to secret talks between Israel and the PLO, culminating in the Oslo Accords of 1993. The first face-to-face talks between Israelis and Palestinians, Oslo resulted in a Declaration of Principles that mandated the evacuation of the Israel Defense Forces from parts of the West Bank and the Gaza Strip and the creation of a self-governing Palestinian National Authority in those evacuated areas. Oslo did not settle all outstanding differences. The nettlesome issues of Jerusalem, Palestinian refugees, Israeli settlements, and borders remain unresolved to this day. But Oslo did, at the time, mark a major step forward and create a framework for future negotiations.

The most fruitful talks between Israelis and Palestinians since 1948, Oslo brought together representatives of the two sides who applied reason and restraint to issues usually treated emotionally and contentiously. One person involved in the Oslo process was Hanan Ashrawi, a graduate from the American University of Beirut (AUB) who served as spokesperson for the Palestinians and became one of their most recognized and articulate voices.

Born into a West Bank Christian Arab family in 1946 (her father, an AUB graduate and physician, had treated wounded *Haganah* soldiers during the 1948 Arab-Israeli war), Ashrawi attended a Quaker girls' school in Ramallah before enrolling at AUB.[4] She was in her senior year at AUB when the Six-Day War broke out in June 1967. Ashrawi frantically tried to return home to her family, but was denied reentry to the Israeli-occupied West Bank. Ashrawi became an exile—and a committed Palestinian nationalist. She worked in Palestinian refugee camps in south Beirut before moving to the United States in 1970, where one of her sisters lived. She resumed her education and earned a PhD in comparative literature at the University of Virginia.

The Israeli government finally allowed Ashrawi to return to the West Bank in 1973. She joined the English department faculty of Birzeit University and became active in Palestinian politics. An articulate woman in a male-dominated world, Ashrawi brought a compassionate element to the contentious realm of Palestinian politics. She saw the emotional complexities of life in the Middle East. While many Israelis and Palestinians were locked in a fatal embrace of mutual distrust and hostility, Ashrawi developed friendships with Israeli women and quietly but tirelessly helped to lay the foundation for coexistence based on a human—not a political—understanding between Arabs and Jews. Yael Dayan, daughter of Moshe Dayan and deputy mayor of Tel Aviv, publicly praised Ashrawi's courage and commitment to the peace process.[5] And when PLO Chairman Yasser Arafat and Israeli Prime Minister Yitzhak Rabin stood beside President Bill Clinton on the south lawn of the White House on September 13, 1993, shook hands, and signed the historic Oslo Accords, Ashrawi had worked out the last-minute details that finally made it possible.

* * *

The 1990s raised hopes for Middle East peace, but it proved a difficult decade for AUB. Lebanon's civil war had battered the school for fifteen years with the continuing traumas of fear, violence, destruction, and death. Those who had remained faced the task of rebuilding in an atmosphere where political and religious differences had not been resolved. The US government ceased funding scholarships at AUB. Countries in the region like Jordan and the Gulf states developed their own national universities, and non-Lebanese parents did not want to send their children to a war zone. Once a magnet for students across the Middle East and central Asia, the school now held only a small minority of AUB students from outside Lebanon. AUB also faced competition from new American schools in the region. Institutions such as the American University of Kuwait and Education City in Qatar (a consortium of US universities sharing a regional campus) sprouted up to satisfy Arabs' abiding hunger for a Western education, which they still saw as a prime route to a better future.

This new generation of Middle Eastern students "objected to many things in American policy," remarked an Arab educator, "except for one thing: American-style education."[6] "Even radical Islamists are not shy about sending their children to be educated in the United States," noted another contemporary observer.[7] They saw such education as their children's ladder to success. They recognized the technological and information revolutions sweeping the world, and they did not want their children left behind. Middle Easterners keenly wanted American-style instruction for their children. Despite these and the many other challenges it faced, AUB's mission remained as important and relevant as it had ever been.

This led John Waterbury, a Princeton political economist specializing in the Middle East, to become the first resident president of AUB since 1984. Waterbury had been deeply moved by Malcolm Kerr's assassination; Kerr had been a personal friend and a fellow political scientist.[8] After Kerr's death and the subsequent US State Department ban on Americans traveling to and living in Lebanon, AUB had been run from the school's Manhattan office, with a deputy in day-to-day charge in Beirut. When the state department finally lifted its travel ban in 1997, Waterbury accepted the AUB presidency. "The opportunity to take the helm of this venerable university after a long period of near life-and-death challenges generated by the civil war in Lebanon was very attractive," he noted.[9]

Waterbury's decision took courage: his two immediate predecessors in Beirut had been kidnapped (David Dodge) and murdered (Malcolm Kerr). Anonymous extremists hurled two sticks of dynamite from a speeding car over the campus wall along Bliss Street during Waterbury's visit to the campus in October 1997, shattering the windows of two buildings. If the incident was intended to intimidate Waterbury, it did not succeed. He came to Beirut, moved into Marquand House, and took up duties as AUB president in January 1998.

Serious and scholarly, Waterbury had not been "known to be one of the more flamboyant men on the Princeton faculty," said a colleague without understatement.[10] But Waterbury was a savvy administrator who used a low-key style, quiet humor, and a gentle insistence on civility to reestablish AUB as a haven for differing ideas and open debate in a volatile environment, understanding that much of the most valuable education at AUB took place outside of the classroom. He stressed responsible freedom of speech, critical thinking cultivating skepticism toward received wisdom, and an analytical approach to problem solving that taught students to wrestle with issues in terms and language they could mutually understand and respect. Trailed by a security guard on campus and by a Lebanese soldier off campus, Waterbury successfully led the university for the next ten years. His work doubled the enrollment of non-Lebanese students, restored AUB's image in the region, and once again made it the best and most respected university in the Arab world.

These years spanned momentous events for the United States and its relationship to the Middle East. None loomed larger than those of September 11, 2001. Waterbury took an Amtrak® commuter train that morning from his home in Princeton, New Jersey, to New York City, where he planned to spend the day working at AUB's midtown office before returning to Beirut for the start of the fall semester. At Newark, many of the passengers got off and transferred to a train that ferried them across the marshes of upper Newark Bay and then underneath the Hudson River to their jobs at the World Trade Center in Lower Manhattan. After reaching New York's Penn Station, Waterbury passed a nearby New York City Fire Department (FDNY) station with firefighters out front drinking coffee and sharing jokes.

Later that morning, operatives of the radical Islamic terrorist organization al Qaeda flew hijacked commercial airliners into the World Trade Center towers, the icons of American prosperity.[11] The assault on the World Trade Center was part of a larger assault on the US homeland that day that killed nearly three thousand Americans, more than had died in any previous attack in the country's history.[12] The leader of al Qaeda, Osama bin Laden, a privileged Saudi radicalized by his years as a *mujahideen* (Islamic resistance fighter) against the Soviets in Afghanistan in the 1980s and by the stationing of one-half-million US troops on the soil of the Arabian Peninsula during the Gulf War of 1991, praised the hijackers for thrusting the "sword of Islam" into the United States as punishment for the "Crusader-Zionist" occupation of the Islamic holy lands (which, by tradition, is a placed barred to infidels). Traumatized by 9/11, America hunted for bin Laden for nearly a decade until US soldiers found and killed him in a raid on his secret safe house in Pakistan on May 1, 2011.

The events of September 11, 2001, revealed the alarming growth of religious extremism in the Muslim world, where radical Islamists had begun to challenge rulers over internal governance and their ties to American power. Operating in the shadows, al Qaeda extremists saw themselves as true believers locked in a millennial struggle with unbelieving "crusaders." They rejected modernizing Arab regimes like those in Egypt and the Gulf states as impious and un-Islamic, and they branded Arab leaders who cooperated with the West as betrayers of the *umma*, the universal Islamic community. They viewed the United States as the latest in a long line of Western Christian precedessors carrying out yet another infidel effort to dominate the Islamic world by spreading idolatry in the form of secularism. Just as the Prophet Mohammed had fought the *jahiliyyah* (the ignorance of pre-Islamic Arabia), so modern Muslims must use every means at their disposal to resist the modern *jahiliyyah* of the West led by the United States. This meant a relentless *jihad* to eliminate America's presence in the region. Such a result would spell the end of apostate regimes allied with the West and hasten the Islamic revolution in the Muslim world.

Panic gripped the United States on September 11. Waterbury returned home by train that afternoon, lost in stunned silence like the other passengers on his commuter train. When his train passed a mosque near Princeton, Waterbury saw a huge American flag draped on its wall, put there to blunt the danger of a hysterical vendetta by angry citizens against Muslim symbols in America. A huddle of police officers stood guard outside the mosque.

Waterbury later learned that ten of the firefighters he had seen outside the FDNY station that morning had perished in the collapse of the World Trade Center Towers.

Waterbury recounted these events in vivid detail to AUB students after returning to Beirut a short time later. "Why do I tell you all this?" he said to his rapt audience. "Because these events make me feel our common links, our shared fears and hopes, our common humanity." Waterbury wanted AUB students to feel what he had felt—and to draw the inescapable conclusion for themselves. "The sacred texts tell us that it is human to hate, human to crave revenge, indeed human to kill. But a university, like a mosque, or a church, or a temple, must lift us above our humanness and connect us to our humanity."[13]

* * *

September 11, 2001, marked a watershed in recent US history. A bolt out of the blue, the events of that day represented America's greatest public trauma since the attacks on Pearl Harbor sixty years earlier. The events of 9/11 rocked the nation, creating a mood of outrage followed by a surge of combative patriotism. The US government, like the American people, had been caught off guard. Threats and vulnerabilities had always lurked *beyond* the homeland. Stung by the attacks, President George W. Bush resolved to do whatever necessary to combat terrorism and prevent another 9/11. One month after 9/11, US military forces in alliance with regional warlords struck against Taliban-ruled Afghanistan, which had given sanctuary to al Qaeda. The irony was intense: the United States had covertly trained and supplied al Qaeda and the Taliban during their war against the Soviets in Afghanistan in the 1980s. In the 1990s, these allies-of-convenience had turned into the worst of enemies.

In the charged post-9/11 atmosphere, Bush and his national security team, led by Vice President Richard "Dick" Cheney, suspected Iraq's Saddam Hussein of complicity with al Qaeda without conclusive proof. The Bush administration also believed Saddam possessed weapons of mass destruction. It presumed guilt on both counts. These fallacious assumptions—along with the expansive belief that destroying Saddam's regime in Iraq would remodel the Middle East along democratic lines—drove America's invasion of Iraq. Fear and hubris overrode caution and prudence. "We're an empire now and when we act, we create our own reality," a Bush adviser told a journalist.[14] The Bush administration prepared a campaign to topple Saddam in the name of "preemption" and "regime change." US military forces invaded Iraq in March 2003.

The US invasion quickly toppled Saddam, but it also ushered in a host of unanticipated and unattractive consequences. The postwar occupation of Iraq proved much more difficult and bloody than Bush and his self-confident advisers expected. The American presence ultimately quelled much of the violence in Iraq and laid the groundwork for a new and more democratic political and social order, but the country remained mired in sectarianism, and anti-Americanism flared across the Middle East. Many in the region had previously criticized the United States for unconditionally supporting Israel and tolerating repressive Arab regimes. Now, anger toward America became more general and strident. Sentiment on the Arab street increasingly viewed US policy in the Middle East as overbearing in its application of military power and selective in its application of democracy—in short, of being arrogant and hypocritical. While many in the Arab world did not like Saddam Hussein, many also saw Bush's targeting of Saddam not as the removal of a brutal, threatening dictator but as the first step in an effort to impose a new imperial order in the region. Most ironic of all, al Qaeda arrived in Iraq *after* the US invasion.

After the 2003 US invasion, AUB became a beacon for a former US serviceman seeking to make sense of the modern Middle East and America's impact there. Andrew Exum had joined the US Army Rangers after studying classics at the University of Pennsylvania, and he experienced combat in both Afghanistan in 2001–2002 and Iraq in 2003–2004. Exum retired from the army in the fall of 2004 with many questions on his mind. "I had just invaded my second country the year before whose language I didn't speak and whose history, politics, and culture I didn't understand." He promptly decided to enroll at "the best university in the Arabic-speaking world" in order to find answer to his questions.[15] AUB did just that—and much more—for Exum. "It was a tremendous journey of exploration for me," he recalled. Exum threw himself into an environment of many different perspectives and voices. Interacting with a broad range of scholars and students on and off campus, he learned to view Middle Eastern culture from the inside out and to understand how Lebanese and other students perceived the United States. Exum brought these insights back with him to the United States, when he joined a Washington think tank at the beginning of the Obama administration and advised Generals David Petraeus and Stanley McChrystal on US policy in Iraq and Afghanistan.

* * *

During these years, Islamic militancy grew across the Middle East and central Asia. Rooted in an Islamic religious movement called the *Salafiyya* (the venerable forefathers), referring to the generation of the Prophet Mohammed and his companions. Salafism took many forms, most of which did not approach the violent extremism of al Qaeda. Salafist movements included Wahhabism founded in Arabia in the eighteenth century, the Muslim Brotherhood founded in Egypt in the 1920s,[16] and the Taliban founded in Afghanistan in the 1980s.[17]

In Muslim countries, the tension between religion and secularism was never far from the surface. Authoritarianism meant the mosque functioned as the only acceptable forum for political expression. The disorienting effects of globalization intensified inequalities of wealth without increasing economic opportunities. Fundamentalist organizations—not the state—provided the only effective social services to suffering urban masses. Modernization brought not greater freedom but continued poverty, powerlessness, and political dysfunction that intensified frustration and anger, especially when modern communications technologies like satellite television and the Internet brought home the contrast between conditions in their countries and those in the United States and elsewhere in the West.

Animus toward the United States became one way of coping with the hard, disillusioning limits of life on the Muslim street in the age of globalization absent viable political parties, a free press, and pathways for dissent. Radical Islamism became a means for the oppressed in Middle Eastern countries to articulate their frustrations and grievances against corrupt government. The politics of protest, couched in culturally familiar and therefore popular language, took many forms: civic art and cell phone anthems celebrating resistance, religious banners proclaiming *jihad*, exhortations to martyrdom, and the flourishing of fundamentalist *madrasas* preaching anti-Americanism and churning out angry young men who viewed the modern world and non-Muslims with intense suspicion. They feared being governed by infidels and found the idea profoundly disturbing. Would Muslims lose their cultural and religious identity and be swamped by foreign traditions different from those in which Islam had arisen and persisted for more than one thousand years? Would they lose touch with their roots? An aggressively defensive strain had entered Muslim thinking.

Such manifestations underscored the rising tide of militant Islam from Lebanon in the west to Afghanistan and Pakistan in the east. A telltale sign of all that had changed came in January 2006, when Hamas—the radical Islamist rival to the PLO within the Palestinian movement—resoundingly won parliamentary elections in the West Bank and wrested control of the Gaza Strip from the PLO the following year. Hamas refused to recognize the Jewish state or to accept the framework agreement negotiated in Oslo between Israel and the PLO. Like Hezbollah in Lebanon and the Taliban in Afghanistan and Pakistan, Hamas drew its power from the disaffected and disillusioned among Palestinians who believed the Oslo Accords had turned the PLO leadership into a tool of Israel in suppressing their own people and who embraced the anti-American, anti-Israeli message of militant Islam.

A moderate Sunni Muslim who supported the West's struggle against Islamic extremism and sought to bring about change in his own country was Rafiq al-Hariri, a self-made Lebanese billionaire and philanthropist who became prime minister in 1992 and served in that role for ten of the next twelve years. A wealthy and cautious businessman, Hariri guided Lebanon through economic development rather than political radicalism. Utilizing extensive contacts in Saudi Arabia and the Gulf states,[18] he rebuilt Beirut's once beautiful and historic city center, which had been devastated during the civil war. The project's success became a symbol of rebirth for the entire country. Hariri also brought rejuvenation to Lebanon by attracting foreign investment and funding hundreds of AUB scholarships for students from across the Middle East.

Hariri's growing popularity in Lebanon and the region made powerful enemies. On February 14, 2005, he was killed in a huge explosion that destroyed his motorcade on the corniche road as it passed Beirut's swank St. George's Yacht Club on the seafront just down the hill from AUB—in the very district his construction company had remade from rubble. Hariri's assassination triggered popular demonstrations against Syria, which many blamed for the killing. These protests culminated in a massive demonstration at the Place des Martyrs on March 14, attended by more than one million Lebanese—one-quarter of the country's entire population, bridging sectarian divisions—that became known as the Cedar Revolution.[19] It represented the largest public rally in the Middle East since four million Egyptians turned out to bury their legendary singer Umm Kulthūm in 1975. The Cedar Revolution forced Damascus to withdraw the remaining troops it had sent to Lebanon in 1976. For the first time in thirty years, Lebanon emerged free from foreign occupation.

Meanwhile, in southern Lebanon, Hezbollah continued its rocket attacks and kidnap missions against Israel. Skirmishes between the two sides continued even after liberal prime minister Ehud Barak withdrew all remaining IDF forces from south Lebanon in May 2000. In mid-July 2006, Israel, now led by conservative prime minister Ehud Olmert (who had succeeded an incapacitated Ariel Sharon) reinvaded Lebanon in retaliation for ongoing Hezbollah ambushes and rocket attacks on the Jewish state. This time, Israel aimed to cripple Hezbollah in a "quick and decisive" military operation and turn the Lebanese people against the popular Shiite organization for provoking Israeli retaliation.[20] The IDF pounded Hezbollah positions throughout Lebanon, severely damaged the country's infrastructure (despite Olmert's promise to Washington at the start of the war not to do so), displaced almost one million civilians, and killed more than one thousand.[21] In response to all the attacks, Lebanese prime minister Fouad Siniora told the Israelis: "You're destroying us and strengthening Hezbollah."[22]

War once again took its toll on Beirut and AUB. Another wave of Shiite refugees flooded the southern suburbs. Israeli bombing destroyed roads and facilities throughout the city. AUB took in hundreds of Lebanese left homeless by the destruction. The wounded found their way to the AUB hospital, which depended on dwindling fuel oil supplies amid Israel's naval blockade of Lebanon's coast. AUB faculty used their knowledge and skills to help those hurt by the war—especially the young, the most innocent in any conflict. A theater professor, Sharif Abdunnur, taught traumatized children penned up in cramped shelters to cope with their fears through laughter and games, which put them at a safe distance from their experiences. Maronite leader Samir Jaaja said, "Most of the nation feels that our present and future can be compared to a feather floating in the wind."[23]

The war ended when a UN-sponsored ceasefire finally took effect in mid-August. Despite Israel's overwhelming military superiority, the 2006 war proved a disappointment for the Jewish state. Hezbollah rocket attacks displaced nearly one-half of the population of northern Israel (approximately 500,000 people); Hezbollah withstood Israel's military might; confidence among Israelis in the IDF's effectiveness fell to an all-time low;[24] Hezbollah's leader, Hassan Nasrallah, became the most popular figure on the Arab street;[25] the people of Lebanon—Christian, Druse, Shiite, and Sunni—united in resentment toward Israel for damaging their country; and radical Islamism increased in influence throughout the Middle East. Hezbollah continued after 2006 to boost its military capacity, and its leaders developed the belief that it could win another war with Israel. This, in turn, increased Israeli fears and the prospect of another attack that would again devastate Lebanon's infrastructure, harm its civilians, and reignite widespread Lebanese antipathy toward Israel and the United States.

In 2011, Hezbollah engineered the replacement of the Sunni-based, American-backed government of Saad al-Hariri, son of Rafiq al-Hariri. Saad had supported a United Nations tribunal, set up in 2007 to investigate his father's assassination, that Hezbollah fiercely opposed. After struggling with Hezbollah, many of Hariri's government officers left their positions, and Hariri was replaced as prime minister. The new Lebanese government marked the culmination of Shias' generation-long ascent from a shadowy group to the country's preeminent political force with a powerful militia and a sprawling social network serving south Lebanon's majority Shiite community. It represented a new era for a combustible country whose internal conflicts mirrored the rivalry between Iran and the United States in the region.

* * *

A new era dawned also in the United States in November 2008, when voters elected Barack Obama (whose father was born into a Kenyan Muslim family), its first African American president. President Obama shared the Blisses' and the Dodges' missionary commitment to ambitious global reform. A graduate of Honolulu's elite Punahou School, founded by New England missionaries in 1841 and dubbed by one writer as "the Exeter of the Pacific,"[26] Obama imbibed the school's ethic of humanitarian service that was reinforced during his years at Harvard Law School, and which he applied as president. Obama the establishment reformer shared the New England faith in the equality and essential similarity of all people around the world.

Obama summoned the wealth and power of the United States to solve the problems and dangers associated with Islamic militancy. He shifted the focus of the US war against terrorism from Iraq (which he considered an unwise "war of choice") to Afghanistan, a "war of necessity" that the United States had been slowly losing since toppling the Taliban in October 2001. Obama declared during the 2008 presidential campaign that America had "a fundamental strategic interest in making sure Afghanistan doesn't revert to being a safe haven for al Qaeda."[27]

America had initially triumphed in Afghanistan after its post-9/11 invasion of the country, but it had failed to build a lasting peace there. The Bush administration's preoccupation with Iraq after 2003 meant that little was accomplished while Afghans still welcomed US troops and aid workers. "Huge resources were devoted to Iraq, which focused away from nation building in Afghanistan," said former UN secretary-general Kofi Annan. "The billions spent in Iraq were the billions that were not spent in Afghanistan."[28] America's neglect led to the revival of the Taliban, which gave sanctuary to al Qaeda, and the opium trade that funded it.

Obama resolved to turn things around in Afghanistan. He would use American wealth and power to vanquish the Taliban and build a peaceful and stable Afghanistan. Just as the Blisses and the Dodges believed that given American values and education, Middle Easterners would build their own version of democracy, so too did Obama believe that, given enough American support, Afghans would build a viable state that would ultimately lead to peace and stability in the region. It was a deeply traditional, American, diplomatic vision that stretched back beyond the life of Daniel Bliss: a strong United States applying a moral vision tempered by pragmatism. But history also taught American presidents before Obama how difficult it could be to reshape other societies and governments.

Afghanistan became "Obama's War." In this effort, Obama confronted a host of deep-seated problems—not least, the military challenges of counterinsurgency warfare and the political challenges of nation building. A remote, landlocked, mountainous country the size of Texas, Afghanistan had never submitted to the will of outsider powers, including Alexander the Great, the Mongols, and the Persians, and had never been fully integrated as a nation. A complex matrix of tribal politics ruled. Afghans had kept two great empires, Britain and the Soviet Union, at bay during the nineteenth and twentieth centuries. As British and Soviet forces had grown, so had Afghan resistance to them until the British and the Soviets gave up and left. The United States had supported Afghan resistance to the Soviet occupation during the 1980s, then abruptly turned away afterward. The country fell into chaos and, in the mid-1990s, under the control of the Taliban.

Following the 2001 US invasion, the American-supported regime of Hamid Karzai took power, but it became dysfunctional and corrupt, focused more on extracting revenues for private gain than on governing for the public good. In 2009, as President Obama deepened America's military involvement in Afghanistan, the country remained a nation devastated by a generation of war; fragmented by deep divisions of language, ethnicity, and geography; and confronting a Taliban insurgency comprised of Pashtuns scattered across both sides of the rugged 1,600-mile Afghan-Pakistani border. Astride this border lived twelve million Pashtuns in Afghanistan, and more than double that number in Pakistan.[29]

The increased US military effort in Afghanistan under Obama, moreover, did little to mitigate America's political problems in the larger Muslim world. Next door in Pakistan, the second most populous Muslim country and a key US ally in the Afghanistan War (as well as a base area and recruiting ground for al Qaeda and the Taliban in its frontier provinces), a majority of people viewed America as the greatest threat to their country, even greater than Pakistan's longtime adversary, India.[30] Deep suspicion underlay every American move in Pakistan. Ninety percent of the $10 billion in US aid provided to Pakistan since 9/11 went to the military (whose intelligence service had, ironically, given elements of the Taliban refuge, arms, and money over the years) rather than to economic development and the strengthening of democracy and civil society. A powerful political force in the country, Pakistan's army included officers and soldiers sympathetic to conservative Islam and even, in some cases, the very militants the army faced in battle.

America faced an uphill struggle to persuade alienated and poverty-stricken Pakistanis to resist the siren call of Islamic extremism. Many Pakistanis began to lose hope—a dangerous portent of future trouble in a country much more populous than Afghanistan and in possession of a nuclear arsenal. A poll of young Pakistanis conducted in the spring of 2009 found that only one in ten expressed confidence in their government. Barely one in five had full-time jobs. One in four could not read or write. Fewer than four in ten received an education.[31] The deep frustration and sense of abandonment felt by a rapidly growing population disillusioned with corrupt politics, few jobs, and lack of education made them despondent about the future and tempted them to turn their energies toward militant Islam in pursuit of social justice. Militant Islam made disaffected young Pakistanis feel powerful in a world that ignored them. "Out there I'm a useless guy, unemployed and cursed by my family," said one Pakistani militant. But "here I'm a commander. My words have weight."[32] The feelings and trends in the thwarted, resentful society of Pakistan are broadly representative of trends across much of the Muslim world.

* * *

For generations, paternalistic strongmen throughout the Islamic world used fear, patronage, intimidation, tribal politics, and crony capitalism to stifle meaningful political evolution and debase everyday transactions. Rulers treated people as subjects rather than citizens. Police brutality, rigged elections, and rampant corruption made life harder and harder as the rich elite grew richer and the poor masses grew poorer. Arab economies expanded, yet the number of Arabs in poverty increased. By the early twenty-first century, half of the population of the Middle East lived on less than two dollars a day, while privileged Arabs connected to regimes in power insulated themselves and their families behind gated communities.

Decades of accumulated resentment exploded in the spring of 2011, when millions of Arabs of all backgrounds and faiths took to the streets to challenge authoritarian rule on an unprecedented scale. The popular protest movement, known as *al-Nahda* (The Awakening), transformed widespread discontent into a ringing collective call for change. The protests astonished and captivated and exhilarated the Arab world. Ordinary Arabs demonstrated they would no longer accept the old rules of repression. They started to see themselves differently; they suddenly found their voice. They felt compelled to express their own views and believed these views deserved respect. They felt enormous pride in speaking up, even in the face of danger and violence. "People are learning that the yearning for freedom, for dignity, for justice and for employment is a legitimate ambition," wrote Lebanese columnist Sateh Noureddine. "This is a historic moment, and it is teaching the Arab world everything. They are learning that if they take to the streets they can accomplish their goals."[33]

The protests began in Tunisia, spread to Egypt, and then moved throughout the entire Arab world, exciting passions and a sense of empowerment across the Middle East through social networks made possible by the Internet. *Al-Nahda* utilized new media technologies like Facebook® and Twitter®, but it reflected fundamental, unifying values nurtured among Arab students over generations at AUB: freedom, democratic and accountable government, the rule of law, social justice, and economic opportunity. The protesters felt they had turned a corner. Said a protester in Yemen: "The street is not afraid of governments anymore. It is the opposite. Governments and their security forces are afraid of the people now. The new generation wants their full rights, and a dignified life."[34] "We've discovered ourselves," said another protester in Egypt. "It's not the end, it's the beginning."[35]

* * *

Al-Nahda confronted America with an acute challenge: how to reconcile pro-testers' demands with US strategic interests and Washington's desire since the end of World War II to avert instability in the Middle East. One way has worked well in the past. For 150 years—far longer than the United States has backed authoritarian Arab regimes, protected the flow of Persian Gulf oil, or deployed combat troops in Arabia, Iraq, and Afghanistan—AUB has edu-cated tens of thousands of Middle Easterners of all faiths and backgrounds, broadened their horizons and opportunities, and exposed them to enduring values of individual dignity, self-determination, and toleration. For the greater part of these 150 years, AUB brought Arabs and Jews along with Americans and Muslims together, transforming, or at least substantially altering, their perceptions of one another. Unlike the stereotypes to which each has become accustomed in recent decades, when Arabs and Jews lived in sealed narrative bubbles and seemed almost incapable of hearing one another, at AUB, Arabs and Jews, and Americans and Muslims, saw that the other was neither alarming nor strange. The power of caricature and dehumanization—defense mechanisms that protect one's psyche from something difficult to accept—gave way to reality. Initially self-conscious, unsympathetic toward one another, and quick to blame the other for their troubles, at AUB, Arabs, Jews, Americans, and Muslims became humanly familiar to each other through dialogue and learned tolerance, and therefore politically plausible partners to each other. They developed a feeling for who the other was and where the other had been. They tended to believe, rather than to doubt, each other. They became more thoughtful about themselves, one another, and the future of the Middle East. By doing so, they dispelled the notion of an intractable dispute between Arabs and Jews and Americans and Muslims. Students of all backgrounds learned at AUB that truth could not be imposed by force and that intellectual conformity was incompatible with true faith.

That any of these things should come as a revelation to anyone is a com-ment on our times.

The possibilities that AUB embodies are still alive. Most Muslims—half of whom were college-age or younger at the beginning of the twenty-first century[36]—still hunger for these possibilities in their lives. Most Middle Easterners do not want to be defined by religious or political extremists.

Muslim societies have many problems, but hating democracy is not among them. They admire and aspire to the same political freedoms that Americans enjoy. To them, AUB represents the positive side of America because it sustains values of cooperation and coexistence in a contentious region of the world. AUB still promotes moderation and understanding—the most powerful and enduring antidotes to extremism of any kind. It still helps to build democracy and open society in the Muslim world—not by prescribing answers, but by teaching its students and future leaders to ask the right questions. AUB can still help Arabs and Jews, and Americans and Muslims, to open their minds and hearts to the opportunities of a shared future by breaking down psychological barriers that block a shift in perception and a reconceptualization of relations. AUB cannot change Arabs and Jews any more than it can change Americans and Muslims, but it can help change their human understanding of one another, thereby laying the groundwork for a future that is better than the bitterness and distrust of the past and the present. This road is long and difficult, with many obstacles along the way. It is there, however.

Naysayers and cynics will assert all of this is naïve if not dangerously impossible, given the passions aroused in the Middle East by the inflamed and complex Israeli-Palestinian dispute, the explosive politics of the region, and the traumatic events of September 11, 2001, and after. Others, especially extremists and rejectionists, will fight hard to deny even this possibility. Such a possibility would indeed take time—perhaps considerable time. But is there a better or more practical alternative in the long run, given the importance of the issues involved and the consequences of failure for all involved?

The Blisses and the Dodges came to understand this central truth. Suffused with the ambition and arrogance, the idealism and ignorance typical of Americans venturing abroad, Daniel Bliss came to the Middle East in February of 1856 full of superior preconceptions and resolved to remake the region in America's image according to American rhythms. Hard and sometimes bitter experience taught Bliss and his descendents, who built the American University of Beirut, a very different wisdom. They learned to engage Middle Easterners on their own terms in their own land. They stopped condescending to the heirs of great world civilizations and learned to work with them, focusing on young people rather than political elites. Through education, not blandishments or coercion, the Blisses and the Dodges offered, rather than imposed, the best of American values: individual freedom wedded to civic responsibility, respect for toleration as well as tradition, uninhibited but orderly exchange of ideas, and opportunities for a better future informed by an understanding of past and present challenges. By sharing these principles with Middle Easterners through trial and tumult, the Blisses and the Dodges helped to transform the region in terms of access and opportunity as well as economic and social achievement. They also made AUB an enduring symbol of what America, in its better moments, can offer to the rest of the world.

President Obama understood this point when he declared at Cairo University on June 4, 2009: "So long as our relationship is defined by our differences, we will empower those who sow hatred rather than peace, those who promote conflict rather than the cooperation that can help all of our people achieve justice and prosperity. . . . There must be a sustained effort to listen to each other; to learn from each other; to respect one another; and to seek common ground."[37]

There is an old saying in the Middle East that "you can fight someone you don't know, but you can't make peace with him."[38] AUB and the United States can still help to resolve this dilemma. It's been done before. It can be done again.

Appendix

PROMINENT LIVING AUB ALUMNI (AS OF 2011)*

NAME	NATIONALITY	AFFILIATION
Abu-Ghazaleh, Talal	Jordan	Jordanian Senate
Ahady, Anwar ul-Haq	Afghanistan	Transportation Minister
Ajarimah, Ahmad	Saudi Arabia	Aramco
Akbar, Ali	Bangladesh	Health Education Bureau
Alami, Lamis	Palestine	Education Minister
Allawi, Mohammed	Iraq	Former Communications Minister
Ansari, Amtul-Latif	Pakistan	Pakistani Senate
Araji, Assem	Lebanon	Lebanese Parliament
Armenian, Haroutune	United States	Johns Hopkins Public Health School
Arrayed, Jalil	Bahrain	Education Ministry
Asfur, Mohammed	Jordan	Jordanian Cabinet
Ashrawi, Hanan	Palestine	Palestinian Legislative Council
Ayyub, Afif	Lebanon	Ambassador to Oman
Azar, Wasef	Jordan	Jordanian Cabinet
Badri, Gasim	Sudan	Ahfad University for Women
Baramki, Gabriel	Palestine	Birzeit University
Barmania, Zubeida	South Africa	Gender Equality Commission
Bassam, Abdulhamid	United Arab Emirates	Gulf Cooperation Council
Batayneh, Aref	Jordan	Jordanian Senate
Bayyati, Hilal	Iraq	National Computer Center

193

Bu-Allay, Kassim	Bahrain	Former Foreign Minister
Budayr, Isam	Jordan	Jordanian Senate
Bu-Habib, Abdallah	Lebanon	World Bank
El-Khair, Kazem	Lebanon	Lebanese Parliament
Fakhro, Ali	Bahrain	Arab Open University
Falah, Fouad	Kuwait	Kuwait University
Farhan, Amal	Jordan	Jordanian Cabinet
Fayyad, Salam	Palestine	Finance Minister
Folios, Christos	Greece	Greek Cabinet
Gatkuth, Faruk	Sudan	Sudanese Parliament
Ghani-Ahmadzai, Mohammed-Ashraf	Afghanistan	Former Kabul University Chancellor
Gharaybeh, Abdel-Karim	Jordan	University of Jordan
Gosaibi, Khalid	Saudi Arabia	National Economy Minister
Hajj-Ali, Nasr	Sudan	Khartoum University
Hitti, Nasif	Lebanon	Arab League Ambassador to France
Husayn, Hamzah	Kuwait	Central Bank of Kuwait
Jamsheer, Abdul-Rahman	Bahrain	Shura Council
Jebejian, Robert	Syria	Jebejian Eye Hospital
Jumblat, Walid	Lebanon	Druse Leader
Kabariti, Abdul-Karim	Jordan	Chief of the Royal Court
Kassis, Nabil	Palestine	Planning Minister
Khalilzad, Zalmay	United States	Former Ambassador to Afghanistan & Iraq
Khatib, Maha	Jordan	Jordan River Foundation
Khiyami, Sami	Syria	Ambassador to Great Britain
Kittis, Constantinos	Cyprus	Former Finance Minister
LeBaron, Joseph	United States	Ambassador to Qatar
Masri, Taher	Jordan	Former Prime Minister
Mikati, Mohammed-Najib	Lebanon	Former Prime Minister

Naimy, Ali	Saudi Arabia	Aramco
Nusaybah, Hazem	Jordan	Former Foreign Minister
Owais, Wajih	Jordan	Education Minister
Pachachi, Adnan	Iraq	Iraqi Cabinet
Pashtun, Mohammed-Yousef	Afghanistan	Urban Development Minister
Sabah, Hissah	Bahrain	Arab Women's Labor Union
Saeed, Khawaja	Pakistan	University of the Punjab
Safadi, Mohammed	Lebanon	Lebanese Parliament
Saidi, Nasser-Amin	United Arab Emirates	Finance Ministry (Dubai)
Salehi, Ali-Akbar	Iran	Foreign Minister
Satti, Awad	Sudan	Ambassador to Great Britain
Siniora, Fouad	Lebanon	Former Prime Minister
Sulyati, Hamad	Bahrain	Shura Council
Tukan, Khalid	Jordan	Atomic Energy Agency Chairman
Yasin, Mohammed	Afghanistan	Agriculture & Land Reform Minister

*Information in this list has been provided to the author courtesy of American University of Beirut.

NOTES

INTRODUCTION

1. Daniel Bliss to Bev Gordon, Sûq al-Gharb, February 11, 1862, Bliss Family Papers, Amherst College Archives, Robert Frost Library, Amherst College, Amherst, Massachusetts.

2. R. Wayne Anderson, quoted in the *Boston Globe*, August 12, 1985, p. 41.

PROLOGUE: SAILING TO BEIRUT

1. The other passengers who boarded the *Sultana* that morning were Mr. George Dickinson, a Boston merchant; Mr. William Hallack, an Amherst student; and six fellow missionaries: Rev. Henry Jessup (who kept a journal during the voyage, on which much of the following account is based); Rev. and Mrs. George Pollard; Miss Mary Tenney; Rev. Tillman Trowbridge; and Miss Sarah West.

2. Quoted in Henry Harris Jessup, "Journal of Personal Journey from Sept. 21, 1855, to Arrival in Syria on Feb. 7, 1856," Henry Harris Jessup Papers, Special Collections, Yale Divinity School Library, Yale University, New Haven, Connecticut (hereafter cited as HHJP, YDSL).

3. Hans Christian Anderson, a friend of Charles's father, read his celebrated fairy tales to the boy on visits to the Watson home.

4. Today known as Izmir, Turkey.

5. Jessup, "Journal of Personal Journey," HHJP, YDSL.

6. Ibid.

7. Ibid.

8. Abby Wood Bliss to Luke Sweetser, January 17, 1856, Bliss Family Papers, Amherst College Archives, Robert Frost Library, Amherst College, Amherst, Massachusetts (hereafter cited as BFP, ACA).

9. The printing press in Malta, founded in 1822, later moved to Beirut and

became the American Press. The Arabic Bible had been translated by the Maronite Bishop of Damascus in 1620 and published in Rome in 1671. A newer, fuller version prepared by American missionaries Eli Smith and Cornelius Van Dyck appeared in 1865.

10. See Daniel Bliss to Mary Sweetser, January 19, 1856, BFP, ACA.

CHAPTER 1: DANIEL BLISS AND AMERICAN MISSION

1. Alexis de Tocqueville, "On the Principal Causes Tending to Maintain a Democratic Republic in the United States," *Democracy in America* (New York: Harper & Row, 1969), v. 1, chapter 9.

2. Quoted in Edward Hitchcock, *Reminiscences of Amherst College, Historical, Scientific, Biographical, and Autobiographical: Also, of Other and Wider Life Experiences* (Northampton, MA: Bridgman & Childs, 1863), pp. 160–61.

3. Amherst graduated an average of eighteen missionaries a year—compared with ten from Yale, eight from Middlebury, seven each from Harvard and Williams, five each from Brown and Princeton. See Claude Moore Fuess, *Amherst: The Story of a New England College* (Boston: Little, Brown, 1935), pp. 138–39; and Hitchcock, *Reminiscences of Amherst College*, pp. 189, 191.

4. Quoted in Grace Dodge Guthrie, *Legacy to Lebanon* (privately published, 1984), p. 4.

5. Robert D. Kaplan, *The Arabists: The Romance of an American Elite* (New York: Free Press, 1993), p. 33.

6. Daniel Bliss to Joseph Adams, Sûq al-Gharb, February 11, 1862, Bliss Family Papers, Amherst College Archives, Robert Frost Library, Amherst College, Amherst, Massachusetts (hereafter cited as BFP, ACA).

7. Daniel Bliss to Mary Bliss, September 22, 1873, in Daniel Bliss, *Letters from a New Campus: Written to His Wife Abby and Their Four Children during Their Visit to Amherst, Massachusetts, 1873–1874*, ed. Douglas Rugh and Belle Dorman Rugh with Alfred H. Howell (New York: Syracuse University Press, 1994), p. 87.

8. Quoted in Alfred Kazin, *An American Procession* (New York: Alfred A. Knopf, 1984), pp. xvi–xvii.

9. Ibid., p. 26.

10. Quoted in Kaplan, *Arabists*, p. 32.

11. Ibid., p. 18.

12. The wife of Bliss's professor of New Testament Greek was Harriet Beecher Stowe, who published *Uncle Tom's Cabin* the same year Bliss began studying there.

13. William R. Hutchison, *Errand to the World: American Protestant Thought and Foreign Missions* (Chicago: University of Chicago Press, 1987), p. 45; see also Michael Oren, *Power, Faith, and Fantasy: America in the Middle East, 1776 to the Present* (New York: W. W. Norton, 2007), p. 41–44.

14. James A. Field Jr., "Near East Notes and Far East Queries," in John K. Fairbank, ed., *The Missionary Enterprise in China and America* (Cambridge, MA: Harvard University Press, 1974), pp. 31–33; and A. L. Tibawi, "The Genesis and Early History of the Syrian Protestant College," Part I, *Middle East Journal* 21, no. 1 (Winter 1967): 2.

15. William Goodell, "Hints and Cautions Addressed to Missionaries Destined to the Mediterranean," (1834–1835), cited in Fairbank, *Missionary Enterprise*, pp. 265–66.

16. Daniel Bliss, "Claims of the Missionary Work upon the Mental Strength of the Ministry," *Missionary Tracts*, no. 14 (Boston: American Board of Commissioners for Foreign Missions, 1856), p. 16. Abby Wood Bliss wrote of Muslims while en route to the Middle East in 1856: "It is hard to realize that some of them have souls." Abby Wood Bliss to Howard Sweetser, January 30, 1856, BFP, ACA.

CHAPTER 2: AMERICA ENCOUNTERS THE MIDDLE EAST

1. Abby Wood Bliss to Howard Sweetser, January 30, 1856, Bliss Family Papers, Amherst College Archives, Robert Frost Library, Amherst College, Amherst, Massachusetts (hereafter cited as BFP, ACA).

2. Mulberry trees that fed silkworms claimed half of the cultivated land in the surrounding mountains.

3. Ussama Makdisi, *Artillery of Heaven: American Missionaries and the Failed Conversion of the Middle East* (Ithaca, NY: Cornell University Press, 2008).

4. Quoted in Daniel Bliss, *The Reminiscences of Daniel Bliss* (New York: Revell, 1920), pp. 105–106.

5. Quoted in James Thayer Addison, *The Christian Approach to the Moslem: A Historical Study* (New York: Columbia University Press, 1942), p. 118.

6. Women were not taught to read and write, and the majority of Ottoman subjects—particularly in the countryside—were illiterate.

7. See Ussama Makdisi, "'Anti-Americanism' in the Arab World: An Inter-

pretation of a Brief History," *Journal of American History* 89, no. 2 (September 2002); and Makdisi, *Artillery of Heaven.*

8. Quoted in Michael B. Oren, *Power, Faith, and Fantasy: America in the Middle East, 1776 to the Present* (New York: W. W. Norton, 2007), p. 214.

9. Daniel Bliss letters, October 15, 1856, and August 28, 1857, published in the *Missionary Herald* 53 (1857): 19, 399.

10. Headquarters' strategy produced meager results. In 1870, after forty-seven years of preaching, 245 Lebanese had converted to Protestantism. See Addison, *Christian Approach to the Moslem*, p. 120.

11. Bustāni went on to assist Eli Smith in preparing the first modern Arabic translation of the Bible; to compile a two-volume dictionary of the Arab language, *Muhit al-Muhit*; the first nonpartisan political journal published in Syria, *Nafir Suriya*; and—his magnum opus—a ten-volume Arabic encyclopedia, *Dairat al-Ma'aref*. See George Antonius, *The Arab Awakening: The Story of the Arab National Movement* (1938; repr., New York: Capricorn Books: 1965), pp. 47–49.

12. Abby Wood Bliss to Abby Sweetser, May 30, 1856, BFP, ACA; and Fouad Ajami, *The Dream Palace of the Arabs: A Generation's Odyssey* (New York: Vintage Books, 1999), p. 44.

13. Abby Wood Bliss to Abby Sweetser, September 14, 1856, BFP, ACA.

14. Ibid.

15. Quoted in *Reminiscences of Daniel Bliss*, p. 123.

16. Leila Tarazi Fawaz, *An Occasion for War: Civil Conflict in Lebanon and Damascus in 1860* (Berkeley: University of California Press, 1994), passim.

17. See "Population of Beirut Table," in Leila Tarazi Fawaz, *Merchants and Migrants in Nineteenth-Century Beirut* (Cambridge, MA: Harvard University Press, 1983), pp. 127–29.

18. Mark Twain, *The Innocents Abroad; or, the New Pilgrim's Progress* (Hartford, CT: American Publishing Company, 1869), p. 433.

19. Quoted in Fouad Ajami and Eli Reed, *Beirut: City of Regrets* (New York: W. W. Norton, 1988), p. 17.

20. Ibid.

21. Daniel Bliss to George ?, Sûq al-Gharb, March 6, 1862, BFP, ACA.

22. Daniel Bliss to Professor William Tyler, Sûq al-Gharb, February 25, 1862, BFP, ACA.

23. ABCFM pamphlet, "Missionary Schools," 1861, quoted in A. L. Tibawi, *American Interests in Syria, 1800–1901: A Study of Educational, Literary and Religious Work* (London: Oxford University Press, 1966), p. 152.

24. Daniel Bliss to Rufus Anderson, Sûq al-Gharb, March 6, 1862, BFP, ACA.

25. Samir Khalaf, "On Doing Much with Little Noise: Early Encounters of Protestant Missionaries in Lebanon," in *Altruism and Imperialism: Western Cultural and Religious Missions in the Middle East*, eds. Eleanor H. Tejirian and Reeva Spector Simon (New York: Middle East Institute, Columbia University, 2002), p. 35.

26. ABCFM secretary Rufus Anderson, Missionary House, Boston, to Syria Mission, March 4, 1862, BFP, ACA.

27. Quoted in Daniel Bliss, "A Few Reminiscences of the Early Days of the Syrian Protestant College," p. 29, undated manuscript, BFP, ACA.

28. He was the direct descendant and namesake of William Dodge, who landed at Salem, Massachusetts, aboard *The Lyon's Whelpe* on July 10, 1629.

29. Beginning the following year, 1864, and until his death, Dodge served as vice-president of the ABCFM. His annual giving to foreign missionary work ranged from five thousand to ten thousand dollars. See Richard Lowitt, *A Merchant Prince of the Nineteenth Century: William E. Dodge* (New York: Columbia University Press, 1954), pp. 341–42.

30. Quoted in Daniel Bliss, "A Few Reminiscences," p. 29, BFP, ACA.

31. Quoted in *Reminiscences of Daniel Bliss*, p. 173.

32. Ibid., p. 172.

33. "V" to Missionary House, Boston, August 21, 1863; forwarded to Daniel Bliss, New York, August 22, 1863, BFP, ACA.

34. Henry Harris Jessup, *Fifty-Three Years in Syria*, vol. 2 (New York: Revell, 1910), pp. 298–99, 302.

35. The Jesuits' Beirut school, l'Université Saint-Joseph, opened in 1874—eight years after the Syrian Protestant College. That same year, the SPC created a Professorship of English Language and Literature "to help counteract the insidious and pernicious views of philosophy, morals, and religion already rapidly spreading in the East, largely through the French language." "Professorship of English at the S.P.C.," 1874, BFP, ACA. There was little contact between the two institutions, which viewed each other with envy and suspicion as rivals.

36. "The Syrian Protestant College," BFP, ACA.

37. Excerpted in *Reminiscences of Daniel Bliss*, p. 198.

38. Tilden later won the Democratic Party's nomination for president in 1876. In an eerie foreshadowing of the 2000 election, Tilden—like Al Gore—received more popular votes but failed to win an electoral majority. Tilden's Republican opponent, Rutherford B. Hayes—like Gore's Republican opponent, George W. Bush—became president.

39. The bill simultaneously provided for the incorporation of Robert College, another American missionary institution under different auspices in Istanbul, Turkey.

40. Daniel Bliss to Bev Gordon, Sûq al-Gharb, February 11, 1862, BFP, ACA; and Daniel Bliss to Rufus Anderson, Sûq al-Gharb, June 13, 1862, BFP, ACA.

41. Daniel Bliss to Rufus Anderson, London, December 16, 1865, in *Papers of the ABCFM* (microfilm), "ABC 16: The Near East, 1817–1919," unit 5, reel 545, 16.8.1, v. 6, "Syrian Mission, 1860–1871, Documents, Reports, Miscellaneous Letters, Letters A–D."

42. Ibid.

43. Quoted in Victor A. Shepherd, "Earl of Shaftesbury" *Sermons and Writings of Victor Shepherd*, October 1993, http://www.victorshepherd.on.ca/Heritage/earlof.htm.

44. Lord Ashley to Edwin Hopper, quoted at "Lord Ashley, Earl of Shaftesbury," Spartacus Educational, http://www.spartacus.schoolnet.co.uk/IRashley.htm.

45. Quoted in Jessup, *Fifty-Three Years in Syria*, p. 282.

46. Lord Ashley to Mr. Haldane, excerpted in Edwin Hodder, *The Life and Work of the Seventh Earl of Shaftesbury, K.G.*, vol. 3, (London: Cassell, 1886), p. 181.

47. One of these first five graduates, Ya'qūb Sarrūf, later moved to Cairo, where he and fellow SPC student Faris Nimr founded *al-Muqattam*, the largest circulation daily newspaper in the Arab world through the mid-twentieth century, and *al-Muqtataf*, the leading Arabic-language scientific journal during the same period.

48. The right of foreigners to own real estate in all parts of the Ottoman Empire, except in the region of the Hijaz, became law in 1867.

49. See William A. Booth, "Sketch of the Early History of the Syrian Protestant College, July 9, 1889," BFP, ACA.

50. See A. L. Tibawi, "The Genesis and Early History of the Syrian Protestant College," Part II, *Middle East Journal* 21, no. 2 (Spring 1967): 201.

51. Daniel Bliss to Abby Bliss, December 24, 1873, in Daniel Bliss, *Letters from a New Campus: Written to His Wife Abby and Their Four Children during Their Visit to Amherst, Massachusetts, 1873–1874*, eds. Douglas Rugh and Belle Dorman Rugh with Alfred H. Howell (New York: Syracuse University Press, 1994), p. 165.

52. In addition to Mary (now sixteen), Frederick (now fourteen), and Howard (now twelve), William Bliss—known in the family as Willie—had been born in 1865.

53. These were later known as College Hall, the Medical Building, and Dodge Hall (greatly enlarged since). College Hall was severely damaged by a car bomb in November 1991 and subsequently rebuilt according to the original plans.

54. Daniel Bliss, Beirut, June 19, 1873, in *Letters from a New Campus*, pp. 38–39.

55. Daniel Bliss, Beirut, September 18, 1873, in *Letters from a New Campus*, pp. 82–83.

56. Daniel Bliss, Beirut, October 12, 1873, in *Letters from a New Campus*, pp. 101–103.

57. Daniel Bliss, Beirut, December 5, 1873, in *Letters from a New Campus*, p. 150.

58. *Reminiscences of Daniel Bliss*, p. 200.

59. Ibid., p. 135.

60. Ibid., p. 132.

61. Ibid., p 142.

62. Ample precedent existed: Arabic had been the principal language of medicine in the West from the time of Umayyad Caliphate in Spain (800 CE) to the Renaissance (1500 CE).

63. Quoted in Kaplan, *Arabists*, p. 37.

CHAPTER 3: TRADITION VERSUS MODERNITY IN THE MIDDLE EAST

1. At this time, Wallace was serving as United States Consul-General to the Ottoman Court in Istanbul (1881–1885).

2. Quoted in Donald M. Leavitt, "Darwinism in the Arab World: The Lewis Affair at the Syrian Protestant College," *The Muslim World* 71, no. 2 (April 1981): 88.

3. Stuart Dodge to Daniel Bliss, March 6, 1882, quoted in John M. Munro, *A Mutual Concern: The Story of the American University of Beirut* (Delmar, NY: Caravan Books, 1977), p. 31.

4. *Annual Reports: Board of Managers, Syrian Protestant College, 1866/67–1901/02*, pp. 251–52, Bliss Family Papers, Amherst College Archives, Robert Frost Library, Amherst College, Amherst, Massachusetts (hereafter cited as BFP, ACA).

5. Excerpted in Munro, *A Mutual Concern*, p. 30.

6. Edward Hitchcock, *The Religion of Geology and Its Connected Sciences* (Boston: Phillips, Sampson, 1852). In March 1860 a favorable review of Darwin's *On the Origin of Species* had appeared in the *American Journal of Science*, a leading periodical in its field founded by Hitchcock's mentor, Benjamin Silliman of Yale.

7. Quoted in Nadia Farag, "The Lewis Affair and the Fortunes of *al-Muqtataf*," *Middle Eastern Studies* 8 (1972): 78.

8. Stuart Dodge to Daniel Bliss, August 1, 1882, quoted in Shafik Jeha, *Darwin and the Crisis of 1882 in the Medical Department of the Syrian Protestant College and the First Student Protest in the Arab World* (Beirut: American University of Beirut Press, 2004), p. 89.

9. Stuart Dodge to Daniel Bliss, August 21, 1882, quoted in ibid., p. 89.

10. Quoted in ibid., p. 43.

11. Quoted in ibid.; and in "Dr. Edwin Rufus Lewis," in *The Founding Fathers of the American University of Beirut: Biographies*, ed. Ghada Yusuf Khoury (Beirut: American University of Beirut Press, 1992), p. 101.

12. William Dodge to Daniel Bliss, November 6, 1882, quoted in Jeha, *Darwin and the Crisis of 1882*, pp. 78–79.

13. William Dodge to Daniel Bliss, November 16, 1882, quoted in Jeha, *Darwin and the Crisis of 1882*, p. 79.

14. Minutes of the Board of Trustees, December 1, 1882, cited in Stephen B. L. Penrose Jr., *That They May Have Life: The Story of the American University of Beirut, 1866–1941* (Princeton, NJ: Princeton University Press, 1941), p. 43. See also Fred Bliss to Howard Bliss, Beirut, December 6, 1882, BFP, ACA.

15. Quoted in Fred Bliss to Howard Bliss, Beirut, December 26, 1882, BFP, ACA.

16. Yusuf Hoyek in *al-Muqtataf* 7 (1882–1883), excerpted in Munro, *A Mutual Concern*, p. 30.

17. Ibid., p. 33.

18. George Antonius, *The Arab Awakening: The Story of the Arab National Movement* (1938; repr., New York: Capricorn Books, 1965) p. 48.

19. L. M. Sa'di, quoted in Penrose, *That They May Have Life*, p. 36.

20. Jurji Zeidan, *Tarajim Mashahir al-Sharq Fi al-Qarn al-Tasi 'Ashar* (2 vols., Matba'at al-Hilal, 1902–1903), vol. 2, p. 43, quoted in Ussama Makdisi, *Faith Misplaced: The Broken Promise of U.S.–Arab Relations, 1820–2001* (New York: PublicAffairs, 2010), p. 76.

21. AUB later recognized Van Dyck's contributions to the school by naming one of its medical buildings in his honor.

22. Excerpted in *Annual Reports: Board of Managers, Syrian Protestant College, 1866/67–1901/02*, BFP, ACA.

23. Fred Bliss to Howard Bliss, Beirut, December 26, 1882, BFP, ACA.

24. Abby Bliss to Howard and Willie Bliss, Beirut, December 7, 1882, "Excerpts from Letters of Abby Wood Bliss to Her Sons," BFP, ACA.

25. Fred Bliss to Howard Bliss, Beirut, December 6, 1882, BFP, ACA.

26. Daniel Bliss to Howard and Willie Bliss, Beirut, February 28, 1883, cited in Leavitt, "Darwinism in the Arab World," p. 91.

27. Excerpted in Jeha, *Darwin and the Crisis of 1882*, pp. 62–63.

28. Cited in Abby Bliss to Howard and Willie Bliss, Beirut, January 10, 1883, "Excerpts from Letters of Abby Wood Bliss to Her Sons," BFP, ACA.

29. Quoted in Leavitt, "Darwinism in the Arab World," p. 93.

30. *The Memoirs of Jurji Zeidan* (in Arabic), pp. 87–88, cited in Jeha, *Darwin and the Crisis of 1882*, p. 65. Zeidan was one of the suspended students.

31. Fred Bliss to Howard Bliss, Beirut, December 26, 1882, BFP, ACA.

32. Fred Bliss to Howard Bliss, Beirut, December 6, 1882, BFP ACA.

33. Abby Bliss to Howard and Willie Bliss, Beirut, December 18, 1882, "Excerpts from Letters of Abby Wood Bliss to Her Sons," BFP, ACA.

34. Cited in Abby Bliss to Howard and Willie Bliss, Beirut, February 27, 1883, BFP, ACA.

35. Abby Bliss to Howard and Willie Bliss, Beirut, December 25, 1882, BFP, ACA.

36. Daniel Bliss to Howard and Willie Bliss, Beirut, May 8, 1883, quoted in Leavitt, "Darwinism in the Arab World," p. 96.

37. Abby Bliss to Howard and Willie Bliss, Beirut, January 1, 1883, "Excerpts from Letters of Abby Wood Bliss to Her Sons," BFP, ACA.

38. Fred Bliss to Howard Bliss, Beirut, December 6, 1882, BFP, ACA.

39. Abby Bliss to Howard and Willie Bliss, Beirut, January 17 and 22, 1883, BFP, ACA.

40. Daniel Bliss to Howard Bliss, Beirut, December 23, 1883, BFP, ACA.

41. Daniel Bliss, "The Race of Life," SPC Baccalaureate Sermon, July 1888 and April 1895, reprinted in Douglas Rugh, ed., *The Voice of Daniel Bliss* (Beirut: American Press, 1956), p. 5.

42. Jurji Zeidan, "Student Rebellion" (in Arabic), *al-Hilal* 33, (1924/25), quoted in Leavitt, "Darwinism in the Arab World," p. 98.

CHAPTER 4: HOWARD BLISS AND AMERICAN NATIONALISM

1. Quoted in Daniel Bliss, *The Reminiscences of Daniel Bliss* (New York: Revell, 1920), p. 214.

2. Quoted in ibid., p. 218.

3. Emigration increased following the opening of the Suez Canal in 1869,

which diverted much Mediterranean commerce away from Beirut to Alexandria in Egypt and dealt a mortal blow to the silk trade, a traditional pillar of the Lebanese economy.

4. See "Statistics of the Syrian Protestant College from 1866 to 1906," Records of the American University of Beirut, Yale Divinity School Library; and Chart of Attendance in Stephen B. L. Penrose Jr., *That They May Have Life: The Story of the American University of Beirut, 1866–1941* (Princeton, NJ: Princeton University Press, 1941), p. 60.

5. Stuart Dodge to Howard Bliss, New York, December 9, 1902, Bliss Family Papers, Amherst College Archives, Robert Frost Library, Amherst College, Amherst, Massachusetts (hereafter cited as BFP, ACA).

6. Today it is known as the Bushy Hill Nature Center in Ivoryton, Connecticut.

7. See W. H. Hall, "Dr. D. Stuart Dodge," *al-Kulliyeh* 7, no. 3 (January 1922): 33–38.

8. Today the statue stands in the main reading room of the Nami Jafet Memorial Library.

9. *Reminiscences of Daniel Bliss*, pp. 211, 213, 220–224.

10. Quoted in Daniel Bliss II, "Epilogue," in Carlton S. Coon Jr., *Daniel Bliss and the Founding of the American University of Beirut* (Washington, DC: Middle East Institute, 1989), p. 86.

11. Municipal authorities later renamed this street Rue Bliss. It remains one of Beirut's major thoroughfares to this day.

12. Daniel Bliss to Howard Bliss, Beirut, December 23, 1883, BFP, ACA.

13. See Stuart Dodge to Daniel Bliss, New York, April 9, 1901, BFP, ACA.

14. Howard Bliss to Daniel, Abby, Fred, and Mary Bliss, Upper Montclair, New Jersey, January 21, 1902, BFP, ACA.

15. Fred Bliss to Howard Bliss, Beirut, January 20, 1902, BFP, ACA.

16. Howard Bliss to Sydney A. Clark, Beirut, December 18, 1912, BFP, ACA.

17. Quoted in *The Outlook*, May 19, 1920.

18. Howard Bliss to Sydney A. Clark, Beirut, December 18, 1912, BFP, ACA.

19. Alfred T. Mahan, "Effects of Asiatic Conditions upon International Policies," *North American Review* (November 1900): 615.

20. Mikha'il Asad Rustum, *Book of a Stranger in the West* (repr., Beirut, 1992), translated and cited in Ussama Makdisi, "'Anti-Americanism' in the Arab World: An Interpretation of a Brief History," *Journal of American History* 89, no. 2 (September 2002).

21. Philip K. Hitti, "America in the Eyes of an Easterner; or, Eight Years in the United States," in Kamal Abdel-Malek, ed., *America in an Arab Mirror: Images of America in Arabic Travel Literature, An Anthology, 1895–1995*, p. 49. See also Philip K. Hitti, *The Syrians in America* (New York: George H. Doran, 1924; repr., Piscataway, NJ: Gorgias Press, 2005), passim.

22. Ameen Rihani, *The Book of Khalid* (New York: Dodd, Mead & Company, 1911), p. 25.

23. "Chapter on the Most Famous of Events and the Most Outstanding of Men," *al-Hilal* 1, (1893): 152, translated and cited in Makdisi, "'Anti-Americanism' in the Arab World."

24. See Nathan Miller, *Theodore Roosevelt: A Life* (New York: William Morrow, 1992), pp. 31–32.

25. The United States had annexed the Philippines in 1899 following the Spanish-American War, in which Theodore Roosevelt had played a central role, first as the assistant secretary of the navy who dispatched Admiral Dewey's fleet to Manila, then as leader of the Rough Riders in Cuba.

26. "The Naulahka," which includes the prophetic lines:

Now it is not good for the Christian's health to hustle the Aryan brown,
For the Christian riles, and the Aryan smiles and he weareth the
    Christian down;
And the end of the fight is a tombstone white with the name of the late
    deceased,
And the epitaph drear: 'A Fool lies here who tried to hustle the East.'

27. Howard Bliss to Amy Blatchford Bliss, Washington, DC, November 23, 1905, BFP, ACA.

28. Taft succeeded Roosevelt as President from 1909 through 1913.

29. Today it is known as the ceremonial East Room.

30. Howard Bliss to Amy Blatchford Bliss, Washington, DC, November 24, 1905, BFP, ACA.

31. "Remarks of President Bliss before the Faculty, April 26, 1909, Regarding the Subject of Required Chapel and Bible Class Attendance," Archives and Special Collections, Nami Jafet Memorial Library AUB, Beirut, Lebanon.

CHAPTER 5: AMERICA CONFRONTS GREAT POWER POLITICS IN THE MIDDLE EAST

1. Quoted in John M. Munro, *A Mutual Concern: The Story of the American University of Beirut* (Delmar, NY: Caravan Books, 1977), p. 65.

2. See George Antonius, *The Arab Awakening: The Story of the Arab National Movement* (1938; repr., New York: Capricorn Books, 1965), passim.

3. Quoted in Lewis Gaston Leary, *Syria: The Land of Lebanon* (New York: McBride, Nast, 1913), p. 149.

4. Charlotte Ward to Home People, Aleih, Lebanon, September 12, 1914, Charlotte Ward Papers, Mount Holyoke College Archives and Special Collections, South Hadley, Massachusetts.

5. See Stephen B. L. Penrose Jr., *That They May Have Life: The Story of the American University of Beirut, 1866–1941* (Princeton, NJ: Princeton University Press, 1941), pp. 162–63; Laurence Evans, *United States Policy and the Partition of Turkey, 1914–1924* (Baltimore: Johns Hopkins, 1965), pp. 21–23, 38–39; and Michael Oren, *Power, Faith, and Fantasy: America in the Middle East, 1776 to the Present* (New York: W. W. Norton, 2007), pp. 344–46.

6. "An Iranian in First World War Beirut: Qasem Ghani's Reminiscences," in *Distant Relations: Iran and Lebanon in the Last 500 Years*, ed. H. E. Chehabi (London: I. B. Taurus, 2006), pp. 125–26.

7. "Historic Diary Written During the Year 1917," Edward F. Nickoley Papers, Box 2, Archives and Special Collections, Nami Jafet Memorial Library, AUB, Beirut, Lebanon.

8. Howard Bliss to Lyman Abbott, Beirut, February 13, 1915, Bliss Family Papers, Amherst College Archives, Robert Frost Library, Amherst College, Amherst, Massachusetts.

9. Quoted in Munro, *Mutual Concern*, pp. 67–68.

10. The following summary account of the Middle East during the Great War is based on David Fromkin, *A Peace to End All Peace: The Fall of the Ottoman Empire and the Creation of the Modern Middle East* (New York: Henry Holt, 1989), passim; Albert Hourani, *A History of the Arab Peoples* (Cambridge, MA: Belknap Press of Harvard University Press, 1991), pp. 315–18; A. H. Hourani, *Syria and Lebanon: A Political Essay* (London: Oxford University Press, 1946), pp. 38–58; K. S. Salibi, *The Modern History of Lebanon* (New York: Frederick A. Praeger, 1965), pp. 159–62; and A. L. Tibawi, *A Modern History of Syria, including Lebanon and Palestine* (London: Macmillan, 1969), pp. 209–82.

11. Quoted in Elie Kedourie, *England and the Middle East: The Destruction of the Ottoman Empire, 1914–1921* (Hassocks, UK: Harvester Press, 1978), p. 69.

12. Quoted in Margaret FitzHerbert, *The Man Who Was Greenmantle: A Biography of Aubrey Herbert* (London: John Murray, 1983), pp. 147–49. See also Roger Adelson, *Mark Sykes: Portrait of an Amateur* (London: Jonathan Cape, 1975), passim.

13. Charles Seymour, ed., *The Intimate Papers of Colonel House*, vol. 3 (New Haven, CT: Yale University Press, 1940), pp. 40–46.

14. See Laurence Evans, *United States Policy and the Partition of Turkey, 1914–1924* (Baltimore: Johns Hopkins, 1965), pp. 54–62.

15. *Foreign Relations of the United States* (hereafter cited as *FRUS*), *1918*, Supplement 1, Part 1, pp. 12–17.

16. Ibid., pp. 8–9.

17. Former Iraqi officers in the Ottoman army comprised much of the commissioned ranks of the Arab army.

18. Meir Zamir, "Faisal and the Lebanese Question, 1918–1920," *Middle Eastern Studies* 27, no. 3 (July 1991): 404–405.

19. *Statements Made on Behalf of His Majesty's Government during the Year 1918 in Regard to the Future Status of Certain Parts of the Ottoman Empire* (London: His Majesty's Stationary Office, 1939), pp. 6–7.

20. Harold Nicolson, *Peacemaking 1919* (London: Constable, 1933), pp. 187–88.

21. See Margaret Macmillan, *Paris 1919: Six Months That Changed the World* (New York: Random House, 2001), pp. xxx, 381–82.

22. "Great Britain and France, The Eastern Question," *Palestine News*, November 1918, BFP, ACA.

23. Quoted in Stephen Bonsal, *Suitors and Suppliants: The Little Nations at Versailles* (New York: Prentice-Hall, 1946), p. 45.

24. *The Outlook*, April 2, 1919.

25. Howard Bliss to Amy Bliss, Paris, February 12, 1919, BFP, ACA.

26. Howard Bliss to President Wilson, Paris, February 7, 1919, in *The Papers of Woodrow Wilson, Volume 54, January 11–February 7, 1919* (hereafter cited as *PWW*), ed. Arthur Link (Princeton, NJ: Princeton University Press, 1986), pp. 551–52; and Wilson to Bliss, Paris, February 11, 1919, *PWW, Volume 55, February 8–March 16, 1919*, p. 81.

27. Quoted in Paul Birdsall, *Versailles Twenty Years After* (New York: Reynal & Hitchcock, 1941), pp. 4–21.

28. Cited in David Hunter Miller, *My Diary at the Conference of Paris, 1918–1919*, vol. 4 (1924), p. 300.

29. See M. E. Yapp, *The Making of the Modern Near East, 1792–1923* (London: Longman, 1987), p. 328; and Macmillan, *Paris 1919*, pp. 421–22.

30. Quoted in Stephen Bonsal, *Suitors and Suppliants: The Little Nations at Versailles* (New York: Prentice-Hall, 1946), p. 43.

31. Edward Mandell House and Charles Seymour, eds., *What Really Happened at Paris: The Story of the Peace Conference, 1918–1919* (New York: Charles Scribner's Sons, 1921), pp. 200–201.

32. "Statement Made by President Howard S. Bliss of the Syrian Protestant College, Beirut, Syria, before the Paris Peace Conference, on Thursday Afternoon, February 13, 1919," BFP, ACA; and "Secretary's Notes of a Conversation Held in M. Pichon's Room at the Quai d'Orsay, Paris, on Thursday, 13 February, 1919, at 3 p.m.," *FRUS: Paris Peace Conference, 1919, Volume III* (Washington, DC: Government Printing Office, 1943), pp. 1013–21.

33. Ibid.

34. Quoted in Paul C. Helmreich, *From Paris to Sevres: The Partition of the Ottoman Empire at the Peace Conference of 1919–1920* (Columbus: Ohio State University Press, 1974), p. 70.

35. Quoted in Christopher M. Andrew and A. S. Kanya-Forster, *The Climax of French Imperial Expansion: 1914–1924* (Stanford, CA: Stanford University Press, 1981), p. 162.

36. *FRUS, The Paris Peace Conference 1919* (Washington, DC: Government Printing Office, 1945), vol. 12, pp. 751–863. The King-Crane Commission report was not made public until excerpts appeared in the *New York Times* on December 3, 1922.

37. "Memorandum by Mr. Balfour Respecting Syria, Palestine, and Mesopotamia, 1919," in Walid Khalidi, ed., *From Haven to Conquest: Readings in Zionism and the Palestine Problem Until 1948* (Washington, DC: Institute for Palestine Studies, 1987), p. 208.

38. President Wilson to Bainbridge Colby, March 29, 1920, *PWW, Volume 65, February 28–July 31, 1920*, p. 141.

39. Robert Lansing, *The Peace Negotiations: A Personal Narrative* (Boston: Houghton Mifflin, 1921), p. 219.

40. Howard S. Bliss, "The Modern Missionary," *Atlantic Monthly* (May 1920): 664–75.

41. Also the burial site of famed early-twentieth-century American novelist Willa Cather.

CHAPTER 6: BAYARD DODGE AND AMERICAN IDEALISM

1. See Eric North to Mary Bliss Dodge, June 4, 1972, Grace Dodge Guthrie Papers (hereafter cited as GDGP), Archives and Special Collections, Nami Jafet Memorial Library, American University of Beirut, Beirut, Lebanon (hereafter cited as A&SC, NJML, AUB).

2. "A Talk with Bayard Dodge," *Saudi Aramco World* 23, no. 4 (July/August 1972).

3. Quoted in Stephen B. L. Penrose Jr., *That They May Have Life: The Story of the American University of Beirut, 1866–1941* (Princeton, NJ: Princeton University Press, 1941), p. 292.

4. "A Talk with Bayard Dodge."

5. Quoted in Jerome Beatty, "Man of the Near East Renaissance," *Reader's Digest* (February 1939): 78.

6. Bayard Dodge Papers (hereafter cited as BDP), A&SC, NJML, AUB.

7. See Mahmoud Haddad, "Syrian Muslims' Attitudes toward Foreign Missionaries in the Late Nineteenth and Twentieth Centuries," in Eleanor H. Tejirian and Reeva Spector Simon, eds., *Altruism and Imperialism: Western Cultural and Religious Missions in the Middle East* (New York: Middle East Institute, Columbia University, 2002), p. 264.

8. Eliahu Elath, *Through the Mist of Time: Reminiscences* (Jerusalem: Yad Izhak Ben-Zvi, 1989), pp. 185, 189, 192, 200–201, and 217. Hebrew translations courtesy of Associate Professor Hezi Brosh, Department of Languages and Cultures, US Naval Academy, Annapolis, MD.

9. Quoted in Laurens Hickok Seelye, "A Philosopher among the Cults of the Near East—II," *The Christian Leader* (January 9, 1937): 41.

10. Penrose, *That They May Have Life*, pp. 287, 300.

11. Jerome Beatty, *Americans All Over* (New York: John Day Company, 1940), p. 81; Grace Dodge Guthrie, interview with author, Falls Church, Virginia, May 7, 2008.

12. See Bayard Dodge, *The American University of Beirut: A Brief History of the University and the Lands Which It Serves* (Beirut: Khayat's, 1958), p. 60.

13. See Fouad Ajami, *The Dream Palace of the Arabs: A Generation's Odyssey* (New York: Pantheon Books, 1998), pp. 14–15.

14. Quoted in Grace Dodge Guthrie, *Legacy to Lebanon* (Richmond, VA: privately printed, 1984), p. 31.

15. Quoted in Penrose, *That They May Have Life*, pp. 292–93.

16. He also published *al-Azhar: A Millenium of Muslim Education* (1961); and *Muslim Education in Medieval Times* (1962).

17. Deiran Berberian to Mary Bliss Dodge, July 5, 1972; Ed and Oline Barr to Mary Bliss Dodge, June 17, 1972; Seelye Bixler to Mary Bliss Dodge, June 15, 1972, GDGP, A&SC, NJML, AUB; and Penrose, *That They May Have Life*, p. ix.

18. "A Talk with Bayard Dodge."

19. Guthrie, *Legacy to Lebanon*, p. 116.

20. See account of Brigadier General J. T. Pierce, commanding officer at the scene, cited in *Al-Kulliyah Review* 10, no. 1 (January 1946): 7.

21. David Dodge, telephone interview with author, Princeton, New Jersey, November 23, 2008.

22. Thomas Schuller to Mary Bliss Dodge, May 31, 1972, GDGP, A&SC, NJML, AUB.

23. In 1921, the British installed Faisal as King of Iraq. He remained on the Iraqi throne until his death in 1933.

24. Quoted in John A. DeNovo, *American Interests and Policies in the Middle East, 1900–1939* (Minneapolis: University of Minnesota Press, 1963), p. 330.

25. See chart in Penrose, *That They May Have Life*, p. 238.

26. Ibid., pp. 219–20.

27. Beatty, "Man of the Near East Renaissance," p. 78.

28. Philip S. Khoury, *Syria and the French Mandate: The Politics of Arab Nationalism, 1920–1945* (Princeton, NJ: Princeton University Press, 1987), p. 4.

29. Albert H. Hourani, *Syria and Lebanon: A Political Essay* (London: Oxford University Press, 1946), p. 84.

30. Bayard Dodge to Dearest {mother] and Dad, January 2, 1920, "Personal Letters," BDP, A&SC, NJML, AUB.

31. See Penrose, *That They May Have Life*, p. 301.

32. David Dodge, telephone interview with author, Princeton, New Jersey, March 29, 2008.

33. Grace Dodge Guthrie, interview.

34. Khoury, *Syria and the French Mandate*, pp. 20–23.

35. The Vichy regime, established after the fall of France, governed the non-occupied area of France in collaboration with Nazi Germany from 1940–1944. Its leadership comprised conservative, procolonial elements in French political and military life.

36. The Free French Movement, under General Charles de Gaulle, opposed collaboration with Nazi Germany, established a government-in-exile in London, and

succeeded to power after the liberation of France in 1944. Palmach forces were made of a Jewish military unit recruited in the neighboring British Mandate of Palestine. It included Moshe Dayan, later a celebrated Israeli general, who lost an eye during the short but bloody campaign.

37. Hourani, *Syria and Lebanon*, pp. 230–40.

38. Khoury, *Syria and the French Mandate*, pp. 583–84, 591–95.

39. Quoted in Michael B. Oren, *Power, Faith, and Fantasy: America in the Middle East, 1776 to the Present* (New York: W. W. Norton, 2007), p. 457.

40. Stephen Hemsley Longrigg, *Syria and Lebanon Under French Mandate* (London: Oxford University Press, 1958), pp. 345–50; and A. L. Tibawi, *A Modern History of Syria* (London: Macmillan, 1969), pp. 376–77.

41. David Dodge, telephone interview with author, Princeton, New Jersey, March 29, 2008.

CHAPTER 7: AMERICA IN THE POSTWAR MIDDLE EAST

1. Hubert Herring, "The Department of State: A Review with Recommendations to the President," *Harper's* (February 1937): 232. See also H. W. Brands, *Into the Labyrinth: The United States and the Middle East, 1945–1993* (New York: McGraw-Hill, 1994), p. xi.

2. Brands, *Into the Labyrinth*, p. xi.

3. See Phillip J. Baram, *The Department of State in the Middle East, 1919–1945* (Philadelphia: University of Pennsylvania Press, 1978), pp. 53–58; 320–24.

4. George Brownell, quoted in Howard M. Sachar, *A History of Israel: From the Rise of Zionism to Our Time* (New York: Alfred A. Knopf, 1976), p. 287.

5. *Time*, September 29, 1947, p. 69.

6. Robert D. Kaplan, *The Arabists: The Romance of an American Elite* (New York: Free Press, 1993), p. 80.

7. See Diary of Bayard Dodge, Bayard Dodge Papers, Archvies and Special Collections, Nami Jafet Memorial Library, American University of Beirut, Beirut Lebanon (hereafter cited as A&SC, NJML, AUB).

8. Bayard Dodge, "Must There Be War in the Middle East?" *Reader's Digest* (April 1948).

9. Ibid.

10. Quoted in ibid., p. 35.

11. Europe and Japan, with fewer oil reserves than the United States, have always depended more on Middle Eastern oil to fuel their industrial economies.

12. See Dodge, "Must There Be War in the Middle East?"

13. Peter Grose, *Israel in the Mind of America* (New York: Alfred A. Knopf, 1983), p. 225.

14. Quoted in ibid., p. 228.

15. Quoted in Dodge, "Must There Be War in the Middle East?" p. 44.

16. David McCullough, *Truman* (New York: Simon & Schuster, 1992), pp. 596–97.

17. Truman went on to defeat his heavily favored Republican opponent, New York governor Thomas Dewey, in a stunning upset that year—but *lost* the states of New York, Pennsylvania, and Illinois.

18. Alfred A. Hero Jr., *American Religious Groups View Foreign Policy* (Durham, NC: Duke University Press, 1973), pp. 360–61; and Grose, *Israel in the Mind of America*, p. 262.

19. President Truman to Henry Morgenthau Jr., December 2, 1947, quoted in Grose, *Israel in the Mind of America*, p. 256.

20. Ussama Makdisi, *Faith Misplaced: The Broken Promise of U.S.–Arab Relations, 1820–2001* (New York: Public Affairs, 2010), p. 6.

21. The following summary of the first Arab-Israeli War is based on Sydney Nettleton Fisher and William Ochsenwald, *The Middle East: A History*, 4th ed. (New York: McGraw-Hill, 1990), pp. 640–47; Albert Hourani, *A History of the Arab Peoples* (Cambridge, MA: Belknap Press of Harvard University Press, 1991), pp. 351–61; Benny Morris, *1948: The First Arab-Israeli War* (New Haven, CT: Yale University Press, 2008), passim; Sachar, *History of Israel*, pp. 315–53; and A. L. Tibawi, *A Modern History of Syria Including Lebanon and Palestine* (New York: Macmillan, 1969), pp. 380–83.

22. Britain's partiality toward the Arabs was also reflected in its embargo on Jewish arms and immigration into Palestine after World War II. Zionists smuggled weapons from the United States, Czechoslovakia, and France.

23. Sachar, *History of Israel*, p. 335.

24. Ibid., p. 333.

25. Bunche's predecessor as UN mediator, Swedish diplomat Folke Bernadotte, had been assassinated in Jerusalem in September 1948 by Jewish *Lehi* extremists. One of the *Lehi* principals who approved the killing was future Israeli Prime Minister Yitzhak Shamir.

26. Earlier, Bunche had been the first African American to gain a PhD in political science from a US university (Harvard, in 1934).

27. Thomas L. Friedman, *From Beirut to Jerusalem* (New York: Farrar, Straus & Giroux, 1989), pp. 126–27.

28. Hourani, *History of the Arab Peoples*, p. 374.

29. See Peter L. Hahn, *Caught in the Middle East: U.S. Policy toward the Arab-Israeli Conflict, 1945–1961* (Chapel Hill: University of North Carolina Press, 2004), p. 250. Ten years later, the number of Palestinian refugees in Lebanon had swelled to 300,000. See Robert Murphy, *Diplomat among Warriors* (Garden City, NY: Doubleday, 1964), p. 396.

30. Dana Adams Schmidt, "Censorship in Lebanon," *New York Times* (January 11, 1948): 3.

31. "Out of Their Own Visions," *Time* (July 15, 1957): 56.

32. Kamal S. Salibi, "Recollections of Lebanon in the 1940s and 1950s," *Bulletin of the Royal Institute for Inter-Faith Studies* 5, no. 2 (Autumn/Winter 2003): 126–30; and John M. Munro, *A Mutual Concern: The Story of the American University of Beirut* (Delmar, NY: Caravan Books, 1977), pp. 112–13, 126.

33. Today Lod, Israel, part of greater Tel Aviv.

34. The *Haganah* explusion order issued by Rabin is quoted in Sandy Tolan, *The Lemon Tree: The True Story of a Friendship Spanning Four Decades of the Israeli-Palestinian Conflict* (London: Bantam Press, 2007), p. 73. See chapter 9, pp. 174–75, on the Oslo Accords.

35. See Benny Morris, *The Birth of the Palestinian Refugee Problem, 1947–1949* (Cambridge, UK: Cambridge University Press, 1987), pp. 204–10.

36. Shmarya Guttman, "Lod Yotzet Lagolah," *Mibifim* 13, no. 3 (November 1948), quoted in Morris, *Palestinian Refugee Problem*, p. 210.

37. See *Tsaror Michtavim*, August 5, 1948, referenced in Morris, *Palestinian Refugee Problem*.

38. Grace Halsell, "A Visit with George Habash: Still the Prophet of Arab Nationalism and Armed Struggle against Israel," *Washington Report on Middle East Affairs* (September 1998).

39. By the late 1960s, more than half of AUB's annual budget revenue came from the US government—a far cry from the financial independence pioneered by Daniel Bliss. See Godfrey Jansen, "Sowing the Wind, Reaping the Whirlwind," *Christian Science Monitor* (June 19, 1971).

40. The "national pact," adopted when Lebanon achieved independence from France in 1943, sought to keep sectarian conflict at bay by representing the demographic distribution of the country's religious groups in national politics. The president had to be a Maronite Christian; the prime minister a Sunni Muslim; and the parliament speaker a Shiite Muslim. It remains in effect to this day.

41. Fouad Ajami and Eli Reed, *Beirut: City of Regrets* (New York: W. W. Norton, 1988), p. 26; and K. S. Salibi, *The Modern History of Lebanon*, (New York: Frederick A. Praeger, 1965), pp. 198–200.

42. US Marines landed in this same area again in 1983, a few months before the tragic barracks bombing of September 1983 that claimed the lives of 243 marines—the bloodiest day in Marine Corps history. See chapter 8, p. 166.

43. Ann Zwicker Kerr, *Come with Me from Lebanon: An American Family Odyssey* (Syracuse, NY: Syracuse University Press, 1994), p. 127.

44. Quoted in Bayard Dodge, *The American University of Beirut: A Brief History of the University and the Lands Which It Serves* (Beirut: Khayat's, 1958), p. 95.

45. In addition to Socal, Aramco included the Texas Company (Texaco), the Standard Oil Company of New Jersey (later Exxon), and the Standard Oil Company of New York (Socony).

46. Quoted in Douglas Little, "Pipeline Politics: America, TAPLINE, and the Arabs," *Business History Review* 64 (Summer 1990): 278.

47. *Tapline: The Story of the World's Biggest Oil Pipeline* (New York: Trans-Arabian Pipe Line Company, 1951).

48. Tapline's capacity would increase to nearly 500,000 barrels per day by 1967. Supertankers that greatly reduced the cost of shipping Saudi crude directly from the Persian Gulf to western Europe and eventually made Tapline obsolete. Tapline ceased operations in 1983.

49. Kamal S. Salibi, "Recollections of Lebanon in the 1940s and 1950s," *Bulletin of the Royal Institute for Inter-Faith Studies* 5, no. 2 (Autumn/Winter 2003): 117–35; and Sandra Mackey, *Lebanon: Death of a Nation* (New York: Congdon &Weed, 1989), pp. 10–13.

50. Mary Leatherbee, "The West Went Thataway—East," *Life* (January 7, 1966).

51. Joseph L. Grabill, *Protestant Diplomacy and the Near East: Missionary Influence on American Policy, 1810-1927* (Minneapolis: University of Minnesota Press, 1971), p. 306.

52. Quoted in "Out of Their Own Visions."

53. Samir Khalaf, *Lebanon's Predicament* (New York: Columbia University Press, 1987), pp. 261–91.

54. Kamal S. Salibi, *A House of Many Mansions: The History of Lebanon Reconsidered* (Berkeley: University of California Press, 1990), pp. 191–92; and Mackey, *Lebanon*, pp. 25–26.

55. Ironically, Post had been a member of the conservative AUB faction fiercely opposed to Edwin Lewis's teaching of evolution during the controversial "Lewis Affair."

56. Charles Malik, *Swift Seasons Roll: A Tribute to Philip K. Hitti* (New York: American Friends of the Middle East, 1954), p. 13.

57. James Morris, "The Impossible City" (1956), in Jan Morris, *Among the Cities* (New York: Oxford University Press, 1985), pp. 55–56.

58. In November 1956, Britain and France, in collaboration with Israel, attacked Egypt in response to Nasser's nationalization of the Suez Canal. President Eisenhower opposed the move and forced London, Paris, and Tel Aviv to call off their attack or else face the cut-off of American financial aid, which they could not afford. Britain, France, and Israel promptly withdrew in humiliation.

59. He later published *al-Azhar: A Millennium of Muslim Learning* (1961) and *Muslim Education in Medieval Times* (1962).

60. Bayard Dodge to Cleveland Dodge, Khartoum, Sudan, November 19, 1956, quoted in Grace Dodge Guthrie, *A Legacy to Lebanon* (Richmond, VA: privately printed, 1984), p. 58.

61. El Al is Israel's national airline.

62. Leila Khaled, *My People Shall Live: The Autobiography of a Revolutionary* (London: Hodder & Stoughton, 1973).

63. Quoted in Kaplan, *Arabists*, p. 184.

64. Faith M. Hanna, *An American Mission: The Role of the American University of Beirut* (Boston: Alphabet Press, 1979), pp. 51–61.

65. "Guerrilla U.," *Newsweek* (October 5, 1970): 68–69.

66. Quoted in Hanna, *American Mission*, p. 65.

67. See Eva and Charles Malik to Mary Bliss Dodge, June 15, 1972, Grace Dodge Guthrie Papers (hereafter cited as GDGP), A&SC, NJML, AUB; and *AUB Bulletin* (June 8, 1972).

68. Ibid.

69. Sam Rea to Mary Bliss Dodge, June 15, 1972, GDGP, A&SC, NJML, AUB.

70. Dodge, *American University of Beirut*, pp. 116–17.

CHAPTER 8: DAVID DODGE AND AMERICAN FRUSTRATION

1. Quoted in Robert D. Kaplan, *The Arabists: The Romance of an American Elite* (New York: Free Press, 1993), p. 15.

2. Malcolm Kerr, quoted in Susan Kerr van de Ven, *One Family's Response to Terrorism: A Daughter's Memoir* (Syracuse, NY: Syracuse University Press, 2008), p. 109.

3. Ann Kerr-Adams, interview with author, Los Angeles, California, July 12, 2009.

4. No census had been taken in Lebanon since 1932 because Maronite-dominated governments feared what it might reveal. The 1932 census showed Maronites and other Christian sects composing just more than 51 percent of Lebanon's population. After 1932, the Muslim community of Sunni, Shia, and Druse grew much faster than the Christian community. Half a century later, demographers estimated Lebanon's Shiite population at 1,400,000—considerably larger than the Sunni and Maronite populations, each estimated at 800,000. See Ahmad Nizar Hamzeh, *In the Path of Hizbullah* (Syracuse, NY: Syracuse University Press, 2004), p. 13.

5. Jean Said Makdisi, *Beirut Fragments: A War Memoir* (New York: Persea Books, 1990), pp. 47–48.

6. Quoted in Fouad Ajami and Eli Reed, *Beirut: City of Regrets* (New York: W. W. Norton, 1988), pp. 31–32.

7. Thomas L. Friedman, *From Beirut to Jerusalem* (New York: Farrar, Straus & Giroux, 1989), p. 23.

8. Burton I. Kaufman, *The Arab Middle East and the United States: Inter-Arab Rivalry and Superpower Diplomacy* (New York: Twayne Publishers, 1996), p. 122.

9. When the invasion started, Begin assured Washington the IDF would advance only forty kilometers (twenty-four miles) into Lebanon, in order to put PLO artillery out of range of Israeli settlements in the Galilee. Kaufman, *Arab Middle East*, p. 124.

10. Israeli shelling inadvertently hit the roof of the synagogue in Wadi Abu Jamil, where the remnants of Beirut's tiny Jewish population still lived. See Robert Fisk, *Pity the Nation: The Abduction of Lebanon* (New York: Atheneum, 1990), p. 315.

11. Malcolm Kerr, quoted in Kerr van de Ven, *One Family's Response to Terrorism*, p. 115.

12. The method of assassination—a remote-controlled bomb that shattered a multistory building housing Phalangist headquarters in Achrafiye—closely resembled that which took the life of popular former Lebanese Prime Minister Rafiq Hariri outside the St. George Hotel and Yacht Club on West Beirut's corniche on February 14, 2005.

13. Today, the one-square-kilometer Shatila camp houses over twelve thousand Palestinian and Lebanese Shiite refugees in squalid conditions.

14. Friedman, *From Beirut to Jerusalem*, p. 159. Sharon later revived his career, becoming foreign minister in Benyamin Netanyahu's government from 1998 to 1999 and, eventually, prime minister from 2001 until a series of incapacitating strokes in early 2006.

15. Makdisi, *Beirut Fragments*, pp. 35–36.

16. Quoted in Robert D. Kaplan, "Tales from the Bazaar," *Atlantic*, August 1992, p. 47.

17. David Evans, quoted in Larry Pintak, *Beirut Outtakes: A TV Correspondent's Portrait of America's Encounter with Terror* (Lexington, MA: Lexington Books, 1988), p. 241.

18. Quoted in Burton Bollag, "American University of Beirut Rebuilds Its Identity," *Chronicle of Higher Education*, June 10, 2005, p. A32.

19. Quoted in Friedman, *From Beirut to Jerusalem*, pp. 29, 228.

20. Secrecy had been a traditional Shiite practice to protect followers from persecution by the Sunni majority ever since the martyrdom of Hussein at Karbala in 680 CE.

21. See Magnus Ranstorp, *Hizb'allah in Lebanon: The Politics of the Western Hostage Crisis* (New York: St. Martin's Press, 1997), pp. 25–30. The ties between Lebanese Shia and Iran dated back to the sixteenth century, when the Safavids established Shia Islam as the official religion of their empire.

22. Friedman, *From Beirut to Jerusalem*, pp. 505–506; and Ranstorp, *Hizb'allah in Lebanon*, pp. 70, 79. Iran's ambassador to Syria from 1982 to 1986, Ali-Akbar Mohtashemi, had been Ayatollah Khomeini's personal secretary during Khomeini's exile in Paris from 1978 to 1979.

23. Quoted in Kerr van de Ven, *One Family's Response to Terrorism*, p. 106.

24. Salwa Es-Said, quoted in ibid., p. 150.

25. They were never seen again.

26. Melissa Dodge, e-mail to author, June 8, 2010.

27. The following account is based on the author's telephone interview with David Dodge, March 29, 2008; Kerr-Adams interview; Con Coughlin, *Hostage: The Complete Story of the Lebanon Captives* (London: Little, Brown, 1992); Kerr van de Ven, *One Family's Response to Terrorism*; Ranstorp, *Hizb'allah in Lebanon*; and Ronald Reagan, *The Reagan Diaries*, ed. Douglas Brinkley (New York: HarperCollins, 2007), p. 168.

28. Doris Dodge to President Reagan, August 1, 1982, White House Subject File FG006-01, Casefile 156534; and President Reagan to Mrs. David Dodge, January 3, 1983, White House Subject File HO016-01, Casefile 111565, Ronald Reagan Presidential Library, Simi Valley, California (hereafter cited as RRPL).

29. David Dodge to President Reagan, August 7, 1983, White House Subject Files, JL003-02, Casefiles 092592 and 1746979, RRPL.

30. Quoted in "David Dodge, an Early Lebanon Hostage, Dies at 86," *New York Times*, January 30, 2009.

31. Ranstorp, *Hizb'allah in Lebanon*, p. 37, citing *International Herald-Tribune*, January 1, 1984.

32. Ryan Crocker, "Eight Years On: A Diplomat's Perspective on the Post-9/11 World," *Newsweek* (September 14, 2009): 40. Crocker went on to become US ambassador to Lebanon (1990–1993), Syria (1998–2001), Pakistan (2004–2007), and Iraq (2007–2009).

33. Anthony H. Cordesman, *The Iran-Iraq War and Western Security, 1984–1987: Strategic Implications and Policy Options* (London: Jane's Publishing, 1987), p. 79.

34. Kerr van de Ven, *One Family's Response to Terrorism*, p. 101.

35. Fouad Ajami, *The Dream Palace of the Arabs: A Generation's Odyssey* (New York: Pantheon Books, 1998), p. 100.

36. Kerr-Adams, interview.

37. Malcolm Kerr to Elsa Kerr, February 1, 1983, excerpted in Ann Zwicker Kerr, *Come with Me from Lebanon: An American Family Odyssey* (Syracuse, NY: Syracuse University Press, 1994), p. 223.

38. Malcolm Kerr to Susan Kerr van de Ven, September 1983, excerpted in Zwicker Kerr, *Come with Me from Lebanon*, p. 259.

39. Malcolm Kerr to John and Susan Zwicker, October 1983, excerpted in Zwicker Kerr, *Come with Me from Lebanon*, p. 262.

40. Malcolm Kerr, "Rich and Poor in the Arab Order," *Journal of Arab Affairs* (October 1981).

41. Zwicker Kerr, *Come with Me from Lebanon*, pp. 164, 191.

42. Kerr van de Ven, *One Family's Response to Terrorism*, p. 103.

43. Quoted in Con Coughlin, *Hostage: The Complete Story of the Lebanon Captives* (London: Little, Brown, 1992), p. 17.

44. Fisk, *Pity the Nation*, p. 531.

45. Terry Anderson, *Den of Lions: Memoirs of Seven Years* (repr.; New York: Ballantine Books, 1994), p. 62n.

46. See AUB Newsletter on Kerr's assassination, last modified December 23, 1998, http://aub.edu.lb/themes/1999/Kerr/newletter.html.

47. Ajami, *Dream Palace of the Arabs*, p. 105; and Kerr van de Ven, *One Family's Response to Terrorism*.

48. Quoted in Friedman, *From Beirut to Jerusalem*, p. 207.

49. Ronald Reagan, *An American Life* (New York: Simon & Schuster, 1990), p. 467.

50. Samir Khalaf, *Lebanon's Predicament* (Columbia University Press, 1987), p. 284.

51. Eleanor Dorman Johnson, interview with author, Beirut, Lebanon, December 28, 2008. See also Gladys Mouro, *An American Nurse Amidst Chaos*, 2nd ed. (Beirut: American University of Beirut Press, 2001).

CHAPTER 9: AMERICA IN THE CONTEMPORARY MIDDLE EAST

1. See James A. Baker III, *The Politics of Diplomacy: Revolution, War and Peace, 1989–1992* (New York: Putnams, 1995), p. 336.

2. Iraq had been a key Soviet ally in the Middle East during the Cold War.

3. Saddam Hussein remained in power in Iraq until deposed by the US invasion of 2003.

4. "The students were a mixture of Muslims and Christians," Ashrawi later wrote, regarding the Quaker girls' school, "but we did not know who was what, and it was not an issue." Hanan Ashrawi, *This Side of Peace: A Personal Account* (New York: Simon & Schuster, 1995), p. 24.

5. Yael Dayan, quoted in Antony Loewenstein, *My Israel Question* (Carlton, AUS: Melbourne University Press, n.d.) pp. 11–12.

6. AUB dean of student affairs Maroun Kisirwam, quoted in Burton Bollag, "American University of Beirut Rebuilds Its Identity," *Chronicle of Higher Education*, June 10, 2005, p. A31.

7. John Waterbury, "Hate Your Policies, Love Your Institutions," *Foreign Affairs*, January/February 2003, p. 61.

8. A week after Kerr's death, Waterbury received a letter from him recommending an AUB student for graduate study at Princeton. John Waterbury, e-mail to author, November 2, 2009.

9. Ibid.

10. Former Princeton president and AUB trustee Robert Goheen, quoted in Katherine Zoepf, "An American in Beirut," *Princeton Alumni Weekly*, January 24, 2007.

11. Al Qaeda advocated the creation of a pan-Islamic state through the use of indiscriminate violence—utterly contrary to the mainstream interpretation of Islam, which condemns the slaughter of innocents and prohibits suicide.

12. Terrorists flew another jetliner into the Pentagon near Washington, DC, and commandeered a fourth one—which they apparently intended to fly into the Capitol. The fourth jet's passengers bravely aborted the hijacking, crashing the plane into the ground near Shanksburg, Pennsylvania.

13. Quoted in Zoepf, "An American in Beirut."

14. Quoted in Ron Suskind, "Without a Doubt," *New York Times*, October 17, 2004.

15. This and subsequent quotes are from author interview with Andrew Exum, Washington, DC, August 4, 2010.

16. The deputy leader of al Qaeda, Ayman al-Zawahiri, had belonged to the Muslim Brotherhood and had helped plot its assassination of Egyptian leader Anwar al-Sadat in October 1980.

17. Afghanistan's devastation during the 1980s opened the way for the Taliban's eventual rise to power in 1994. The Taliban ruled Afghanistan until being toppled by a United States–led invasion in late 2001. See Ahmed Rashid, *Taliban: Militant Islam, Oil and Fundamentalism in Central Asia* (New Haven, CT: Yale University Press, 2000).

18. Beginning in the 1970s, the Saudi royal family used Hariri's construction company in most of their lucrative development projects. The royal family rewarded Hariri with Saudi citizenship.

19. The Place des Martyrs in downtown Beirut memorializes Lebanese journalists hanged by the Ottoman Turks for advocating independence in World War I.

20. Israeli sources, quoted in Augustus R. Norton, *Hezbollah: A Short Story* (Princeton, NJ: Princeton University Press, n.d.) p. 139.

21. See Amos Harel and Avi Issacharoff, *34 Days: Israel, Hezbollah, and the War in Lebanon* (New York: Palgrave Macmillan, 2008), p. 81.

22. Quoted in ibid., p. 105.

23. Katherine Zoepf, "In Lebanon, A Professor Uses Theater to Help Traumatized Children," *Chronicle of Higher Education*, September 8, 2006, pp. A39–40. Quote is in Harel and Issacharoff, *34 Days*, p. 250.

24. The IDF chief of staff, General Dan Halutz, resigned after the war.

25. A favorability survey of 1,700 Egyptians conducted soon after the war yielded these results: Hassan Nasrallah, 82 percent; Iranian president Mahmoud Ahmadinejad, 73 percent; Hamas's Khaled Mashal, 60 percent; al Qaeda's Osama bin Laden, 52 percent; and the Muslim Brotherhood's Mohammed Mahdi Akef, 45 percent. See Saad Eddine Ibrahim, "The 'New Middle East' Bush Is Resisting," *Washington Post*, August 23, 2006.

26. Walter Russell Mead, "Honolulu, Harvard, and Hyde Park," *Foreign Affairs*, July/August 2010.

27. Quoted in Jonathan Alter, *The Promise: President Obama, Year One* (New York: Simon & Schuster, 2010), p. 374.

28. Quoted in Ahmed Rashid, *Descent into Chaos: The United States and the Failure of Nation Building in Pakistan, Afghanistan, and Central Asia* (New York: Viking, 2008), p. xli.

29. "Welcome to 'Pashtunistan,'" *Week*, February 12, 2010, p. 15. The border arbitrarily dividing Pashtuns in Afghanistan from those in Pakistan was drawn by an outsider, British diplomat Mortimer Durand, in 1893.

30. Talat Masoon in the *Islamabad News*, October 2009, cited in *Week*, November 6, 2009, p. 18.

31. Sabrina Tavernise, "Survey of Pakistan's Young Predicts 'Disaster' if Their Needs Aren't Addressed," *New York Times*, November 22, 2009, citing Nielsen survey of 1,226 Pakistanis aged eighteen to twenty-nine, conducted in March and April 2009.

32. Quoted in Sabrina Tavernise and Waqar Gillani, "Frustrated Strivers in Pakistan Turn to Jihad," *New York Times*, February 28, 2010.

33. Quoted in Anthony Shadid, "Egypt's Protesters Have Passion, but No Clear Leadership," *New York Times*, February 1, 2011.

34. Quoted in the *New York Times*, February 3, 2011.

35. Quoted in the *New York Times*, February 12, 2011.

36. Homi Kharas, "American Education in the Middle East: Smart Power for a New Era," November 21, 2008, www.brookings.edu/events/2008/1121_me_education.aspx (accessed October 14, 2011).

37. President Obama, "A New Beginning," address at Cairo University, Egypt, June 4, 2009, in *The New Arab Revolt*, Council on Foreign Relations (New York: Council on Foreign Relations, 2011), p. 383.

38. Quoted in Lawrence Wright, "Letter from Gaza," *New Yorker*, November 9, 2009.

BIBLIOGRAPHY

PRIMARY SOURCES

Unpublished

Archives and Special Collections, Nami Jafet Memorial Library, American University of Beirut, Beirut, Lebanon:
    Bayard Dodge Papers.
    Daniel Bliss Papers.
    Grace Dodge Guthrie Papers.

Robert Frost Library, Amherst College, Amherst, Massachusetts:
    Abby Wood Bliss Papers.
    Daniel Bliss Papers.
    Frederick Bliss Papers.
    Howard Bliss Papers.
    Willie Bliss Papers.

Special Collections, Mount Holyoke College, South Hadley, Massachusetts:
    Charlotte Allen Ward Papers (MS 0595).

Ronald Reagan Presidential Library, Simi Valley, California
    Burns, William: Files.
    Clark, William: Files.
    Crisis Management Center, National Security Council (NSC): Records.
    Earl, Robert L.: Files.
    Executive Secretariat, NSC:
        Country Files: Lebanon.
        NSC Meeting Files: Records.

Fortier, Donald R.: Files.
McFarlane, Robert: Files.
Poindexter, John: Files.

Yale Divinity School Library, Yale University, New Haven, Connecticut:
    Papers of the American Board of Commissioners for Foreign Missions
        (microfilm).
    Records of the American University of Beirut, 1895–1958 (HR 520).
    Henry Harris Jessup Papers, 1851–1912 (RG 117).

Published

Anderson, Rufus. *History of the Missions of the American Board of Commissioners for Foreign Missions to the Oriental Churches.* 2 vols. Boston: Congregational Publishing Society, 1873.

Anderson, Terry. *Den of Lions: Memoirs of Seven Years.* New York: Ballantine Books, 1994.

Ashrawi, Hanan. *This Side of Peace: A Personal Account.* New York: Simon & Schuster, 1995.

"A Talk with Bayard Dodge." *Saudi Aramco World* 23, no. 4 (July/August 1972): 11–17.

Bird, Isaac. *Bible Work in Bible Lands; or Events in the History of the Syria Mission.* Philadelphia: Presbyterian Board of Missions, 1872.

Bird, Kai. *Crossing Mandelbaum Gate: Coming of Age between the Arabs and Israelis, 1956–1978.* New York: Scribner, 2010.

Bliss, Daniel. *The Reminiscences of Daniel Bliss.* New York: Revell, 1920.

Bliss, Frederick Jones. *The Religions of Modern Syria and Palestine.* New York: Charles Scribner's Sons, 1912.

Bliss, Howard S. "The Modern Missionary." *Atlantic Monthly* (May 1920): 664–75.

Chehabi, H. E. "An Iranian in First World War Beirut: Qasem Ghani's Reminiscences." In H. E. Chehabi, ed. *Distant Relations: Iran and Lebanon in the Last 500 Years.* London: I. B. Taurus, 2006.

Coon, Carleton S., Jr., ed. *Daniel Bliss and the Founding of the American University of Beirut.* Washington, DC: Middle East Institute, 1989.

Copeland, Miles. *The Game of Nations: The Amorality of Power Politics.* New York: Simon & Schuster, 1969.

Cortas, Wadad Makdisi. *A World I Loved: The Story of an Arab Woman*. New York: Nation Books, 2009.

Dodge, Bayard. *The American University of Beirut: A Brief History of the University and the Lands Which It Serves*. Beirut: Khayat's, 1958.

———. "Must There Be War in the Middle East?" *Reader's Digest*, April 1948, pp. 34–45.

Guthrie, Grace Dodge. *Legacy to Lebanon*. Privately published, 1984.

Jacobsen, David, with Gerald Astor. *Hostage: My Nightmare in Beirut*. New York: Donald I. Fine, 1991.

Jessup, Henry Harris. *Fifty-Three Years in Syria*. 2 vols. New York: Revell, 1910.

Hitchcock, Edward. *Reminiscences of Amherst College, Historical, Scientific, Biographical and Autobiographical: Also, of Other and Wider Life Experiences*. Northampton, MA: Bridgman & Childs, 1863.

House, Edward Mandell, and Charles Seymour, eds. *What Really Happened at Paris: The Story of the Peace Conference, 1918–1919*. New York: Charles Scribner's Sons, 1921.

Kerr, Ann Zwicker. *Come with Me from Lebanon: An American Family Odyssey*. Syracuse, NY: Syracuse University Press, 1994.

Kerr, Malcolm H. "Arab Society and the West." In Patrick Seale, ed. *The Shaping of an Arab Statesman: Sharif Abd al-Hamid Sharaf and the Modern Arab World*. London: Quartet Books, 1983.

Khaled, Leila. *My People Shall Live: The Autobiography of a Revolutionary*. London: Hodder & Stoughton, 1973.

Khoury, Ghada Yusuf, ed. *The Founding Fathers of the American University of Beirut: Biographies*. Beirut: American University of Beirut Press, 1992.

Lansing, Robert. *The Peace Negotiations: A Personal Narrative*. Boston: Houghton Mifflin, 1921.

Leary, Lewis Gaston. *Syria: The Land of Lebanon*. New York: McBride, Nast & Company, 1913.

Makdisi, Jean Said. *Beirut Fragments: A War Memoir*. New York: Persea Books, 1990.

———. *Teta, Mother and Me: An Arab Woman's Memoir*. London: Saqi, 2005.

Malik, Charles. *Swift Seasons Roll: A Tribute to Philip K. Hitti*. New York: American Friends of the Middle East, 1954.

McGilvary, Margaret. *The Dawn of a New Era in Syria*. New York: Revell, 1920.

Mouro, Gladys. *An American Nurse amidst Chaos*. 2nd ed. Beirut: American University of Beirut Press, 2001.

Murphy, Robert. *Diplomat among Warriors*. Garden City, NY: Doubleday, 1964.

Reagan, Ronald. *An American Life*. New York: Simon & Schuster, 1990.
————. *The Reagan Diaries*. Edited by Douglas Brinkley. New York: HarperCollins, 2007.
Rizk, Salom. *Syrian Yankee*. Garden City, NY: Doubleday, 1943.
Rugh, Douglas, ed. *The Voice of Daniel Bliss*. Beirut: American Press, 1956.
Rugh, Douglas, and Belle Dorman Rugh with Alfred H. Howell, eds. *Letters from a New Campus: Written to His Wife Abby and Their Four Children during Their Visit to Amherst, Massachusetts, 1873–1874*. New York: Syracuse University Press, 1994.
Salibi, Kamal S. "Recollections of Lebanon in the 1940s and 1950s." *Bulletin of the Royal Institute for Inter-Faith Studies* 5, no. 2 (Autumn/Winter 2003): 117–35.
Seelye, Laurens Hickcok. "A Philosopher among the Cults of the Near East." *The Christian Leader*. January 2 and 9, 1937.
Shultz, George P. *Turmoil and Triumph: My Years as Secretary of State*. New York: Charles Scribner's Sons, 1993.
Strong, William E. *The Story of the American Board: An Account of the First Hundred Years of the American Board of Commissioners for Foreign Missions*. Boston: Pilgrim Press, 1910.
Sutherland, Tom, and Jean Sutherland. *At Your Own Risk: An American Chronicle of Crisis and Captivity in the Middle East*. Golden, CO: Fulcrum Publishing, 1996.
Tabbara, Lina Mikdadi. *Survival in Beirut: A Diary of Civil War*. London: Onyx Press, 1979.
Tapline: The Story of the World's Biggest Oil Pipe Line. New York: Trans-Arabian Pipe Line Company, 1951.
Thomson, W. M. *The Land and the Book; or, Biblical Illustrations Drawn from the Manners and Customs, the Scenes and Scenery of the Holy Land*. 2 vols. New York: Harper & Brothers, 1858.
Waterbury, John. "Hate Your Policies, Love Your Institutions." *Foreign Affairs*, January/February 2003, pp. 58–68.
————. "A President's Beirut Diary." *The Chronicle of Higher Education*, September 8, 2006, sec. B, pp. 10–11.
Zurayk, Constantine. "U.S. College in the Near East." *Life*, March 23, 1953, pp. 134–40.

Interviews

Dodge, David. Telephone interview with the author, Princeton, New Jersey, March 29 and November 23, 2008.

Dodge, Melissa. E-mail to the author, June 8, 2010.

Exum, Andrew. Interview with the author, Washington, DC, August 4, 2010.

Guthrie, Grace Dodge. Interview with the author, Falls Church, Virginia, May 7, 2008.

Johnson, Eleanor Dorman. Interview with the author, Beirut, Lebanon, December 28, 2008.

Kerr-Adams, Ann. Interview with the author, Los Angeles, California, July 13, 2009.

Waterbury, John. E-mail and written responses to the author, Princeton, New Jersey, November 2, 2009.

SECONDARY SOURCES

Abouchdid, Eugenie Elie. *Thirty Years of Lebanon and Syria, 1917–1947*. Beirut: Sader-Rihani Printing, 1948.

Achcar, Gilbert, with Michel Warschawski. *The 33-Day War: Israel's War on Hezbollah in Lebanon and Its Consequences*. Boulder: Paradigm Publishers, 2007.

Addison, James Thayer. *The Christian Approach to the Moslem*. New York: Columbia University Press, 1942.

Ajami, Fouad. *The Arab Predicament: Arab Political Thought and Practice since 1967*. Cambridge, UK: Cambridge University Press, 1981.

———. *Beirut: City of Regrets*. New York: W. W. Norton, 1988.

———. *The Dream Palace of the Arabs: A Generation's Odyssey*. New York: Pantheon Books, 1998.

———. "The Sentry's Solitude." *Foreign Affairs*, November/December 2001, pp. 2–16.

Alhstrom, Sydney E. *The American Protestant Encounter with World Religions*. Beloit, WI: Beloit College Press, 1962.

———. *A Religious History of the American People*. New Haven, CT: Yale University Press, 1972.

Alter, Jonathan. *The Promise: President Obama, Year One*. New York: Simon & Schuster, 2010.

Antonius, George. *The Arab Awakening: The Story of the Arab National Movement.* New York: G.P. Putnam, 1946; repr., New York: Capricorn Books, 1965.

Baktiaya, Adil. "Syrian Protestant College's Struggle for Legitimacy as Reflected in Archival Sources," *International Review of Turkology* 1, no. 2 (Summer 2008): 25–41.

Baram, Phillip J. *The Department of State in the Middle East, 1919–1945.* Philadelphia: University of Pennsylvania Press, 1978.

Beale, Howard K. *Theodore Roosevelt and the Rise of America to World Power.* Baltimore: Johns Hopkins Press, 1956.

Beatty, Jerome. "Man of the Near East Renaissance." *Reader's Digest*, February 1939.

Bollag, Burton. "American University of Beirut Rebuilds Its Identity." *Chronicle of Higher Education*, June 10, 2005.

Bonsal, Stephen. *Suitors and Suppliants: The Little Nations at Versailles.* New York: Prentice-Hall, 1946.

Boorstin, Daniel J. *The Americans: The Democratic Experience.* New York: Random House, 1973.

Brands, H. W. *Into the Labyrinth: The United States and the Middle East, 1945–1993.* New York: McGraw-Hill, 1994.

Brecher, F. W. "Charles R. Crane's Crusade for the Arabs, 1919–1939." *Middle Eastern Studies* 24 (1998).

Bryson, Thomas A. *Seeds of Mideast Crisis: The United States Diplomatic Role in the Middle East during World War II.* Jefferson, NC: McFarland, 1981.

Buhite, Russell. *Patrick J. Hurley and American Foreign Policy.* Ithaca, NY: Cornell University Press, 1973.

Chehabi, H. E., ed. *Distant Relations: Iran and Lebanon in the Last 500 Years.* London: I. B. Tauris, 2006.

Council on Foreign Relations. *The New Arab Revolt.* New York: Council on Foreign Relations, 2011.

Daniel, Robert L. *American Philanthropy in the Near East, 1820–1960.* Athens: Ohio University Press, 1970.

———. "The Friendship of Woodrow Wilson and Cleveland H. Dodge." *Mid-America: An Historical Review* 43, no. 3 (July 1961): 182–96.

Davis, John. *The Landscape of Belief: Encountering the Holy Land in Nineteenth-Century American Art and Culture.* Princeton, NJ: Princeton University Press, 1996.

Deeb, Marius. *The Lebanese Civil War.* New York: Praeger Publishers, 1980.

DeNovo, John A. *American Interests and Policies in the Middle East, 1900–1939.* Minneapolis: University of Minnesota Press, 1963.

Dodge, Phyllis B. *Tales of the Phelps-Dodge Family: A Chronicle of Five Generations.* New York: New-York Historical Society, 1987.

Doran, Michael Scott. "Somebody Else's Civil War." *Foreign Affairs*, January/February 2002, pp. 22–42.

Earle, Edward Mead. "American Missions in the Near East." *Foreign Affairs* 7, no. 3, April 1929, pp. 398–417.

Evans, Laurence. *United States Policy and the Partition of Turkey, 1914–1924.* Baltimore: Johns Hopkins Press, 1965.

Fairbank, John K., ed. *The Missionary Enterprise in China and America.* Cambridge, MA: Harvard University Press, 1974.

Farag, Nadia. "The Lewis Affair and the Fortunes of al-Muqtataf," *Middle Eastern Studies* 8 (1972): 73–83.

Fawaz, Leila Tarazi. *Merchants and Migrants in Nineteenth-Century Beirut.* Cambridge, MA: Harvard University Press, 1983.

———. *An Occasion for War: Civil Conflict in Lebanon and Damascus in 1860.* Berkeley: University of California Press, 1994.

Fedden, Robin. *The Phoenix Land: The Civilization of Syria and Lebanon.* New York: George Braziller, 1965.

Field, James A., Jr. *America and the Mediterranean World, 1776–1882.* Princeton, NJ: Princeton University Press, 1969.

Finnie, David H. *Pioneers East: The Early American Experience in the Middle East.* Cambridge, MA: Harvard University Press, 1967.

Firro, Kais M. *Inventing Lebanon: Nationalism and the State under the Mandate.* London: I. B. Tauris, 2003.

Fisher, Sydney Nettleton, and William Ochsenwald. *The Middle East: A History.* 4th ed. New York: McGraw-Hill, 1990.

Fisk, Robert. *Pity the Nation: The Abduction of Lebanon.* New York: Atheneum, 1990.

Friedman, Thomas L. *From Beirut to Jerusalem.* New York: Farrar Straus Giroux, 1989.

———. "Have You Heard?" *New York Times*, April 12, 1995.

Fromkin, David. *A Peace to End All Peace: The Fall of the Ottoman Empire and the Creation of the Modern Middle East.* New York: Henry Holt, 1989.

Fuess, Claude Moore. *Amherst: The Story of a New England College.* Boston: Little, Brown, 1935.

Fuller, Graham E. "The Future of Political Islam." *Foreign Affairs*, March/April 2002, pp. 48–60.

Gelvin, James. "The Ironic Legacy of the King-Crane Commission." In David W.

Lesch, ed., *The Middle East and the United States: A Historical and Political Reassessment*. Boulder: Westview Press, 1996.

Gendzier, Irene L. *Notes from the Minefield: United States Intervention in Lebanon and the Middle East, 1945–1958*. New York: Columbia University Press, 1997.

Gibb, H. A. R., and Harold Bowen. *Islamic Society and the West: A Study of the Impact of Western Civilization on Moslem Culture in the Near East*. London: Oxford University Press, 1957.

Gordon, David C. *The Republic of Lebanon: Nation in Jeopardy*. Boulder: Westview Press, 1983.

Grabill, Joseph L. "Cleveland H. Dodge, Woodrow Wilson, and the Near East." *Journal of Presbyterian History* 48 (Winter 1970): 249–64.

———. *Protestant Diplomacy and the Near East: Missionary Influence on American Policy, 1810–1927*. Minneapolis: University of Minnesota Press, 1971.

Grose, Peter. *Israel in the Mind of America*. New York: Alfred A. Knopf, 1983.

Hahn, Peter L. *Caught in the Middle East: U.S. Policy Toward the Arab-Israeli Conflict, 1945–1961*. Chapel Hill: University of North Carolina Press, 2004.

———. *Crisis and Crossfire: The United States and the Middle East since 1945*. Washington, DC: Potomac Books, 2005.

Hamzeh, Ahmad Nizar. *In the Path of Hizbullah*. Syracuse, NY: Syracuse University Press, 2004.

Hanna, Faith M. *An American Mission: The Role of the American University of Beirut*. Boston: Alphabet Press, 1979.

Hanssen, Jens. *Fin de Siecle Beirut: The Making of an Ottoman Provincial Capital*. Oxford: Clarendon Press, 2005.

Harel, Amos, and Avi Issacharoff. *34 Days: Israel, Hezbollah, and the War in Lebanon*. New York: Palgrave Macmillan, 2008.

Harris, Paul William. *Nothing but Christ: Rufus Anderson and the Ideology of Protestant Foreign Missions*. New York: Oxford University Press, 1999.

Heikal, Mohamed. *The Road to Ramadan*. New York: Quadrangle/The New York Times Book Company, 1975.

Heimert, Alan. *Religion and the American Mind*. Cambridge, MA: Harvard University Press, 1966.

Hitti, Philip K. *History of Syria Including Lebanon and Palestine*. London: Macmillan, 1951.

———. *Lebanon in History: From the Earliest Times to the Present*. 3rd ed. London: Macmillan, 1967.

————. *The Syrians in America*. New York: George H. Doran, 1924; repr., Piscataway, NJ: Gorgias Press, 2005.

Hodder, Edwin. *The Life and Work of the Seventh Earl of Shaftesbury, K.G.* Vol. 3. London: Cassell, 1886.

Hopkins, Charles Howard. *The Rise of the Social Gospel in American Protestantism, 1865–1915*. New Haven, CT: Yale University Press, 1940.

Hourani, Albert. *Arabic Thought in the Liberal Age: 1798–1939*. Cambridge, UK: Oxford University Press, 1962.

————. *A History of the Arab Peoples*. Cambridge, MA: Belknap Press of Harvard University Press, 1991.

————. *Syria and Lebanon: A Political Essay*. Cambridge, UK: Oxford University Press, 1946.

Howard, Harry N. "An American Experiment in Peace-Making: The King-Crane Commission." *Moslem World* 32 (April 1942): 122–46.

————. *The King-Crane Commission: An American Inquiry in the Middle East*. Beirut: Khayat's, 1963.

Hutchison, William R. *Errand to the World: American Protestant Thought and Foreign Missions*. Chicago: University of Chicago Press, 1987.

Jansen, Godfrey. "Sowing the Wind, Reaping the Whirlwind," *Christian Science Monitor*, June 19, 1971.

Jeha, Shafik. *Darwin and the Crisis of 1882 in the Medical Department of the Syrian Protestant College and the First Student Protest in the Arab World*. Beirut: American University of Beirut Press, 2004.

Kaplan, Robert D. *The Arabists: The Romance of an American Elite*. New York: Free Press, 1993.

————. "Tales from the Bazaar." *Atlantic* 270, no. 2 (August 1992): 37–61.

Kassir, Samir. *Beirut*. Berkeley: University of California Press, 2010.

Kaufman, Burton I. *The Arab Middle East and the United States: Inter-Arab Rivalry and Superpower Diplomacy*. New York: Twayne Publishers, 1996.

Kedourie, Elie. "The American University of Beirut." *Middle Eastern Studies* 3, no. 1 (October 1966): 74–90.

————. *Arabic Political Memoirs and Other Studies*. London: Frank Cass, 1974.

Khalaf, Samir. "Leavening the Levant: New England Puritanism as a Cultural Transplant." *Journal of Mediterranean Studies* 7, no. 2 (1997): 268–92.

————. *Lebanon's Predicament*. New York: Columbia University Press, 1987.

Khalidi, Rashid. *Resurrecting Empire: Western Footprints and America's Perilous Path in the Middle East*. Boston: Beacon Press, 2004.

Khater, Akram Fouad. *Inventing Home: Emigration, Gender, and the Middle Class in Lebanon, 1870–1920*. Berkeley: University of California Press, 2001.

Khoury, Philip S. *Syria and the French Mandate: The Politics of Arab Nationalism, 1920–1945*. Princeton, NJ: Princeton University Press, 1987.

Kidd, Thomas S. *American Christians and Islam: Evangelical Culture and Muslims from the Colonial Period to the Age of Terrorism*. Princeton, NJ: Princeton University Press, 2009.

Kuklick, Bruce. *Puritans in Babylon: The Ancient Near East and American Intellectual Life, 1880–1930*. Princeton, NJ: Princeton University Press, 1996.

Labelle, Maurice, Jr. "'We Have a Campaign of Hatred against Us': Arab Anti-Americanism, U.S. Street Diplomacy, and the 1958 Lebanon Crisis." Presentation, Society for Historians of American Foreign Relations Conference, Falls Church, VA, June 25, 2009.

Landau, Rom. *Search for Tomorrow: The Things Which Are and the Things Which Shall Be Hereafter*. London: Nicholson and Watson, 1938.

Latourette, Kenneth Scott. *Missions and the American Mind*. Indianapolis: National Foundation Press, 1949.

Leavitt, Donald M. "Darwinism in the Arab World: The Lewis Affair at the Syrian Protestant College." *The Muslim World* 71, no. 2 (April 1981): 85–98.

LeDuc, Thomas. *Piety and Intellect at Amherst College, 1865–1912*. New York: Columbia University Press, 1946.

Littell, Robert. "Our Best Investment in the Arab World." *Reader's Digest*, February 1963, pp. 240–46.

Little, Douglas. *American Orientalism: The United States and the Middle East since 1945*. Chapel Hill: University of North Carolina Press, 2002.

———. "Pipeline Politics: America, TAPLINE, and the Arabs," *Business History Review* 64 (Summer 1990): 255–85.

Lohbeck, Don. *Patrick J. Hurley*. Chicago: Henry Regnery, 1956.

Longrigg, Stephen Hemsley. *Syria and Lebanon under French Mandate*. Cambridge, UK: Oxford University Press, 1958.

Lowitt, Richard. *A Merchant Prince of the Nineteenth Century: William E. Dodge*. New York: Columbia University Press, 1954.

Mackey, Sandra. *Lebanon: Death of a Nation*. New York: Congdon & Weed, 1989.

MacMillan, Margaret. *Paris 1919: Six Months That Changed the World*. New York: Random House, 2001.

Makdisi, Ussama. "'Anti-Americanism' in the Arab World: An Interpretation of a Brief History." *Journal of American History* 89, no. 2 (September 2002).

————. *Artillery of Heaven: American Missionaries and the Failed Conversion of the Middle East*. Ithaca, NY: Cornell University Press, 2008.

————. *The Culture of Sectarianism: Community, History, and Violence in Nineteenth-Century Ottoman Lebanon*. Berkeley: University of California Press, 2000.

————. *Faith Misplaced: The Broken Promise of U.S.–Arab Relations, 1820–2001*. New York: Public Affairs, 2010.

————. "Reclaiming the Land of the Bible: Missionaries, Secularism, and Evangelical Modernity." *American Historical Review*, June 1997, pp. 680–713.

Marr, Timothy. *The Cultural Roots of American Islamicism*. Cambridge, UK: Cambridge University Press, 2006.

McCullough, David. *Truman*. New York: Simon & Schuster, 1992.

McPhee, John. *The Headmaster: Frank L. Boyden, of Deerfield*. New York: Farrar, Straus & Giroux, 1966.

Mead, Walter Russell. *God and Gold: Britain, America, and the Making of the Modern World*. New York: Alfred A. Knopf, 2007.

————. "Honolulu, Harvard, and Hyde Park." *Foreign Affairs*, July/August 2010.

————. *Special Providence: American Foreign Policy and How It Changed the World*. New York: Alfred A. Knopf, 2001.

Morris, Benny. *The Birth of the Palestinian Refugee Problem, 1947–1949*. Cambridge, UK: Cambridge University Press, 1987.

————. *1948: The First Arab-Israeli War*. New Haven, CT: Yale University Press, 2008.

Morris, Jan. *Among the Cities*. Oxford: Oxford University Press, 1985.

Munro, John M. *A Mutual Concern: The Story of the American University of Beirut*. Delmar, NY: Caravan Books, 1977.

Nevakivi, Jukka. *Britain, France and the Arab Middle East, 1914–1920*. London: Athlone Press, 1969.

Norton, Augustus Richard. *Hezbollah: A Short History*. Princeton, NJ: Princeton University Press, 2007.

Oren, Michael B. *Power, Faith, and Fantasy: America in the Middle East, 1776 to the Present*. New York: W. W. Norton, 2007.

Penrose, Stephen B. L., Jr. *That They May Have Life: The Story of the American University of Beirut, 1866–1941*. Princeton, NJ: Princeton University Press, 1941.

Picard, Elizabeth. *Lebanon, a Shattered Country: Myths and Realities of the Wars in Lebanon*. New York: Holmes & Meier, 2002.

Pintak, Larry. *Beirut Outtakes: A TV Correspondent's Portrait of America's Encounter with Terror*. Lexington, MA: Lexington Books, 1988.

Qasim, Na'im. *Hizbullah: The Story from Within*. Translated from Arabic by Dalia Khalil. London: Saqi, 2005.

Rahman, Fazlur. *Islam and Modernity*. Chicago: University of Chicago Press, 1982.

Ranstorp, Magnus. *Hizb'allah in Lebanon: The Politics of the Western Hostage Crisis*. New York: St. Martin's Press, 1997.

Rashid, Ahmed. *Descent into Chaos: The United States and the Failure of Nation Building in Pakistan, Afghanistan, and Central Asia*. New York: Viking, 2008.

Roberts, Jon H. *Darwinism and the Divine in America: Protestant Intellectuals and Organic Evolution, 1859–1900*. Madison: University of Wisconsin Press, 1988.

Sachar, Howard M. *A History of Israel: From the Rise of Zionism to Our Time*. New York: Alfred A. Knopf, 1976.

Sa'di, Lufti M. "Al-Hakim Cornelius Van Alen Van Dyck." *Isis* 27 (1937): 20–45.

Salibi, Kamal. *A House of Many Mansions: The History of Lebanon Reconsidered*. Berkeley: University of California Press, 1988.

———. *The Modern History of Lebanon*. New York: Frederick A. Praeger, 1965.

Sarton, George. *The Incubation of Western Culture in the Middle East*. Washington, DC: Library of Congress, 1951.

Scholz, Norbert J. "Foreign Education and Indigenous Reaction in Late Ottoman Lebanon: Students and Teachers at the Syrian Protestant College in Beirut." PhD diss., Georgetown University, UMI Dissertation Services, 1997.

Seale, Patrick. *Asad of Syria: The Struggle for the Middle East*. Berkeley: University of California Press, 1989.

Shwadran, Benjamin. *The Middle East, Oil, and the Great Powers*. New York: Praeger, 1965.

Talbott, Strobe, and Nayan Chanda, eds. *The Age of Terror: America and the World after September 11*. New York: Basic Books, 2001.

Tejirian, Eleanor H., and Reeva Spector Simon, eds. *Altruism and Imperialism: Western Cultural and Religious Missions in the Middle East*. New York: Middle East Institute, Columbia University, 2002.

Tibawi, Abdul Latif. *American Interests in Syria, 1800–1901: A Study of Educational, Literary and Religious Work*. Oxford, Oxford University Press, 1966.

———. "The Genesis and Early History of the Syrian Protestant College: Part I." *Middle East Journal* 21, no. 1 (Winter 1967): 1–15.

———. "The Genesis and Early History of the Syrian Protestant College: Part II." *Middle East Journal* 21, no. 2 (Spring 1967): 199–212.

———. *A Modern History of Syria including Lebanon and Palestine*. London: Macmillan, 1969.

Traboulsi, Fawwaz. *A History of Modern Lebanon*. London: Pluto Press, 2007.

Tuveson, Ernest Lee. *Redeemer Nation: The Idea of America's Millennial Role*. Chicago: University of Chicago Press, 1968.

Varg, Paul A. "Motives in Protestant Missions, 1890–1917." *Church History* 23 (March 1954): 68–82.

Vitalis, Robert. *America's Kingdom: Mythmaking on the Saudi Oil Frontier*. Stanford, CA: Stanford University Press, 2007.

Wood, Forrest G. *The Arrogance of Faith: Christianity and Race in America from the Colonial Era to the Twentieth Century*. New York: Alfred A. Knopf, 1990.

Wright, Robin. *In the Name of God: The Khomeini Decade*. New York: Simon & Schuster, 1989.

———. *Sacred Rage: The Crusade of Modern Islam*. New York: Linden Press/Simon & Schuster, 1985.

Yapp, M. E. *The Making of the Modern Middle East, 1792–1923*. London: Longman, 1987.

Yergin, Daniel. *The Prize: The Epic Quest for Oil, Money, and Power*. New York: Simon & Schuster, 1991.

Zakaria, Fareed. "Why Do They Hate Us?" *Newsweek*, October 15, 2001.

Zamir, Meir. *Lebanon's Quest: The Road to Statehood, 1926–1939*. London: I. B. Tauris, 1997.

Zeine, Zeine N. *The Struggle for Arab Independence: Western Diplomacy & the Rise and Fall of Faisal's Kingdom in Syria*. London: Khayat's, 1960.

Zoepf, Katherine. "An American in Beirut." *Princeton Alumni Weekly*, January 24, 2007.

INDEX